Mom's Family
RECIPES

THE COMPLETE MENU COOKBOOK

- Family style recipes for the whole family
- Simple detailed instructions & cooking glossary

◢▮▮▮Kappa Books, Inc.

Ambler, Pennsylvania 19002
Printed in the U.S.A.

TABLE OF CONTENTS

Notes:_____

APPETIZERS

& UNIQUE DIPS

LAYERED CATFISH DIP

3 cups water
1 lb. U.S. farm-raised catfish fillets
12 ozs. cream cheese, softened
2 tbs. mayonnaise
2 tbs. Worcestershire sauce
1 tbs. lemon juice
dash garlic salt
1 sm. onion, chopped
1 bottle (12 oz.) chili sauce
parsley (optional)

In a large skillet bring water to a
boil. Add catfish. Return to boil;
reduce heat. Cover and simmer
gently for 5 to 7 minutes until fish
flakes easily. Remove from water.
Cool slightly. Flake catfish; set
aside. In a mixing bowl stir
together cream cheese,
mayonnaise, Worcestershire
sauce, lemon juice and garlic salt.
Stir in chopped onion.

To assemble, spread cheese
mixture over bottom of a 12 inch
plate or shallow serving bowl.
Spread chili sauce over cheese
layer. Top with cooked catfish.
Garnish with parsley, if desired.
Serve with sturdy crackers.

Yields: 12 servings

MUSHROOM PIE

1 lb. fresh from Pennsylvania mushrooms
1/2 cup butter
1/4 lb. ham, thickly sliced
and cut into strips
1 round Boursin cheese with
fine herbs, cut into sm.
pieces

Philo dough
salt and pepper

Coarsely chop mushrooms and
set aside. Preheat oven to 375
degrees F. Melt butter and sauté
mushrooms. Remove mushrooms
and set aside. Lightly coat a pie
pan with some of the melted butter
and cover with 1 philo leaf. Dab
the leaf with melted butter. Repeat
until there are four leaves on the
bottom of the pie pan.

Add mushrooms to the pie pan.
Season with salt and pepper to
taste. Sprinkle with cheese evenly
over the mushrooms. Season to
taste. Sprinkle ham over cheese
season to taste.

Cover with four more philo
leaves, again spreading melted
butter between each leaf. Roll the
corners of the leaves in toward the
center of the pie. Brush top of pie
with melted butter. Bake for 20
minutes at 375° F. or until pastry
puffs up. This mushroom pie can
be served hot or at room
temperature.

Yields: 4 servings

MARINATED MAINE SARDINES

3 cans (3 3/4 or 4 ozs.
each) Maine sardines
3/4 cup sour cream
1/4 cup half and half cream
1/4 cup tarragon vinegar
2 tbs. lemon juice
2 tbs. dry white wine, optional
1 clove garlic, crushed
1/2 tsp. horseradish
1/2 tsp. salt
1/2 cup thinly sliced onion

1 cup thinly sliced peeled
cucumber
6 lettuce cups
paprika

Drain sardines and arrange in a
single layer in a shallow baking
dish. Combine cream, vinegar,
lemon juice, wine, garlic,
horseradish, and salt. Separate
onion slices into rings. Add onion
and cucumber. Mix thoroughly.
Spread over sardines. Chill
overnight. Arrange in lettuce cups
and sprinkle with paprika.

Yields: 6 servings

ANTIPASTO MINI-SANDWICHES

12 ozs. thinly sliced cooked
lean roast beef
1/2 cup Italian dressing,
divided
1 loaf Vienna bread,
unsliced (8 ozs.)
2 tbs. chopped ripe olives
6 Boston lettuce leaves
6 tomato slices cut 1/4 inch
thick
6 onion slices cut 1/8 inch
thick
6 green bell pepper rings
cut 1/4 inch thick
6 slices provolone cheese (4
ozs. total)

Place beef in plastic bag. Add
1/3 cup of the dressing, turning
to coat beef. Close bag securely;
marinate in refrigerator 1 – 2
hours.

Cut bread lengthwise in half.
Combine remaining dressing and
olives; spoon over bottom half of
bread.

5

To assemble, place lettuce, tomato, onion, green pepper and cheese in layers on bottom half of bread. Remove beef from marinade; arrange over cheese. Cover with top half of bread. To serve, cut into slices.

Yields: 6 servings

INFORMAL FONDUE PARTY

3 tbs. butter or margarine
1 cup finely chopped onion
1 clove garlic, minced or juice
2 cups cooked dry baby limas
2 cans (8 oz.) tomato sauce or 1 can each green chile salsa and tomato sauce
1/2 lb. (2 cups) diced or coarsely shredded sharp cheese
1 to 2 dashes bottled hot salsa

In a large heavy saucepan on a range burner, cook onion and garlic in butter until translucent, don't burn. Mash 1 cup of the beans with a fork and add, along with the remaining whole beans, to the onions. Add tomato sauce and salsa. Over a low heat stir in cheese, a handful at a time. Keep stirring until cheese is melted and mixture is hot.

Transfer mixture to a fondue pot over low to medium heat. Serve with fondue forks and chunks of French bread and an assortment of other dunkables such as cocktail franks, strips of green pepper, celery, carrot sticks and chunks of apple and let everyone dip in.

Yields: 5 super size or up to 10 snack size servings

ARTICHOKE AND BEEF SKEWERS

1 lb. deli roast beef, sliced 1/8 inch thick
1/4 cup prepared fat-free Italian dressing
2 cans (14 ozs. each) quartered artichoke hearts
1 basket cherry tomatoes, cut in half
1 can (6 ozs.) sm. pitted ripe olives, drained (optional)
1/4 cup prepared fat-free Italian dressing

Place deli roast beef in utility dish; add 1/4 cup dressing, turning to coat.

In large bowl, combine artichoke hearts, tomatoes, olives, if desired, and remaining dressing; toss to coat.

Remove beef from dressing (1 slice at a time); roll up tightly from wide end. Cut into 3/4 inch wide pinwheels.

To assemble, alternately thread two beef pinwheels, two artichoke pieces, two tomato halves and two olives, if desired, on each of twenty-four 6 inch bamboo skewers. Serve immediately or cover and refrigerate until serving time.

Yields: 24 appetizers

PETITE BURRITO FRIJOLES

1 lb. dried Idaho red beans, cooked and mashed
2 cups chopped sweet Spanish onions
2 cloves garlic, minced
1/2 cup bacon drippings
1 tsp. Tabasco sauce
salt
1/2 lb. Monterey jack cheese
3 doz. (8 inch) flour tortillas
oil for deep fat frying

Fry beans, onions and garlic in hot bacon drippings until dry and crispy. Season with Tabasco sauce and salt to taste. Cut cheese into 1/2 x 3/8 x 1 inch pieces. Cut each tortilla into four pie shaped wedges. Shape beans into oval shapes around cheese cubes. Wrap with tortillas fastening with toothpicks. Fry in deep fat at 400 degrees F for 3 to 5 minutes, until lightly browned. Remove toothpicks before serving.

To cook beans: Cover beans with 6 cups water and soak overnight. Or, for quick method, bring to boil and boil 2 minutes; cover and let stand 1 hour. Add 2 teaspoons salt and simmer beans until tender, 1 1/2 to 2 hours. Drain.

Yields: 12 dozen burritos

MEATBALLS IN RED PEPPER SAUCE

1 recipe cooked appetizer-size Savory Meatballs
1 tbs. olive oil
1 med. onion, finely chopped
3 cloves garlic, crushed
1 cup ready-to-serve beef broth
2 tsps. cornstarch
2 jars (7 ozs. each) roasted red peppers, rinsed, drained, finely chopped
1/2 cup dry white wine
2 tbs. tomato paste
3/4 tsp. dried thyme leaves
Savory meatballs:
2 lbs. lean ground beef
1 cup soft bread crumbs
2 eggs
1/4 cup finely chopped onion
2 cloves garlic, crushed
1 tsp. salt
1/4 tsp. pepper

In large nonstick skillet, heat oil over medium heat until hot. Add onion and garlic; cook and stir 2 to 3 minutes or until tender.

Combine broth and cornstarch; add to skillet with red peppers, wine, tomato paste and thyme. Bring to a boil; reduce heat to medium-low. Simmer 10 to 12 minutes or until slightly thickened, stirring occasionally.

Add meatballs to skillet; continue to cook until meatballs are heated through, stirring occasionally.

Savory meatballs: Heat oven to 350 degrees F. In large bowl, combine all ingredients, mixing lightly but thoroughly.

For 64 appetizer-size meatballs: Shape beef mixture into 64

(1 inch) meatballs; place on rack in broiler pan.

Bake in 350 degrees F oven 18 to 20 minutes or until no longer pink and juices run clear.

Yields: 64 appetizers

PINTO PARTY PATE'

1 1/2 cups mashed cooked Idaho pinto beans
1 package (3 oz.) cream cheese, softened
1/4 cup minced green onion
2 ozs. chopped green chilies
1 tsp. Worcestershire sauce
1/8 tsp. Tabasco sauce
1/2 tsp. salt
1/8 tsp. garlic salt
chopped parsley

Combine pinto beans with cream cheese, onion, chilies and seasonings. Chill in a bowl lined with wax paper. Shape into a ball. Roll in chopped parsley. Serve as a spread with crisp crackers.

Yields: 8 to 10 servings

BEEF BUTTERFINGERS

12 boneless beef chuck top blade steaks, cut 3/4 inch thick
1 1/2 lbs. fresh mushrooms, sliced
1/2 cup unsalted butter, divided
1/4 cup warm brandy
2 tbs. Madeira wine
2 tbs. dry sherry
2 tbs. all-purpose flour
1 tbs. prepared mustard
1/2 tsp. garlic salt
1/2 tsp. pepper
Please DO eat the daisies garnish:
12 green onions
12 slivers carrot (1/4 x 1/16 inch)

Prepare "please DO eat the daisies garnish. Divide each steak into 2 pieces, following natural seam and removing connective tissue between pieces. Refrigerate.

Cook mushrooms in 1/4 cup butter in large frying pan, 8 to 10 minutes, stirring occasionally. Add reserved chopped green onion; continue cooking 1 to 2 minutes, stirring constantly. Add warm brandy; carefully ignite. Shake pan until flame is extinguished. Add Madeira and sherry; stir in flour, mustard, garlic salt and pepper. Cook over low heat, stirring constantly, until slightly thickened. Keep warm.

Quickly brown steaks (in batches) in remaining butter in large frying pan over medium heat 3 minutes per side for rare. Transfer steaks to warm serving platter.

Add 3 tablespoons water to drippings in frying pan, stirring constantly. Stir in mushroom sauce; heat through. Pour over steaks. Scatter onion daisies over steaks and serve immediately.

Please DO eat the daisies garnish: Cut each green onion into 6 inch length; chop remaining green ends and reserve for sauce. Remove outer skin from onions and carefully cut off tip of bulb. Cut thin slits lengthwise in bulb of each onion to fringe, forming "petals." Insert a sliver of carrot into the center of each fringed onion (for the "stamen"). Place onions, blossom side down, in ice eater and refrigerate (to crisp onion and curl petals).

Yields: 6 servings

CHINESE BEANS PASTRIES

2 cups cooked Idaho red or pinto beans
1/2 cup sugar
1/4 tsp. salt
2 tbs. butter
1/4 cup milk
1 1/2 cups flour
1/2 tsp. salt
1/2 cup shortening
5 to 6 tbs. water
1 egg yolk, beaten with 2 tbs. water

For filling, mash and strain beans. Combine with sugar, and 1/4 teaspoon salt, butter and milk. Cook, stirring until sugar dissolves.

Cool. For pastry, sift flour with 1/2 teaspoon salt. Cut in shortening. Add warm water to form ball. Divide into 8 parts. Roll each into a 4 inch square. Top with mound of bean filling. Fold in all corners and seal. Place on cookie sheet. Brush with egg yolk mixture. Bake at 425 degrees F for 15 to 20 minutes or until golden. Cool.

Yields: 8 pastries

FRENCH HERB PATTIES

1/2 lb. ground beef (80 percent lean)
1/4 tsp. each coarse ground black pepper, dried rosemary and thyme leaves
1 tbs. butter
2 sm. onions, sliced and separated into rings
1 tbs. Dijon-style mustard

Shape ground beef into 2 patties, each 1/2 inch thick. Combine pepper, rosemary and thyme; gently press into both sides of patties.

Melt butter in small nonstick skillet over medium heat. Add onions; cook 6 to 8 minutes or until transparent and tender. Stir in mustard. Divide onions evenly between 2 plates; keep warm.

Place patties in same pan; cook 4 minutes. Pour off drippings. Turn patties; continue cooking 4 minutes or to desired doneness. Season with salt, if desired. Place patties over onions; top with additional Dijon-style mustard, if desired.

Yields: 2 servings

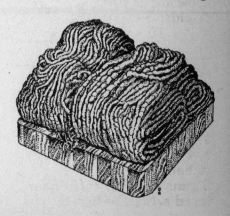

TWO-BITE LITTLE BEAN CROQUETTES

2 cups cooked Idaho red, pink or pinto beans, drained and mashed white hot
2 tbs. minced onion
1/2 tsp. oregano
1 can (4 oz.) peeled green chilies, drained and chopped fine
1/4 cup grated parmesan cheese
1/4 lb. sharp-aged natural cheddar, provolone or Monterey jack cheese
fine bread crumbs for breading
1 egg, beaten with 1 tbs. water
oil or shortening for deep frying

Combine mashed beans, seasonings, parmesan cheese, adding salt if necessary. Put in refrigerator to chill thoroughly before shaping into small balls. Place a small cube of cheese of your choice in the center of each. Cover cheese with bean mixture. Roll these small balls in bread crumbs, then in egg-water mixture, and again in bread crumbs. This may be done early in the day or the day before. Just before serving, fry in deep fat or oil heated to 380 degrees F. When brown, drain on paper towels. May be served from chafing dish or container over candle warmer so they will be hot. Provide cocktail picks. This mixture may be made into 6 to 8 croquettes to be used as a main course dish.

Yields: 6 to 8 servings

BLACK-EYE SALAD

1 lb. (2 cups) dry black-eyed peas cooked the savory way
2 jars (4 oz. size) marinated artichoke hearts
1 cup sliced raw radishes and/or carrots
1 cup thinly sliced celery
1/2 cup sliced green onions

Put beans in bowl and drizzle artichoke marinade over them. Cut hearts to bite size and add to beans with radishes, carrots, celery and onion. Add your favorite French or Italian dressing to cover; pepper to taste. Chill before serving, and spoon onto lettuce leaves.

Savory cooking method: Drain and rinse soaked black-eyed peas (4 to 5 cups); add 6 cups hot water, 2 tablespoons shortening, 2 teaspoons onion salt and 1/2 teaspoon garlic salt, 1 tablespoon chicken stock base, and 1/4 teaspoon white pepper. Simmer gently until barely tender. Drain while hot; cool beans quickly, uncovered.

Yields: 8 servings

BEEF AND PASTA SATAY

1 lb. boneless beef top sirloin or top round steak, cut 1 inch thick or flank steak
2 tbs. prepared teriyaki sauce
6 ozs. uncooked vermicelli or thin spaghetti
vegetable cooking spray
1/2 cup seeded and chopped cucumber
Peanut butter sauce:
3 tbs. prepared teriyaki sauce
2 tbs. creamy peanut butter
1 tbs. water
1/8 to 1/4 tsp. ground ginger
1/8 to 1/4 tsp. crushed red pepper

Trim fat from beef steak. Cut steak lengthwise in half and then crosswise into 1/8 inch thick strips. Add 2 tablespoons teriyaki sauce to beef; toss to coat.

Cook vermicelli according to package directions. Meanwhile in medium bowl, combine sauce ingredients, mixing until well blended. Add hot vermicelli; toss to coat. Keep warm.

Spray large nonstick skillet with cooking spray. Heat over medium-high heat until hot. Add beef (1/2 at a time) and stir-fry 1 to 2 minutes or until outside surface is no longer pink. (Do not overcook.) Add to vermicelli mixture; toss lightly. Sprinkle with cucumber; serve immediately.

Yields: 5 servings

HONEY NUT BRIE

1/4 cup honey
1/4 cup coarsely chopped pecans
1 tbs. brandy (optional)
1 wheel (14 ozs.) Brie cheese (about 5 inch diameter)

Combine honey, pecans and brandy, if desired, in small bowl. Place cheese on large round ovenproof platter or 9 inch pie plate.

Bake in preheated 500 degrees F oven 4 to 5 minutes or until cheese softens. Drizzle honey mixture over top of cheese. Bake 2 to 3 minutes longer or until topping is thoroughly heated. Do not melt cheese.

Tip: Serve as a party dish with crackers, tart apple wedges and seedless grapes.

Yields: 16 to 20 servings

BEAN SALAD, CAESAR STYLE

1 1/2 cups cooked Idaho Great Northern (lg. white) beans
3 med. heads romaine lettuce
1 cup garlic-flavored olive oil
3 tbs. red wine vinegar
2 to 3 tbs. lemon juice (1 lemon)
1 one-minute coddled egg
freshly ground pepper
salt
dash of Worcestershire
6 tbs. grated parmesan cheese
1 cup Caesar croutons
7 or 8 anchovy strips

Beans: Why not cook enough to have beans soup or a casserole of beans? Soak overnight 2 cups Idaho Great Northern beans in 6 cups cold water. In a hurry? Add the beans to measured amount of water, bring rapidly to the boiling point. Boil 2 minutes. cover. Let stand 1 hour. To cook, for either method, bring beans and soaking water to boiling point, adding 1 tablespoon butter to keep down foaming and 2 teaspoons salt. Reduce heat. Cover tightly. Simmer until tender but not mushy, a bit over an hour. Drain well, reserving liquid. Take out 2 cups cooked beans, cover, chill in refrigerator. Return liquid to the remaining 4 cups of beans to use in other ways.

Greens: the original Caesar salad uses romaine lettuce, brittle-crisp and clean-tearing, with distinct flavor. Other greens or a mixture of greens may be used but likely choice will depend on what is in the market. Iceberg lettuce has good texture and flavor. It combines well with romaine. Wash greens 24 hours earlier if possible. Gently shake off moisture using a tea towel. Wrap in fresh towels and refrigerate. Leaves will be dry and crisp the next day. When serving times comes, tear greens rather than cutting. Chill bowl and salad plates.

Garlic-flavored salad oil: slice 6 cloves of garlic lengthwise into quarters. Let stand 1 or 2 days in 1 cup olive oil or vegetable oil or half of each. Strain.

Caesar croutons: remove crusts from sliced sandwich bread. Cut each slice in 5 strips one way, then across 5 times to make squares. Spread on cookie sheet. Pour just a little of the garlic oil over. Heat in a very slow oven (250 degrees F) an hour or more or until very dry, so that they will stay crunchy when tossed with the other ingredients. Sprinkle with parmesan cheese. Store in covered jar in refrigerator. Heat in oven just before using. Some like to use sour dough French bread.

The egg: some like to use the raw egg in the making of the salad. It should be "cackle-fresh." Others like a coddled egg, which is a "boiled egg," whatever method you like, with time shortened to 1 minute only. Do this just before needed.

Yields: 4 to 6 servings

CALICO BEAN SALAD

2 cups cooked Great Northern or sm. white beans
2 cups cooked or canned dark or light red kidney beans
2 cups canned or cooked garbanzos
1 1/2 to 2 cups French, Italian or vinaigrette dressing (bottled or homemade)
salt and coarse black pepper
tomato wedges
onion rings

Drain beans, mix together lightly, cover with dressing. Refrigerate for several hours. When ready to serve, mix again. Taste and add more seasonings or a little vinegar if needed. Serve in a large bowl and garnish with tomato wedges and onion rings.

Yields: 8 to 10 servings

MAINE SARDINE CANAPÉS

3 cans (3 3/4 or 4 ozs. each) Maine sardines
1/2 cup butter or margarine, softened
2 tbs. prepared mustard
10 slices sandwich bread
pimiento strips

Drain sardines and split in half lengthwise. Combine butter and mustard. Spread bread with mustard-butter. Remove crusts. Cut each slice of bread into thirds. Place a sardine half on each piece of bread. Garnish with pimiento strips.

Yields: 30 canapés

RED BEANS SALAD, IDAHO STYLE

2 to 2 1/2 cups grown in Idaho cooked or canned red beans
1 1/2 cups coarsely cut celery
1 cup sliced on the bias sweet Spanish onions
1/2 cup sweet pickles, sliced
1/2 cup sm. cubes of sharp cheddar cheese, if desired
1 tbs. sweet pickle liquid
1/2 cup French dressing

Drain cooked or canned red beans. Combine with other ingredients, adding coarse grind black pepper and salt as needed. Allow to stand in the refrigerator several hours or overnight. Garnish with onion rings, hard cooked eggs slices, if desired.

Yields: 4 servings

BUFFET SALAD

2 cups cooked and drained beans
1 clove of garlic, minced
1/4 cup olive oil
1/4 cup snipped parsley
2 tbs. diced green or sweet red pepper or canned pimiento
2 tbs. dry white table wine
1 tsp. red or white wine vinegar
salt and coarse-grind black pepper, to taste
salami, cut in thin strips

Add garlic to olive oil. Add other ingredients except salami, mixing carefully. Cover and chill. To serve, garnish with strips of salami and ripe olives.

Yields: 3 to 4 servings

BREADS
MUFFINS & ROLLS

RAISIN SCONES

3 cups Bisquick Original
baking mix
1/2 cup raisins
1/3 cup sugar
4 eggs
sugar

Heat oven to 400 degrees F. Mix baking mix, raisins, 1/3 cup sugar and 3 eggs until moistened. Turn dough onto surface well dusted with baking mix; roll lightly in baking mix to coat. Roll dough into 9 inch circle. Cut into 12 wedges with knife dipped in baking mix. Place wedges, alternating wide and narrow ends, about 2 inches apart on ungreased cookie sheet. Beat remaining egg with fork; brush over tops of wedges. Sprinkle with sugar.

High altitude directions (3500 to 6500 feet): Heat oven to 425 degrees F.

Yields: 12 scones

BANANA-NUT BREAD

1 1/3 cups mashed bananas
(about 2 lg.)
2/3 cup sugar
1/3 cup vegetable oil
1/4 cup milk
3 eggs
1/2 tsp. vanilla
2 cups Bisquick Original
baking mix
1/2 cup Gold Medal all-
purpose flour
1/2 cup chopped nuts

Heat oven to 350 degrees F. Grease bottom only of loaf pan, 9 x 5 x 3 inches. Mix bananas, sugar, oil, milk, eggs and vanilla in large bowl. Stir in remaining ingredients. Pour into pan. Bake about 1 hour or until toothpick inserted in center comes out clean. Cool 10 minutes. Loosen sides of loaf from pan; remove from pan. Cool completely before slicing.

High altitude directions: (3500 to 6500 feet): Heat oven to 375 degrees F. Decrease sugar to 1/3 cup and baking mix to 1 3/4 cups. Increase flour to 2/3 cup. Bake about 45 minutes.

Yields: 8 to 10 servings

HONEY CLOVERLEAFS

1 package (16 oz.) hot roll
mix
6 tbs. honey, divided
1/4 cup butter or margarine
1 tsp. grated lemon peel
1 cup sliced almonds

Prepare hot roll mix in large bowl according to package directions, adding 2 tablespoons honey to liquid. Cover kneaded dough with bowl and let rest 5 minutes.

Melt butter in small saucepan over medium heat. Add remaining 4 tablespoons honey; stir in lemon peel.

Roll dough into 36 balls (about 1 to 1 1/2 inch diameter each). Form clusters of three balls; dip each in honey mixture then in almonds. Place each cluster in well greased muffin cup. Cover and set in warm place to rise about 30 minutes or until doubled in bulk.

Bake in preheated 350 degrees F oven 15 to 20 minutes or until lightly browned. Brush with honey mixture, if desired. Remove from pan and cool slightly on wire rack. Serve warm or cool.

Variation: Dough may be dipped in honey mixture then in chopped parsley, rosemary or other fresh herbs.

Yields: 1 dozen rolls

COLUSA CORN MUFFINS

3/4 cup plain yogurt
1/3 cup butter or marga-
rine, melted
1/2 cup honey
2 eggs
3/4 cup all-purpose flour
3/4 cup whole wheat flour
3/4 cup cornmeal
2 1/2 tsps. baking powder
1/2 tsp. salt
1/2 tsp. baking soda

Beat together yogurt, butter, honey and eggs in small bowl. Set aside. Combine flours, cornmeal, baking powder, salt and baking soda in large bowl. Add honey mixture. Stir just enough to barely moisten flour. Do not overmix. Spoon batter into paper-lined or greased muffin cups.

Bake in preheated 350 degrees F oven 20 to 25 minutes or until wooden toothpick inserted near center comes out clean. Remove from pan; cool slightly on wire racks. Serve warm.

Yields: 1 dozen muffins

KOLACKY

1/2 cup wheat germ
1 package (16 oz.) roll mix

1 cup warm milk (110 degrees F to 115 degrees F)
2 eggs
2 cups pitted chopped prunes
1 med. orange, unpeeled, chopped (about 2/3 cup)
1/3 cup honey
3/4 cup water
honey for glaze (optional)

Add wheat germ to flour mixture from hot roll mix in medium bowl. Dissolve yeast from hot roll mix in warm milk in large bowl; add eggs and mix well. Beat in flour mixture. Knead dough on floured board 5 to 10 minutes or until smooth and elastic. Shape dough into a ball and place in greased medium bowl; turn to grease all sides. Cover bowl and set in warm place to rise about 1 hour or until doubled in bulk.

Combine prunes, orange, honey and water in small saucepan. Cook and stir over medium heat until mixture comes to a boil; simmer 10 minutes or until thickened. Cool.

Punch down dough and cut into 18 pieces. Pat each piece of dough into 3 inch rounds and place on greased baking sheet. Make indentation in center of each round; fill with heaping tablespoonfuls of cooled prune mixture. Cover and set in warm place to rise about 30 minutes or until doubled in bulk.

Bake in preheated 375 degrees F oven 10 minutes or until dough browns. Brush with honey while still warm, if desired. Serve warm or cool.

Yields: 1 1/2 dozen buns

HONEY OATMEAL RICOTTA MUFFINS

1 egg
1 cup whole milk ricotta cheese
3/4 cup honey
1/3 cup butter or margarine, softened
1 1/4 cups quick-cooking rolled oats, divided

2 tbs. grated orange peel
1/2 tsp. baking soda
1 cup self-rising flour

Beat egg in large bowl; stir in ricotta cheese, honey and butter. Mix in 1 cup oats, orange peel and baking soda. Slowly stir in flour. Spoon batter into greased and floured or paper-lined muffin cups. Sprinkle remaining 1/4 cup oats over muffins.

Bake in preheated 375 degrees F oven about 25 minutes or until wooden toothpick inserted near center comes out clean. Remove from pan; cool slightly on wire racks. Serve warm.

Yields: 1 1/2 dozen muffins

HONEY CURRANT SCONES

2 1/2 cups all-purpose flour
2 tsps. grated orange peel
1 tsp. baking powder
1/2 tsp. baking soda
1/2 tsp. salt
1/2 cup butter or margarine
1/2 cup currants
1/2 cup dairy sour cream
1/3 cup honey
1 egg, slightly beaten

Combine flour, orange peel, baking powder, baking soda and salt in large bowl; mix well. Cut in butter until mixture resembles size of small peas. Add currants. Combine sour cream, honey and egg in medium bowl; mix well. Stir honey mixture into dry mixture to form soft dough. Knead dough on lightly floured surface 10 times. Shape dough into 8 inch square.

Cut into 4 squares; cut each square diagonally into 2 triangles. Place triangles on greased baking sheet.

Bake in preheated 375 degrees F oven 15 to 20 minutes or until golden brown. Serve warm.

Yields: 8 scones

BUSY BEE BRAN MUFFINS

3 eggs
1/2 cup honey
1/2 cup vegetable oil
3 1/2 cups bran cereal
1 1/2 cups milk
2 1/4 cups all-purpose flour
4 tsps. baking soda
1 tsp. ground cinnamon

Beat eggs, honey and oil in small bowl until blended; set aside. Combine bran cereal with milk in large bowl; let stand 5 minutes. Add egg mixture to cereal mixture and mix lightly. Combine flour, baking soda and cinnamon in medium bowl; mix well. Stir into bran mixture. Do not overmix. Spoon batter into paper-lined or greased muffin cups.

Bake in preheated 350 degrees F oven 25 to 30 minutes or until wooden toothpick inserted near center comes out clean. Remove from pan; cool slightly on wire rack. Serve warm.

Yields: about 1 1/2 dozen muffins

FOCACCIA (ITALIAN FLATBREAD)

2 1/2 to 3 cups Gold Medal Better for Bread flour
1 tbs. dried rosemary leaves, crushed, or 2 tbs. snipped fresh rosemary
2 tsps. salt
1 package regular or quick-acting active dry yeast (If using quick-acting yeast, omit first rise. After kneading, cover dough and let rest 10 minutes. Press dough in pan; continue as directed.)
3 tbs. olive or vegetable oil

1 cup hot water (120 degrees F to 130 degrees F)
olive or vegetable oil
ground pepper, if desired

Mix 1 1/2 cups of the flour, the rosemary, salt and yeast in large bowl. Add 3 tablespoons oil and the hot water. Beat on low speed 30 seconds, scraping bowl constantly. Beat on medium speed 1 minute, scraping bowl frequently. Stir in enough remaining flour to make dough easy to handle.

Turn dough onto lightly floured surface. Knead 5 to 8 minutes or until smooth and elastic. Place in greased bowl; turn greased side up. Cover; let rise in warm place about 1 hour or until double. (Dough is ready if indentation remains when touched.)

Punch down dough. Brush 12 inch pizza pan or large cookie sheet with oil. Press dough in pizza pan or flatten into 12 inch circle on cookie sheet. Make depressions, with fingers about 2 inches apart, into dough. Brush with oil; sprinkle with pepper. Let rise uncovered in warm place 30 minutes.

Heat oven to 400 degrees F. Bake 20 to 25 minutes or until golden brown. Brush with additional oil. Serve warm.

High altitude directions (3500 to 6500 feet): Rising times may be slightly shorter.

Yields: 1 focaccia

BLUEBERRY BREAD

Heat oven to 400 degrees F. Grease bottom only of loaf pan, 8 1/2 x 1/2 x 2 or 9 x 5 x 3 inches, with shortening. Prepare 1 package Betty Crocker wild blueberry muffin mix as directed on package for muffins—except decrease water to 3/4 cup. Pour into pan. Bake 8-inch loaf 40 to 50 minutes, 9-inch loaf 35 to 45 minutes or until toothpick inserted in center comes out clean and top of loaf is deep golden brown. Cool 15 minutes; remove from pan.

Cool completely before slicing.

Blueberry-banana bread: Prepare blueberry bread as directed—except fold in 1/2 cup mashed ripe banana with the blueberries.

Blueberry-lemon-poppy seed bread: Prepare blueberry bread as directed—except fold in 1 tablespoon poppy seed and 1 teaspoon lemon juice with the blueberries.

High altitude directions (3500 to 6500 feet): No changes needed.

Yields: 6 to 8 servings

HOMESTYLE WHITE BREAD

2 packages active dry yeast
1 1/4 cups water (105 degrees F to 115 degrees F)
1 cup warm water
3 tbs. sugar
1 tbs. salt
3 tbs. shortening
6 to 6 1/2 cups Gold Medal Better for Bread flour
margarine or butter, softened

Dissolve yeast in 1 1/4 cups warm water in large bowl. Stir in 1 cup warm water, the sugar, salt, shortening and 3 1/2 cups of the flour. Beat until smooth. Mix in enough remaining flour to make dough easy to handle.

Turn dough onto lightly floured surface; knead about 10 minutes or until smooth and elastic. Place in greased bowl; turn greased side up. Cover; let rise in warm place about 1 hour or until double. (Dough is ready if indentation remains when touched.)

Grease 2 loaf pans, 9 x 5 x 3 inches. Punch down dough; divide in half. Round up; place on lightly floured surface. Cover with inverted bowls; let rest 15 to 20 minutes. Roll each half into rectangle, 18 x 9 inches. Fold into thirds. Roll dough into rectangle, 13 x 8 inches, pressing out as many air bubbles as possible. Roll up tightly, beginning at 8 inch end. Pinch edge of dough into roll to

seal well; press in ends of roll. Press each end with side of hand to seal; fold ends under. Place loaves, seam sides down, in pans. Brush lightly with margarine. Let rise about 1 hour or until double.

Heat oven to 425 degrees F. Place loaves on low rack so that tops of pans are in center of oven. Pans should not touch each other or sides of oven. Bake 25 to 30 minutes or until loaves are deep golden and sound hollow when tapped. Immediately remove from pans. Brush tops of loaves with margarine; cool on wire racks.

Cinnamon-raisin bread: Mix in 1 1/2 cups raisins with the second addition of flour. Mix 1/4 cup sugar and 2 teaspoons ground cinnamon. Sprinkle each rectangle, 13 x 8 inches, with 1 tablespoon water and half of the sugar mixture.

Raisin bread: Mix in 1 1/2 cups raisins with the second addition of flour.

High altitude directions (3500 to 6500 feet): Decrease flour to 5 1/2 to 6 cups. Rising times may be slightly shorter.

Yields: 2 loaves

SAN LUIS POTATO BREAD

2 tbs. sugar
2 packages active dry yeast
8 cups all-purpose flour (about)
1/4 cup butter or margarine
1 1/2 cups mashed Colorado potatoes
1 tsp. salt
1/2 cup water
1 1/2 cups milk
2 eggs

In large bowl, combine sugar, salt, yeast and 1 1/2 cups flour. In 2 quart saucepan, mix water, mashed potatoes and 1 1/2 cups milk; add butter; over low heat, heat until very warm (120 degrees F to 130 degrees F), stirring often. (Butter does not need to melt.)

With mixer at low speed, gradually beat liquid into dry ingredients just until blended; beat in eggs. At medium speed, beat 2 minutes, occasionally scraping bowl. Beat in 1 cup flour to make a thick batter; continue beating 2 minutes, scraping the bowl often. Stir in enough additional flour (about 3 1/4 cups) to make a soft dough.

On well floured surface, knead dough about 10 minutes, until smooth and elastic, kneading in about 1 1/2 cups flour. Shape into ball; place in greased large bowl, turning to grease top. Cover; let rise until doubled, about 1 hour.

Punch down dough; turn onto lightly floured surface; cut in half; cover; let rise 15 minutes.

Grease two 2 quart round, straight-sided, shallow casserole. Shape 1 piece of dough into ball; place in casserole. Cut 2 parallel slashes on top. Repeat. Cover; let rise until doubled, about 1 hour.

Preheat oven to 400 degrees F. Brush each loaf with milk. Bake 40 minutes or until well browned and loaves sound hollow when tapped with fingers. Remove loaves to cool on wire racks.

Yields: 2 loaves

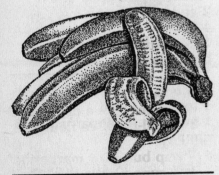

HONEY WHOLE WHEAT BREAD

2 packages active dry yeast
2 1/4 cups warm water
(105 degrees F to 115 degrees F), divided
3 cups whole wheat flour
1 cup finely shredded carrots
1 cup mashed ripe bananas
1/2 cup butter or margarine, softened
1/3 cup honey
1 tbs. salt
1/2 tsp. ground cinnamon
4 to 6 cups all-purpose flour
2 tbs. melted butter or margarine

Dissolve yeast in 1/2 cup warm water in large bowl. Stir in whole wheat flour, remaining 1 3/4 cups warm water, carrots, bananas, 1/2 cup softened butter, honey, salt and cinnamon; beat until smooth using an electric mixer. Mix in enough all-purpose flour to make a soft dough.

Knead dough on lightly floured surface about 10 minutes or until smooth and elastic. Shape dough into a ball. Place in greased large bowl; turn to grease all sides. Cover bowl and set in warm place to rise about 1 hour or until doubled in bulk.

Punch down dough; divide into two equal pieces. Roll each piece on lightly floured surface into 18 x 9 inch rectangle. Overlap the sides, folding into thirds to form 6 x 9 inch rectangle. Roll each piece tightly from 6 inch side, jelly roll style. Pinch ends and seams to seal; place in greased 9 x 5 x 3 inch loaf pan. Brush tops with 2 tablespoons melted butter. Cover and set in warm place to rise about 1 hour or until doubled in bulk.

Bake in preheated 375 degrees F oven 40 to 45 minutes or until loaves sound hollow when tapped and crust is brown. Remove from pans and cool on wire racks.

Yields: 2 loaves

DENVER BISCUITS

2 cups scalded milk
1 package yeast
1/2 tsp. baking powder
6 to 7 cups flour
1/2 cup mashed Colorado potatoes
1/2 cup shortening
1 tsp. salt
1/2 cup water
1/2 tsp. soda

Scald milk and shortening and let cool to 115 degrees F. Add yeast, salt, sugar and let stand until foamy (about 5 minutes). Add mashed potatoes and flour, making a soft dough. Let rise 2 hours. Add soda and baking powder and knead as for bread, leaving the dough soft. Set aside one hour. Roll out about 3/4 inch thick and cut with a biscuit cutter. Let rise again for 30 minutes. Bake in a 350 degrees F oven until light brown.

Yields: 5 to 6 dozen biscuits

ROCKY MOUNTAIN ICE BOX ROLLS

3 tbs. shortening
2 cups hot water
6 1/2 to 7 cups flour
1 cup mashed Colorado potatoes
1 package dry yeast, dissolved in 1/4 cup lukewarm water
1/2 cup sugar
1 egg
1 tsp. salt

Beat sugar, egg and shortening. Add potatoes and hot water, salt and a little flour. Then add yeast and the rest of the flour. Let rise until doubled and punch dough down. The dough then can be refrigerated and used as needed. To bake, shape dough into rolls as you desire. Let rise and bake in a 350 degrees F oven for 20 to 25 minutes until rolls are brown.

Yields: 5 to 6 dozen rolls

ITALIAN BAKED BEAN CASSEROLE

2 cups great northern (lg. white) beans, uncooked
6 cups water for soaking and cooking
1 1/2 to 2 tsps. salt
1/2 cup olive or other salad oil
1 cup chopped onion
2 cloves garlic, minced
1 to 1 1/2 cups coarsely cut celery
2 tbs. snipped parsley
1/2 tsp. dried thyme, crushed
1/4 tsp. dried sweet basil, crushed
1/4 tsp. coarse grind black pepper
1 cup fresh skinned or solid pack canned tomatoes
2/3 cup bean liquid and tomato juice combined
grated parmesan or romano cheese

To prepare beans: Dry beans cooked without soaking take longer to cook and are not so tender as those soaked overnight or by the hot water method. Why waste fuel?

Overnight method: Cover washed beans with the cold water. Allow to stand overnight—12 to 15 hours. Choose method which best fits your schedule.

Morning method: Cover washed beans with the cold water. Bring to the boiling point over high heat. Boil briskly 2 minutes only. Remove from heat. Cover, let stand 1 hour. Another method is to bring the full amount of water to the boiling point; gradually add beans so that boiling will not stop. Boil beans 2 minutes. Let stand. One seems about as effective as the other.

To cook the beans: Use water in which the beans were soaked. Place over high heat. Add 1 teaspoon butter to keep down foaming. Bring to the boiling point; cover and reduce heat so that water will simmer. Stir carefully a time or two. Always add the salt after 1 hour of cooking, allowing 1 1/2 to 2 teaspoons salt to 2 or 2 1/3 cups (1 pound) of dried beans unless salt pork or smoked meats are in the recipe. Then omit salt until all ingredients are added. The taste test is the best bet.

For the casserole dish, simmer beans 1 1/2 hours or until tender but not mushy. Hardness of water, altitude, type of recipe will make a difference in amount of time.

To make the casserole: Drain cooked beans, saving liquid. There will be about 5 cups cooked beans. Cook onion, garlic, celery in the oil over low heat until tender but not browned. Add parsley, herbs (use twice the amount if you have fresh herbs), tomatoes coarsely cut, and bean liquid lengthened out with tomato juice or water to make 2/3 cup. Heat all to boiling point. Lightly mix into the beans. Bits of ham, Italian sausage or salami may be added to make a one-dish meal. Turn into a 1 1/2 quart casserole or baking dish. This may all be done in the morning or even the day before, and refrigerated until about 1 hour before serving.

Bake, covered with lid or foil, about 50 minutes in a 350 degrees F (moderate) oven. Remove from oven, dust top generously with grated parmesan or romano cheese (shredded cheddar cheese may be used), and return to the oven to bake 10 minutes more, uncovered so that cheese will brown a bit.

Serve piping hot with additional cheese as a side dish, to sprinkle over each serving, if desired. Good partners are a tossed mixed green salad, hot garlic buttered French bread along with roast leg of lamb—hot or cold sliced fresh fruit and assorted cheeses for dessert.

Yields: 6 servings

IMPOSSIBLE HAM 'N SWISS PIE

2 cups cut-up fully cooked smoked ham
1 cup shredded natural Swiss cheese (4 ozs.)
1/3 cup chopped green onions or chopped onion
2 cups milk
4 eggs
1 cup Bisquick Original baking mix
1/4 tsp. salt, if desired
1/8 tsp. pepper
1 tomato, sliced
1 green bell pepper, cut into rings

Heat oven to 400 degrees F. Grease glass pie plate, 10 x 1 1/2 inches. Sprinkle ham, cheese and onions in pie plate. Beat remaining ingredients except tomato and green pepper 15 seconds in blender on high, 1 minute with hand beater or until smooth. Pour into pie plate. Bake 35 to 40 minutes or until knife inserted in center comes out clean. Cool 5 minutes; garnish with tomato and green pepper.

High altitude directions (3500 to 6500 feet): Bake about 45 minutes.

Microwave directions: Prepare as directed—except decrease milk to 1 3/4 cups. Pour into greased microwavable pie plate, 10 x 1 1/2 inches; sprinkle top with paprika before microwaving. Microwave on medium-high (70%) 24 to 28 minutes, rotating plate 1/4 turn every 8 minutes, until knife inserted in center comes out clean (center will be slightly soft). Garnish with tomato and green pepper. Cover with waxed paper; let stand on flat, heatproof surface 10 minutes (do not let stand on wire rack). Sprinkle with additional paprika if desired.

High altitude microwave directions (3500 to 6500 feet): Decrease baking mix to 3/4 cup. Microwave 20 to 24 minutes.

Yields: 6 servings

HARVEST CASSEROLE

1 lb. ground beef
1 package Betty Crocker scalloped or au gratin potatoes
2 med. zucchini, thinly sliced (about 2 cups)
1 cup fresh green beans, cut into 1 inch pieces (frozen cut green beans can be substituted for the fresh green beans)
2 tomatoes, chopped
1/4 cup sliced green onions (with tops)
2 cups water
2/3 cup milk
1 tbs. dried basil leaves
2 tsps. dried parsley
1 tsp. salt
1/4 tsp. pepper

Heat oven to 400 degrees F. Cook ground beef, stirring

occasionally, until brown; drain. Mix beef and remaining ingredients in ungreased 3 quart casserole. Cover and bake about 40 minutes, stirring once, until potatoes are tender.

High altitude directions (3500 to 6500 feet): If using fresh beans, cook beans 15 minutes before assembling casserole. If using fresh or frozen beans, use 2 cups hot water. Omit salt. Increase bake time to 45 to 50 minutes. Stir 1 teaspoon salt into casserole before serving.

Yields: 6 servings

MAINE SARDINE RAREBIT

3 cans (3 3/4 or 4 ozs. each) sardines
4 slices bacon, chopped
1/2 cup chopped green pepper
1/2 cup chopped onion
1 can (10 1/2 oz.) condensed tomato soup
1 cup shredded cheese
1/4 cup half and half cream
1/2 tsp. prepared mustard
6 slices toast

Drain sardines. Place on an 18 inch square of aluminum foil. Seal edges by making double folds in the foil. Heat in a moderate oven, 350 degrees F, for 15 minutes. Fry bacon until crisp. Add green pepper and onion and cook until tender. Add remaining ingredients except toast. Heat until cheese melts, stirring constantly. Place sardines on toast and cover with sauce.

Yields: 6 servings

SUNSHINE BEAN CASSEROLE

2 cups each drained cooked or canned red beans, lg. limas and garbanzos
1 lb. ground beef
1 lg. onion, chopped
1 clove garlic, minced

1/4 cup brown sugar
1 to 2 tbs. prepared mustard
1/2 cup catsup
1 tsp. cumin powder (optional)
1/4 cup red wine (or 1/4 cup water with 3 tbs. vinegar)
salt and pepper to taste

Put drained beans into a 2 1/2 quart casserole; mix lightly and set aside. In large skillet cook ground beef, onions and garlic until meat is lightly browned; stir in remaining ingredients. Add skillet mixture to beans in casserole; mix together. Cover and bake for about an hour at 325 degrees F. Or simmer the mixture in an electric slow cooker on low for 3 to 4 hours.

Yields: 6 to 8 servings

MICROWAVE CHEESEY POTATO CASSEROLE

1/2 cup chopped onions
1/2 cup Swiss cheese, shredded
2 tbs. grated parmesan cheese
1 (10 1/2 oz.) cream of celery soup
3 to 4 cups thinly sliced Colorado potatoes (about 3 med.)
1/4 tsp. pepper
1/4 tsp. dill

In bowl mix together soup, onions, cheese, dill and pepper. Pour into 1 1/2 quart casserole. Add potatoes and mix thoroughly. Microwave at high for 9 to 11 minutes, stirring after 5 minutes. Sprinkle cheese on top before serving.

Yields: 6 to 8 servings

THE WORLD'S BEST CHOCOLATE CAKE

2 cups Gold Medal all-purpose flour (If using self-rising flour, omit baking soda, salt and baking powder.)
2 cups sugar
1/2 cup shortening
3/4 cup water
3/4 cup buttermilk
1 tsp. baking soda
1 tsp. salt
1 tsp. vanilla
1/2 tsp. baking powder
2 eggs
4 ozs. melted unsweetened chocolate (cool)

Heat oven to 350 degrees F. Grease and flour 12 cup bundt cake pan, rectangular pan, 13 x 9 x 2 inches, 3 round pans, 8 x 1 1/2 inches, or 2 round pans, 9 x 1 1/2 inches. Beat all ingredients in large bowl 30 seconds on low speed, scraping bowl constantly. Beat on high speed 3 minutes, scraping bowl occasionally. Pour into pan(s). Bake bundt cake 50 to 55 minutes, rectangle 40 to 45 minutes, rounds 30 to 35 minutes or until toothpick inserted in center comes out clean; cool 10 minutes. Invert bundt cake pan onto heatproof serving plate. Remove rounds from pans.

High altitude directions (3500 to 6500 feet): Heat oven to 375 degrees F. Decrease sugar to 1 1/2 cups and baking powder to 1/4 teaspoon. For self-rising flour, not recommended for use.)

Yields: 8 to 10 servings

SWEET YELLOW CAKE

2 1/4 cups Gold Medal all-purpose flour (If using self-rising flour, omit baking powder and salt.)
1 1/2 cup sugar
3 1/2 tsps. baking powder
1 tsp. salt
1 1/4 cups milk
3 eggs
1/2 cup shortening
1 tsp. vanilla

Heat oven to 350 degrees F. Grease and flour 2 round pans, 9 x 1 1/2 inches, or 3 round pans, 8 x 1 1/2 inches, or 1 rectangular pan, 13 x 9 x 2 inches. Beat all ingredients in large bowl on low speed 30 seconds, scraping bowl constantly. Beat on high speed 3 minutes, scraping bowl occasionally. Pour into pan(s). Bake 9 inch rounds 30 to 35 minutes, 8 inch rounds 20 to 25 minutes, rectangle 40 to 45 minutes or until toothpick inserted in center comes out clean or until cake springs back when touched lightly in center. Cool layers 10 minutes; remove from pans.

Cupcakes: Line 36 medium muffin cups, 2 1/2 x 1 1/4 inches. Fill each cup 1/2 full. Bake 20 minutes.

Eggnog cake: Add 1 teaspoon ground nutmeg and 1/4 teaspoon ground ginger; substitute 1 teaspoon rum flavoring for the vanilla.

High altitude directions (3500 to 6500 feet): Heat oven to 375 degrees F. Decrease sugar to 1 1/4 cups and baking powder to 2 1/2 teaspoons. Bake 9 inch rounds 25 to 30 minutes, cupcake 15 to 20 minutes.

Yields: 8 to 10 servings or 36 cupcakes

LIGHT AND AIRY POUND CAKE

2 3/4 cups sugar
1 1/4 cups (2 1/2 sticks) margarine or butter, softened
1 tsp. vanilla
5 eggs
3 cups Gold Medal all-purpose flour
1 tsp. baking powder
1/4 tsp. salt
1 cup evaporated milk

Heat oven to 350 degrees F. Grease and flour 12 cup bundt cake pan or tube pan, 10 x 4 inches. Beat sugar, margarine, vanilla and eggs on low speed 30 seconds, scraping bowl constantly. Beat on high speed 5 minutes, scraping bowl occasionally. Beat in flour, baking powder and salt alternately with milk on low speed. Pour into pan. Bake 70 to 80 minutes or until toothpick inserted in center comes out clean. Cool 20 minutes; remove from pan.

Almond pound cake: Substitute almond extract for the vanilla.

Lemon pound cake: Substitute lemon extract for the vanilla; fold 2 to 3 teaspoons grated lemon peel into batter.

Orange-coconut pound cake: Fold 2 to 3 tablespoons finely shredded orange peel and 1 can (3 1/2 ounces) flaked coconut (1 1/3 cups) into batter.

Yields: 8 to 10 servings

GLAZED RUM-FLAVORED CAKE

1 package Betty Crocker Super Moist yellow cake mix
1 package (4 serving size) vanilla instant pudding and pie filling (dry)
1 1/3 cups water
1/3 cup vegetable oil
2 tsps. rum flavoring
4 eggs
Rum Glaze:
2 tbs. margarine or butter
1 cup powdered sugar
1/2 tsp. rum flavoring
1 tbs. hot water

Heat oven to 350 degrees F. Grease and flour 12 cup bundt cake pan. Beat all ingredients except glaze in large bowl on low speed 30 seconds, scraping bowl constantly. Beat on medium speed 2 minutes, scraping bowl occasionally. Pour into pan. Bake 38 to 43 minutes or until cake pulls away from sides of pan and springs back when touched lightly in center or when toothpick inserted in center comes out clean. Cool 10 minutes; invert onto wire rack or heatproof serving plate. Remove pan; cool cake completely. Spread with glaze, allowing some to drizzle down side.

Rum Glaze: Heat margarine in saucepan over medium heat until melted; cool slightly. Stir in remaining ingredients. If necessary, stir in additional hot water, 1/2 teaspoon at a time, until glaze is thin enough to drizzle.

High altitude directions (3500 to 6500 feet): Generously grease and flour pan. Stir 1/4 cup Gold Medal all-purpose flour into cake mix (dry). Increase water to 1 1/2 cups; decrease oil to 1/4 cup.

Yields: 6 to 8 servings

POTATO CHEESECAKE

Crust:
1/2 cup graham cracker crumbs
1/4 cup butter, melted
3/4 cup sugar
Batter:
2 lbs. cream cheese
4 eggs
3/4 cup sugar
1/4 cup egg yolks
1 cup mashed potatoes
1 capful lemon juice
1/4 cup heavy cream

Crust: Mix together the graham cracker crumbs, butter and sugar. Place in a 10 inch cake or springform pan. Bake 10 to 15 minutes at 350 degrees F; set aside.

Batter: With an electric mixer or food processor, mix the cream cheese, eggs, sugar and egg yolks (add the eggs one at a time until incorporated to avoid lumps). Add the mashed potatoes and mix until smooth. Add the lemon juice, vanilla and heavy cream, mix until smooth. Pour batter into the pre-baked crust and bake in a water bath at 350 degrees F for 1 1/2 to 2 hours.

Yields: 6 to 8 servings

SOUR CREAM CHOCOLATE CAKE

1 cup butter
4 egg yolks, beaten
1/2 tsp. soda
1 tsp. ground ginger
1 cup sour cream
1 cup chopped walnuts
2 squares unsweetened chocolate
1 cup hot mashed Colorado potatoes
4 egg whites, beaten until stiff but not dry
2 cups sugar
3 cups flour
1 tsp. baking powder
1 tsp. cinnamon
1 tsp. vanilla
1 cup raisins
Coconut frosting:
3 egg yolks, beaten
1 cup chopped nuts
1 cup cream or evaporated milk
1 cup butter
2 cups flaked coconut
1 cup sugar

Cream butter, sugar and egg yolks. Sift dry ingredients together and set aside. Add sour cream and dry ingredients alternately until well mixed. Add melted chocolate, potatoes, nuts and raisins. Fold in egg whites and vanilla last. Divide batter among three 8 inch round pans. Bake at 350 degrees F for 40 minutes or until toothpick inserted in center of cakes comes out clean. Frost and fill with coconut frosting.

Coconut frosting: Cook cream, sugar and beaten egg yolks on top of stove until thick. Add butter and stir until it melts. Stir in nuts and coconut last. Fill and frost cooled cake.

Yields: 8 to 10 servings

SPUDIN' SPICE CAKE WITH QUICK CARAMEL FROSTING

1 3/4 cups sugar
1 1/2 tsps. cinnamon
1 tsp. nutmeg
3 eggs, unbeaten
1 tsp. soda combined with 1 cup buttermilk
1 cup cold mashed Colorado potatoes
3/4 cup shortening
1/2 tsp. salt
2 cups flour
Quick caramel frosting:
3/4 cup firmly packed brown sugar
2 cups powdered sugar, sifted
1/4 cup butter
3 tbs. milk

Cream sugar, potatoes, shortening, salt and spices for 4 minutes. Add eggs and beat until thoroughly blended. Add buttermilk alternately with flour, starting and ending with flour. Pour into greased and floured 8 inch pans. Bake at 350 degrees F for 30 to 35 minutes.

Quick caramel frosting:

Melt butter in pan; stir in brown sugar. Cook over low heat 2 minutes. Add milk. Bring to full boil. Cool to lukewarm without stirring. Add powdered sugar. Beat until smooth and of spreading consistency. Frost cooled cake.

Yields: 6 to 8 servings

CHOCOLATE POTATO CAKE

1 cup vegetable shortening
4 eggs
1 tsp. soda
4 tbs. cocoa
1 tsp. vanilla
1 cup warm mashed Colorado potatoes
2 cups sugar
2 cups flour
1/2 tsp. salt
1 cup buttermilk
1 cup chopped pecans
Potato cake icing:
2 cups sugar
3/4 cup evaporated milk
2 tbs. butter
2 tbs. light corn syrup
3 tbs. cocoa
1 cup nuts
1 tsp. vanilla

Cream together sugar and shortening; add eggs one at a time and beat well after each. Add mashed potatoes. Add sifted dry ingredients alternately with buttermilk. Add vanilla and nuts. Pour batter into two 9 inch round pans or one 9 x 13 inch oblong cake pans. Bake at 350 degrees F for 35 to 40 minutes. When cool, frost with potato cake icing.

Potato cake icing: Blend sugar, cocoa, syrup and milk. Boil and stir to soft ball stage (234 degrees F to 240 degrees F). Cool. Add butter, vanilla and nuts.

Yields: 8 to 12 servings

INDOORS S'MORES

8 cups Golden Grahams cereal
5 cups miniature marshmallows
1/4 cup light corn syrup
5 tbs. margarine or butter
1 1/2 cups milk chocolate chips
1 tsp. vanilla
1 cup miniature marshmallows, if desired

Measure cereal into large bowl. Butter rectangular pan, 13 x 9 x 2 inches. Heat 5 cups marshmallows, the corn syrup, margarine and chocolate chips in 3 quart saucepan over low heat until melted; remove from heat. Stir in vanilla. Pour over cereal; quickly toss until completely coated with chocolate. Stir in additional marshmallows.

Press mixture evenly in pan using buttered back of spoon. Let stand at least 1 hour, or refrigerate if a firmer bar is desired. Cut into about 2 inch squares. Store loosely covered at room temperature for no longer than 2 days.

Yields: 24 squares

OUTRAGEOUS CHOCOLATE CHIP COOKIES

1 cup granulated sugar
2/3 cup packed brown sugar
1 cup (2 sticks) margarine or butter, softened
1 cup peanut butter
1 tsp. vanilla
2 eggs
2 cups Robin Hood or Gold Medal all-purpose flour
1 cup quick-cooking or regular oats, if desired (add 2/3 cup flour if omitting oats)
2 tsps. baking soda
1/2 tsp. salt
1 package (12 oz.) semi-sweet chocolate chips

Heat oven to 350 degrees F. Beat sugars, margarine, peanut butter, vanilla and eggs in large bowl vigorously with wooden spoon until creamy and well blended. Mix in flour, oats, baking soda and salt. Stir in chocolate chips. Drop dough by rounded tablespoonfuls about 2 inches apart onto ungreased cookie sheet. Bake 10 to 12 minutes or until golden brown. Cool 1 minute; remove from cookie sheet to wire rack.

Yields: 4 dozen cookies

"M & M'S" COOKIES

1 package Betty Crocker cookie bars with "M & M's" Supreme dessert bar mix
1/3 cup Gold Medal all-purpose flour
1/3 cup margarine or butter, softened
2 eggs

Heat oven to 350 degrees F. Stir all ingredients thoroughly in large bowl. (Dough will be stiff and not smooth.) Drop dough by rounded teaspoonfuls about 2 inches apart onto ungreased cookie sheet. Bake 10 to 14 minutes or until light golden brown; cool. Store cookies in airtight container.

High altitude directions (3500 to 6500 feet): Omit flour. Bake 12 to 16 minutes.

Yields: 3 dozen cookies

CARNIVAL CUP CAKES

3/4 cup mashed cooked Idaho pinto beans (1 cup cooked drained beans)
2 cups sifted all-purpose flour
1 1/4 cups granulated sugar
2 1/2 tsps. baking powder
1 tsp. each salt and cinnamon
1/2 tsp. each ground cloves and nutmeg
1/2 cup shortening
3/4 cup milk
1 tsp. molasses

1 tsp. grated orange rind
2 eggs, unbeaten
1/4 cup milk
1 tsp. vanilla

Using electric mixer or potato masher, mash 1 cup hot well cooked pinto beans. Brush cup cake pans with shortening or softened butter or line with paper baking cups. Preheat oven to 400 degrees F (moderately hot).

Sift all ingredients into large bowl or mixer bowl. Add shortening, 3/4 cup milk, molasses, orange rind; beat 2 minutes. Add eggs, 1/4 cup milk, vanilla, and mashed beans (warm, not hot); beat 2 minutes more. Fill pans 2/3 full. Bake at 400 degrees F for 20 minutes. Cool on wire rack. Frost as desired.

Yields: 14 to 16 cupcakes

FIESTA PUDDING-CAKE

2 cups well-cooked Idaho pinto beans (1 2/3 cups mashed beans)
2 cups finely chopped peeled cooking apples
1/2 cup (1 stick) softened butter
1 cup granulated sugar
2 tsps. vanilla extract
1 egg, unbeaten
1 cup sifted all-purpose flour
1 tsp. soda
1/2 tsp. salt
1 tsp. cinnamon
1/2 tsp. ground cloves
1/2 tsp. allspice
1/2 tsp. mace
1 cup seedless raisins
1/2 cup walnuts or pecans, coarsely chopped

Cook 2 to 4 cups of Idaho pinto beans in water until very soft, about 2 1/2 hours. You'll find other uses for the extra cooked beans. While still hot, using a slotted spoon, lift out 2 cups of the beans. Place in a deep bowl along with 1/4 cup of the hot bean liquid. Using electric mixer, whip until smooth and like very thick mashed potatoes. A potato masher may be used. Cover with foil or a bowl cover while preparing other ingredients. The mashed beans should be warm, not hot, when used.

Cream butter, adding sugar gradually, until mixture is fluffy. Add vanilla and the whole egg. Beat well, then stir in the warm (not hot) beans. Sift in half of the combined ingredients. Add apples, raisins, nuts, and the remaining flour. (There is no liquid.) Stir together, on low speed if using an electric mixer only until mixed. Do not beat. Batter will be quite thick.

Spoon into buttered 9 inch tube pan, smoothing top of the batter. Bake on the middle shelf of oven heated to 350 degrees F (moderate) for 1 hour. Remove from oven. Let stand on wire rack about 10 minutes. Loosen edges of cake with spatula or thin knife blade. Tap bottom of pan and turn out on rack. Using another cake rack or serving plate, invert the cake so that the top side will be up. When cool, frost with hard sauce type frosting or glaze the top, nice for pudding service.

Party idea: Serve as holiday pudding with a hot pudding sauce topped with hard sauce. Or use, thin sliced, with egg nog, fruit punches, and other beverages.

Yields: 8 to 10 servings

FRESH BLUEBERRY COBBLER

1/2 cup sugar
1 tbs. cornstarch
4 cups fresh blueberries
2 tbs. water
1 tsp. lemon juice

1 cup Bisquick Original baking mix
1/4 cup milk
1 tbs. sugar
1 tbs. margarine or butter, melted

Heat oven to 425 degrees F. Mix 1/2 cup sugar and the cornstarch in 2 quart saucepan. Stir in blueberries, water and lemon juice. Heat to boiling, stirring constantly; boil and stir 1 minute. Pour into ungreased 2 quart casserole. Mix remaining ingredients until soft dough forms. Drop dough by 6 tablespoons onto hot blueberry mixture. Bake about 15 minutes or until golden brown.

Fresh cherry cobbler: Substitute 4 cups pitted fresh red tart cherries for the blueberries, increase 1/2 cup sugar to 1 1/4 cups, increase cornstarch to 3 tablespoons and substitute 1/4 teaspoon almond extract for the lemon juice.

Fresh peach cobbler: Substitute 4 cups peeled fresh peach slices for the blueberries and add 1/4 teaspoon ground cinnamon to sugar-cornstarch mixture.

Fresh raspberry or blackberry cobbler: Substitute 4 cups fresh raspberries or blackberries for the blueberries, increase 1/2 cup sugar to 1 cup, increase cornstarch to 3 tablespoons and substitute 1/4 teaspoon almond extract for the lemon juice.

High altitude directions (3500 to 6500 feet): Heat oven to 450 degrees F.

Yields: 6 servings

RICE/POTATO PUDDING

1 quart. milk
3 ozs. rice
1 oz. potato flakes
salt to taste
2 egg yolks
vanilla to taste
sugar
5 ozs. (1/2 cup plus 1 tbs.) heavy cream

Boil milk, rice, potato flakes and salt. Simmer until rice is tender.

Mix together sugar, yolks and vanilla, add to above and cook until thick. Remove from heat and cool. Add cream after it sets.

Yields: 10 servings

POTATO STARTERS

4 tsp. baking powder
1/4 tsp. ground nutmeg
3 lg. eggs
3 tbs. shortening
2 3/4 cups unsifted all-purpose flour
1 cup plain mashed Colorado potatoes
1 tsp. ground mace
1 tsp. salt
3/4 cup sugar
salad oil

In medium bowl, combine flour, baking powder, mace, nutmeg and salt; set aside. In large bowl, with electric mixer at high speed, beat eggs with sugar and shortening 2 minutes, until light and fluffy. At low speed, add potatoes; mix until blended. Add flour mixture gradually; beat at low speed until just combined. Cover bowl with plastic wrap; refrigerate 2 hours.

Place dough on well-floured pastry cloth; roll dough to 1/3 inch thickness; cut with floured 3 inch doughnut cutter, dipping center in flour between cutting. Meanwhile, in electric skillet or heavy, wide saucepan, heat 1 1/2 to 2 inches salad oil to 375 degrees F on a deep fat thermometer. Gently drop three or four doughnuts and several holes into hot oil (adding too many doughnuts at a time reduces the temperature of the fat and causes greasy doughnuts); as doughnuts rise to the surface, turn with slotted spoon. Fry 3 minutes, or until browned on both sides. With slotted spoon, remove doughnuts and holes; drain over pan of oil. Place on paper towel-lined wire rack. Repeat with remaining dough. If desired, shake doughnuts in bag with confectioners sugar or cinnamon-sugar.

Yields: 18 doughnuts

ZUCCHINI POTATO PANCAKES

1/4 cup unsifted all-purpose flour
1/4 tsp. baking powder
dash of ground nutmeg
1 sm. onion, grated
1/4 cup salad oil
additional salad oil
1 1/2 lbs. baking Colorado potatoes, unpared
2 lg. eggs
1/2 tsp. salt
1/8 tsp. pepper
1/2 lb. zucchini
sour cream

Line baking sheet with paper towels. Preheat oven to 250 degrees F. In bowl, mix eggs, flour, baking powder, salt, pepper and nutmeg. Add onion. Shred potatoes and zucchini; stir into egg mixture. Heat oil in 12 inch skillet over medium heat. Drop potato mixture, 1/4 cup at a time, into hot oil; flatten into 3 inch rounds. Cook until golden, about 3 minutes on each side. Garnish with sour cream.

Yields: 1 1/2 dozen pancakes

ASPEN BROWNIES WITH COFFEE ICING

1/2 cup chopped nuts
1 2/3 cups sugar
1/4 tsp. salt
1 cup flour
1 cup mashed Colorado potatoes
3 ozs. unsweetened chocolate
3/4 cup margarine
1 tsp. vanilla
4 eggs
1/2 tsp. baking powder
Coffee icing:
1 cup powdered sugar
1 tbs. cocoa
2 tbs. strong hot coffee
1 tsp. vanilla

Melt chocolate and margarine in saucepan on top of stove, or in a glass dish in the microwave. Cool. Cream sugar, vanilla, salt and eggs. Mix well. Add chocolate mixture and potatoes, flour, baking powder and nuts. Beat until creamy. Pour into greased and floured 9 x 11 inch oblong cake pan. Bake at 350 degrees F about 30 minutes or until done. Frost with coffee icing.

Coffee icing: Mix together and spread on top of cooled brownies.

Yields: 12 brownies

CREAMY POTATO FUDGE

3 ozs. unsweetened chocolate
1/2 cup chopped nuts
1 lb. sifted powdered sugar
1/3 cup mashed Colorado potatoes, unseasoned
3 tbs. butter
1/8 tsp. salt
1 tsp. vanilla

Melt chocolate and butter in top of double boiler. Add potatoes, salt and vanilla. Mix well. Blend in sugar and mix thoroughly. Add nuts and knead until smooth. Press into buttered 8 inch square pan. Cool and cut.

Yields: 1 1/4 lbs.

VINEGAR PIE

4 eggs
1 1/2 cups sugar
1/4 cup butter or margarine, melted
1 1/2 tbs. cider or white vinegar
1 tsp. vanilla extract
9 inch frozen pie shell, defrosted

Preheat oven to 350 degrees F. In a large mixing bowl, combine eggs, sugar, butter, vinegar and vanilla; mix well. Pour into pie shell. Bake until firm, about 50 minutes. Cool on a rack. Serve garnished with chopped nuts or whipped cream, if desired.

Yields: one (9-inch) pie

OLD-FASHIONED RAISIN PIE

2 cups raisins
2 cups water
1/2 cup packed brown sugar
2 tbs. cornstarch
1/2 tsp. cinnamon
1/4 tsp. salt
1 tbs. vinegar
1 tbs. butter or margarine
pastry for double 9 inch crust

Combine raisins and water; boil 5 minutes. Blend sugar, cornstarch, cinnamon and salt. Add to raisins and cook, stirring until clear. Remove from heat. Stir in vinegar and butter. Cool slightly. Turn into pastry-lined pan. Cover with top pastry or lattice strips. Bake at 425 degrees F about 30 minutes or until golden brown.

Yields: one 9-inch pie

CRANBERRY PECAN PIE

2 cups fresh or frozen cranberries
1 cup orange juice
1/2 cup honey
2 tbs. cornstarch
2 tbs. cold water
1/2 tsp. orange extract
1 baked (9 inch) pie shell with fluted rim
Pecan topping:
1/2 cup honey
3 tbs. butter or margarine
1 3/4 cups pecan halves

Combine cranberries, juice and honey in medium saucepan. Cook, covered, over low heat 15 minutes if using fresh cranberries or 20 minutes if using frozen berries. Cool. Puree cranberry mixture in blender; return to saucepan. Combine cornstarch and water in cup. Stir into cranberry mixture. Bring mixture to a boil over high heat and cook until thickened. Stir in orange extract. Cool, then pour into pie shell. Spoon Pecan Topping evenly over cranberry mixture.

To prepare topping: Combine honey and butter in medium saucepan. Cook and stir over medium heat 2 minutes or until mixture is smooth. Add pecan halves and stir until well coated.

Bake in preheated 350 degrees F oven 20 minutes or until top is bubbly. Cool on wire rack. Serve at room temperature or chilled.

Yields: 8 servings

VINEGAR PASTRY

3 cups flour
1 cup shortening
1/2 tsp. salt
1 egg
5 tbs. cold water
1 tbs. white vinegar

Mix flour, shortening and salt with pastry blender until fine crumbs about the size of small peas. Beat egg with fork. Add cold water and vinegar. Combine liquid with flour and shortening mixture until thoroughly mixed. Divide dough into three balls of equal size. Each ball makes one single 9-inch pastry. Roll dough out and bake at 425 degrees F until lightly browned. (If wrapped well in plastic wrap, dough may be stored in refrigerator for approximately two weeks. Also freezes well. Remove from refrigerator several hours before rolling out.)

Yields: three (9-inch) pie shells

HONEY STRAWBERRY TART

1/3 cup honey
1 tbs. lemon juice
1 baked or ready-to-eat (9 inch) pie shell

4 cups halved fresh strawberries
mint sprigs for garnish (optional)

Combine honey and lemon juice in small bowl; mix well. Brush bottom of pie shell with mixture. Fill shell with strawberries. Drizzle remaining honey mixture over berries. Garnish with mint sprigs, if desired.

Tip: Prepare honey glaze and strawberries. Fill shell and glaze strawberries just before serving to prevent shell from becoming soggy.

Yields: 8 servings

RASPBERRY FLAN

1 1/2 cups milk
3 eggs, slightly beaten
1/4 cup honey
1 tsp. grated orange peel
Raspberry sauce:
2 cups fresh or thawed frozen raspberries (substitute blackberries, strawberries or blueberries for raspberries, if desired)
2 tbs. honey
1/2 tsp. grated orange peel

Combine milk, eggs, honey and orange peel in medium bowl; stir until blended. Pour into four 1/2 cup buttered molds or one 3 cup mold. Place molds on rack in pan of hot water.

Bake in preheated 300 degrees F oven 15 to 20 minutes for 1/2 cup molds or 30 to 40 minutes for 3 cup mold or until custard is set and knife blade inserted near center comes of clean.

Cool at room temperature, then refrigerate 2 hours. Run thin blade around edge to loosen; invert flan onto serving plate. Spoon Raspberry Sauce over each serving. Garnish with raspberries and mint sprig, if desired.

To prepare sauce: Reserve 12 whole berries and set aside for garnish, if desired. Place remainder in blender or food processor; process until pureed.

Sieve to remove seeds, if desired. Combine puree with honey and orange peel in small bowl.

Yields: 4 servings

QUEEN BEE APPLE PIE

6 cups pared green tart apple slices
1/4 cup walnuts, coarsely chopped
1/3 cup raisins
1 1/4 cups water, divided
1 cup honey
1 tsp. ground cinnamon
1 tsp. lemon juice
1/4 tsp. ground nutmeg
1/3 cup cornstarch
pastry for 2-crust (9 inch) pie

Combine apples, nuts and raisins in large bowl. Set aside. Combine 1 cup water, honey, cinnamon, lemon juice and nutmeg in small saucepan. Bring to a boil over medium heat, stirring. Mix cornstarch with remaining 1/4 cup water in cup; stir into honey mixture. Cook and stir until mixture thickens and becomes clear. Pour hot honey mixture over apple mixture; toss to coat evenly.

Turn apple mixture into pastry lined 9 inch pie plate. Adjust top crust over filling. Seal and flute edges. Cut slits in top crust so steam can escape.

Bake in preheated 350 degrees F oven 10 minutes. Reduce heat to 300 degrees F; bake 35 minutes more or until golden brown. Cool completely on wire rack.

Yields: 8 servings

OLD FASHIONED OATMEAL PIE

1/2 cup butter or margarine
3/4 cup honey
2 eggs, beaten
3/4 cup quick-cooking rolled oats
3/4 cup flaked or shredded coconut
3/4 cup brown sugar
1/2 cup currants

1/2 cup chopped walnuts
1 unbaked (9 inch) pie shell
whipped cream (optional)

Cream butter with honey in large bowl with electric mixer. Add eggs; mix well. Add oats, coconut, brown sugar, currants and walnuts; mix well. Pour mixture into pie shell.

Place pie on center rack of preheated 350 degrees F oven; bake 40 to 45 minutes or until filling browns and knife blade inserted near center comes out clean. Cool completely on wire rack. Top with whipped cream, if desired, and serve.

Yields: 8 servings

HONEY LEMON PIE

1 cup honey
2 seedless, thin skinned lemons, sliced paper thin (with skins) (If lemons with thick skins are used, grate peel, then remove and discard white membrane. Slice peeled lemons paper thin. Combine honey, lemon peel and lemon slices. Proceed as recipe directs.)
1 cup blanched almonds
pastry for 2-crust (8 inch) pie
4 eggs
1 tbs. all-purpose flour
Honey Whipped Cream:
1 cup heavy cream
3 tbs. honey
1 tsp. vanilla

Combine honey and lemons in small glass bowl; let stand at least 2 hours or overnight. Process almonds in food processor until almonds are ground, but not pasty; set aside.

Spread almond mixture evenly over bottom of pastry lined 8 inch pie plate. Beat eggs and flour in small bowl until blended; stir in honey mixture. Pour over almond mixture. Adjust top crust over filling. Seal and flute edge. Cut slits in top crust so steam can escape.

Place pie on bottom shelf of preheated 425 degrees F oven;

bake 15 minutes. Reduce oven temperature to 350 degrees F. Bake 35 to 40 minutes more or until knife inserted through a slit in top crust comes out clean. Cool completely on wire rack. Top with honey whipped cream.

To prepare cream: Beat cream in medium bowl with electric mixer until soft peaks form. Gradually add honey; beat until mixture forms stiff peaks. Fold in vanilla.

Yields: 8 servings

ORANGE ALMOND CAKE

1/2 cup vegetable shortening
1 cup honey
1 tbs. grated orange peel
3 eggs
1 3/4 cups all-purpose flour
2 tsps. baking powder
1/2 tsp. salt
1/4 cup ground blanched almonds
1/4 cup toasted almonds slices (optional)
orange slices, quartered (optional)
Honey whipped cream:
1 cup heavy cream
3 tbs. honey
1 tsp. vanilla

Cream shortening in large bowl with electric mixer. Gradually add honey, beating until light and fluffy. Add orange peel. Add eggs, one at a time, beating thoroughly after each addition. (Mixture may appear curdled.) Combine flour, baking powder and salt in small bowl; fold dry ingredients into creamed mixture. Mix until blended. Add ground almonds; mix well. Grease bottoms only of two 8 inch round cake pans; pour in cake batter.

Bake in preheated 325 degrees F oven 30 minutes or until wooden toothpick inserted in center comes out clean. Cool in cake pans on wire racks 10 minutes. Remove from pans and cool on wire racks. Frost with honey whipped cream; garnish with toasted almond slices and orange slices.

To prepare cream: Beat cream in medium bowl with electric mixer until soft peaks form. Gradually add honey; beat until mixture forms stiff peaks. Fold in vanilla.

Yields: 10 to 12 servings

CARROT SPICE CAKE

1/2 cup butter or margarine
1 cup honey
2 eggs
2 cups finely grated carrots
1/2 cup golden raisins
1/2 cup chopped nuts
1/4 cup orange juice
2 tsps. vanilla
1 cup whole wheat flour
1 cup all-purpose flour
2 tsps. baking powder
1 1/2 tsps. ground cinnamon
1 tsp. baking soda
1/2 tsp. salt
1/2 tsp. ground ginger
1/4 tsp. ground nutmeg

Cream butter in large bowl with electric mixer until fluffy. Beat in honey in fine stream until blended. Add eggs, one at a time, beating well after each addition. Combine carrots, raisins, nuts, orange juice and vanilla in small bowl; set aside. Combine flours, baking powder, cinnamon, baking soda, salt, ginger and nutmeg in another small bowl. Add dry ingredients to creamed mixture alternately with carrot mixture, beginning and ending with dry ingredients. Turn batter into greased 12 x 8 x 2 inch baking pan.

Bake in preheated 350 degrees F oven 35 to 45 minutes or until wooden toothpick inserted near center comes out clean. Cool cake in pan on wire rack 10 minutes. Remove cake from pan and cool completely on wire rack.

Yields: 10 to 12 servings

DOUBLE CHOCOLATE HONEY RING

1/2 cup butter or margarine
1 cup honey

3 eggs
1 tsp. vanilla
1 3/4 cups all-purpose flour
1/2 cup unsweetened cocoa powder
2 tsps. baking powder
1 tsp. salt
1 tsp. baking soda
1/2 cup dairy sour cream
1 cup semisweet chocolate chips
1/2 cup chopped nuts
additional unsweetened cocoa powder (optional)
edible blossoms (optional)
White Chocolate Glaze:
2 ozs. white chocolate
2 tsps. milk

Cream butter in large bowl with electric mixer; gradually add honey, beating until light and fluffy. Add eggs, one at a time, beating thoroughly after each addition. (Mixture may appear slightly curdled.) Beat in vanilla. Combine flour, 1/2 cup cocoa, baking powder, slat and baking soda in small bowl. Add dry ingredients alternately with sour cream to butter mixture. Fold in chocolate chips and nuts. Pour batter into greased 12 cup fluted tube pan.

Bake in preheated 325 degrees F oven 50 to 55 minutes or until wooden toothpick inserted near center comes out clean. Cool in pan on wire rack 10 minutes. Remove from pan and cool completely on wire rack. Glaze with white chocolate glaze, sprinkle with additional cocoa and garnish with blossoms, if desired.

To prepare glaze: Melt chocolate in top of double boiler. Stir in milk. Drizzle glaze over cake with spoon.

Yields: 12 servings

HONEY RUM CAKE

2 tbs. butter or margarine
2 tbs. honey
1 cup chopped toasted almonds
1 package (18 1/2 oz.) yellow cake mix with pudding

3 eggs
1/3 cup water
1/3 cup vegetable oil
1/3 cup light rum (substitute 1 tsp. rum flavoring for light rum, if desired, and increase water to 2/3 cup)
toasted sliced almonds (optional)
Honey Rum Glaze:
3/4 cup honey
1/3 cup butter or margarine
3 tbs. water
1/3 cup light rum (substitute 1 tsp. rum flavoring for light rum, if desired, and increase water to 2/3 cup)
Honey rum whipped Cream:
1 cup heavy cream
3 tbs. honey
2 tbs. light rum or 1/2 tsp. rum flavoring

Melt butter in small saucepan; add honey and mix well. Divide mixture in half and spread over bottom surfaces of two 8 inch cake pans. Sprinkle half of nuts into each pan; set aside. Combine cake mix, eggs, water, oil and rum in large bowl. Beat with electric mixer at highest speed 2 minutes. Pour batter over nuts in prepared pans.

Place pans on center rack of preheated 350 degrees F oven 30 to 35 minutes or until wooden toothpick inserted near center comes out clean. Prick cakes with fork while still in pans.

Spoon 1/4 honey rum glaze over each cake and let cool 5 minutes. Invert cakes onto racks; spoon remaining glaze over nut side of each cake.

When cool, place one cake nut side up on serving dish; cover top with 2/3 honey rum whipped cream. Add second layer, nut side up, and decoratively pipe remaining cream around top edge of cake. Garnish with almonds, if desired.

To prepare glaze: Combine honey, butter and water in small saucepan. Bring to a boil over medium heat. Cook and stir 5 minutes. Stir in rum.

To prepare cream: Whip cream in medium bowl with electric mixer until soft peaks form. Gradually beat in honey; continue whipping until mixture forms stiff peaks. Fold in rum with rubber spatula. Cover and refrigerate until ready for use.

Yields: 10 to 12 servings

BANANAS FLAMBE

**1 lg. banana
4 tsps. honey
4 tsps. chopped walnuts
4 tsps. brandy (optional)**

Halve unpeeled banana lengthwise; place in small flameproof dish. Drizzle cut surface on each half with 2 teaspoons honey and sprinkle with walnuts. On top rack of preheated oven broiler, broil banana about 5 minutes or until heated but not burnt. Remove from broiler. If desired, pour brandy over top and flame.

Tip: Orange blossom honey is particularly good in this dessert.

Yields: 2 servings

ROASTED HONEY APPLES

**4 med. baking apples
1/2 cup honey
1/4 cup orange juice
1 tbs. lemon juice
1 tsp. grated orange peel
1/2 tsp. ground ginger
(substitute 1 tsp. fresh grated or chopped candied ginger for ground ginger, if desired)
1/3 cup hot water**

Pare top 1/3 of apples and remove core leaving 1/2 inch of core on bottom. Place apples in greased 8 inch square baking dish. Combine honey, orange juice, lemon juice, orange peel and ginger in small bowl; mix well. Spoon over apples allowing mixture to fill centers and coat entire surface. Pour water into baking dish.

Bake, covered with foil, in preheated 400 degrees F oven 15 minutes. Remove cover and bake 30 minutes more or until apples are glazed and tender; baste with liquid from baking dish every 15 minutes.

Tip: If desired, serve honey roasted apples with plain or vanilla yogurt and granola.

To microwave: Pare and core apples and mix glaze ingredients following directions above; omit water in pan. Arrange apples in a circle, 1/2 inch apart, in a microwave safe dish. Cover tightly with plastic wrap. Microwave at high (100%) 8 to 12 minutes (depending on size of apples) until apples are tender; baste apples and rotate dish every 2 to 3 minutes. Let stand 3 to 5 minutes before serving.

Yields: 4 servings

HONEY RUM FRUIT BOAT

**1/2 cup honey
3 to 4 tbs. rum or 1 tsp. rum flavoring
1 fresh ripe pineapple
2 oranges, peeled and sliced
1 cup grapes**

Stir honey and rum together in medium glass bowl until blended; set aside. Cut pineapple in half lengthwise including green top. Carefully carve fruit from center leaving shells intact. Slice pineapple pieces. Add pineapple, oranges and grapes to honey mixture and stir until fruit is well coated. Marinate 1 hour. Stir fruit and arrange in pineapple shells. Serve chilled or at room temperature.

Yields: 4 servings

FROZEN FUDGE POPS

**2 cups milk
1/3 cup honey
3 tbs. unsweetened cocoa powder
2 tbs. cornstarch**

**1 tsp. vanilla
1 tsp. butter or margarine**

Combine milk, honey, cocoa, cornstarch, vanilla and butter in medium saucepan. Cook and stir over low heat until little bubbles appear and mixture thickens. Remove from heat; cool slightly and pour into popsicle molds. Freeze 2 to 4 hours or until firm. Store in freezer.

Yields: 6 to 8 fudge pops

HONEY LIME PEARS

**1/2 cup honey
1/4 cup water
1/4 cup lime juice
1/2 tsp. grated lime peel
2 cored halved pared firm ripe pears**

To microwave: Combine honey, water and lime juice in 2 quart microwave safe dish; microwave at high (100%) 2 1/2 to 3 minutes or until mixture boils. Stir in lime peel. Add pear halves to syrup; cover with vented plastic wrap and microwave at high 7 to 10 minutes or until pears are tender. Serve warm or cold with poaching liquid.

Yields: 4 servings

GOLDEN GRAPEFRUIT DELIGHT

**2 pink or red grapefruit
4 tbs. honey, divided
1 cup plain yogurt
1/4 tsp. almond extract
2 to 3 tbs. sliced almonds, toasted**

Grate grapefruit peel to equal 1/4 teaspoon; reserve. Peel grapefruit and slice into 1/2 inch thick circular pieces. Gently toss grapefruit slices and 2 tablespoons honey in medium glass bowl; refrigerate until ready to serve. Combine yogurt, remaining honey, reserved grapefruit peel and almond extract in small bowl; mix well. Spoon grapefruit into individual dishes. Top with yogurt sauce; garnish with almonds.

Yields: 2 to 3 servings

STRAWBERRY SABAYON

1 1/2 cups half and half
1/4 cup honey
1 tbs. cornstarch
2 eggs, beaten
1 tsp. vanilla
1/2 tsp. grated orange peel
fresh strawberries, sliced, for garnish (optional)
Strawberry Sauce:
1 box (10 oz.) frozen sliced strawberries, thawed
2 to 3 tsps. cornstarch

To microwave: Combine half and half, honey and cornstarch in microwave safe 1 quart container. Microwave at high (100%) 4 to 5 minutes, stirring halfway through cooking time. Blend small amount of hot liquid with eggs; return to hot mixture and mix well. Microwave at high 30 to 60 seconds or until mixture comes to a boil and thickens; stir after 30 seconds. Stir in vanilla and orange peel. Cool, stirring occasionally. Pour into serving dishes; decorate with Strawberry Sauce. Garnish with sliced strawberries, if desired.

To prepare sauce: To microwave: Place strawberries in blender or food processor; process until pureed. Blend in cornstarch. Place mixture in small microwave safe container and microwave at high (100%) 3 to 5 minutes or until thickened, stirring every minute.

Tip: Add 2 tablespoons brandy or cream sherry for a festive touch.

Yields: 4 servings

HONEY OAT BISCOTTI

1/2 cup butter or margarine
3/4 cup honey
2 eggs
1 tsp. vanilla
2 cups all-purpose flour
3 tsps. ground cinnamon
1 tsp. baking powder
1/2 tsp. baking soda
1/2 tsp. salt
2 cups quick-cooking rolled oats
1/2 cup chopped nuts

Cream butter in large bowl with electric mixer; beat in honey, eggs and vanilla. Combine flour, cinnamon, baking powder, baking soda and salt in small bowl; mix well. Stir into butter mixture. Stir in oats and nuts. Shape dough into two 10 x 3 x 1 inch logs on greased baking sheet.

Bake in preheated 375 degrees F oven 12 to 15 minutes or until lightly browned. Remove from oven; cool 5 minutes. Remove to cutting board. Reduce oven temperature to 300 degrees F. Cut each log into 1/2 inch strips; place on cookie sheet. Bake 25 to 30 minutes or until crisp throughout strip. Cool completely on wire racks.

Yields: 3 dozen cookies

OATMEAL CHOCOLATE CHIP COOKIES

1 cup honey
1/2 cup vegetable shortening
1/2 cup butter or margarine
2 eggs
1 tsp. vanilla
2 cups all-purpose flour
1 cup quick-cooking rolled oats
2 tsps. baking powder
1/2 tsp. baking soda
1/4 tsp. salt
1 cup semisweet chocolate chips
1/2 cup chopped pecans

Cream honey, shortening and butter in large bowl with electric mixer until smooth. Beat in eggs, one at a time, then add vanilla. Combine flour, oats, baking powder, baking soda and salt in medium bowl; mix well. Add dry ingredients to honey mixture; mix thoroughly. Stir in chocolate chips and nuts. Drop by heaping teaspoonfuls onto greased cookie sheet.

Place cookie sheet above center of preheated 350 degrees F oven; bake 12 to 16 minutes or until lightly browned. Let cookies stand 1 minute, then remove to wire racks to cool.

Yields: 5 dozen cookies

BUTTERSCOTCH CRISPIES

1 cup butterscotch chips
1/2 cup honey
1/2 cup peanut butter
5 cups crispy rice cereal
1 package (6 oz.) semisweet chocolate chips

To microwave: Combine butterscotch chips, honey and peanut butter in microwave safe 4 cup measure. Microwave at high (100%) 1 to 2 minutes; stir until smooth. Combine cereal and butterscotch mixture in large bowl; mix well.

Press into greased 9 inch square baking dish. Sprinkle evenly with chocolate chips; place under preheated oven broiler 2 minutes or until chips are soft enough to spread. Spread evenly over top of cereal mixture. Cool completely. Cut into squares.

Yields: 16 squares

ALMOND RUGELACH

1 cup butter or margarine, softened
3 ozs. cream cheese, softened
8 tbs. honey, divided
2 cups all-purpose flour
1 tsp. lemon juice
1 tsp. ground cinnamon
1 cup finely chopped almonds
1/2 cup dried cherries or dried cranberries

Cream butter and cream cheese in large bowl with electric mixer until fluffy. Add 3 tablespoons honey and mix well. Mix in flour until dough holds together. Form into a ball; wrap in plastic wrap and refrigerate 2 hours.

Divide dough into fourths; roll out one piece into 9 inch circle on floured surface. Combine 2 tablespoons honey and lemon juice in small bowl or cup; mix well. Brush dough with honey mixture; sprinkle 1/4 teaspoon cinnamon over entire surface. Combine almonds and dried cherries in another small bowl; drizzle remaining 3 tablespoons honey over mixture and mix well. Spread 1/4 of almond mixture onto circle of dough, stopping 1/2 inch from outer edge. Cut circle into 8 triangular pieces. Roll up each triangle from wide outer edge toward tip. Gently bend both ends to form a crescent. Place on oiled parchment paper lined baking sheet and refrigerate 20 minutes or longer. Repeat with remaining dough, cinnamon and filling. Bake in preheated 350 degrees F oven 20 to 25 minutes or until golden brown. Remove from pan and cool on wire racks.

Tip: For longer storage, package unbaked crescents in freezer safe container or bags and freeze until ready to bake. Crescents may be stored in freezer up to 3 months. Thaw before baking.

Yields: 32 cookies

CHEWY HONEY NUT COOKIES

2 cups all-purpose flour
1 tsp. salt
1/2 tsp. baking powder
1/2 tsp. baking soda
1/2 cup butter or margarine
1 cup honey
1/2 cup dairy sour cream
2 tsps. vanilla
2 cups raisins
1 cup quick-cooking rolled oats
1 cup chopped walnuts

Combine flour, salt, baking powder and baking soda in small bowl; mix well and set aside. Cream butter in large bowl with electric mixer; beat in honey in fine stream until blended. Stir in sour cream and vanilla. Blend in flour mixture and raisins, oats and walnuts. Cover and refrigerate dough about 30 minutes.

Drop dough by rounded tablespoonfuls onto well greased cookie sheet. Place cookie sheet above center of preheated 325 degrees F oven 20 to 25 minutes or until lightly browned. Let cookies stand 1 minute, then remove to wire racks to cool.

Yields: 4 dozen cookies

HONEY SHORTBREAD

1 cup butter
1/3 cup honey
1 tsp. vanilla
2 1/2 cups all-purpose flour
3/4 cup chopped pecans

Beat butter, honey and vanilla in large bowl with electric mixer until mixture is light and fluffy. Add flour, 1 cup at a time, beating well after each addition. If dough becomes too stiff to stir, knead in remaining flour by hand. Work in nuts. Pat dough into shortbread mold or ungreased 9 inch cast iron skillet. Score surface with knife so it can be divided into 24 wedges; prick deeply with fork into score marks.

Bake in preheated 300 degrees F oven 35 to 40 minutes. Cool in pan on wire rack 10 minutes. Remove from pan. Cut into wedges while warm.

Yields: 2 dozen wedges

BREAD PUDDING

8 cups day-old egg bread cubes
3 cups milk
1 cup half and half
6 eggs, beaten
1/2 cup honey
1 tbs. grated orange peel
1 tsp. vanilla
1 tsp. ground cinnamon
Honey cream sauce:
1 cup whipping cream
1/4 cup honey
1 tbs. rum or rum flavoring

Arrange bread in bottom of lightly greased shallow 2 quart baking dish. Stir together milk and half and half in large bowl; beat in eggs, honey, orange peel, vanilla and cinnamon, mixing well. Pour mixture over bread cubes in baking dish and let stand 1 hour or until liquid is absorbed by bread.

Bake in preheated 375 degrees F oven 45 to 50 minutes or until knife inserted near center comes out clean.

To prepare sauce: Beat cream in medium bowl with electric mixer until soft peaks form; slowly beat in honey and beat until mixture forms stiff peaks. Fold in rum.

Note: Recipe can be halved; use lightly greased 1 quart baking dish and bake pudding 40 to 45 minutes or until knife inserted near center comes out clean.

Yields: 8 to 12 servings

BAKLAVA

3 cups finely chopped walnuts
2 tsps. ground cinnamon
1/2 tsp. ground nutmeg
dash ground cloves
1 1/2 cups clarified butter, divided (To clarify butter, cut 1 lb. butter into pieces and melt in medium saucepan over medium heat. Skim off foam; strain clear yellow liquid into a bowl, leaving cloudy residue in bottom of pan.)
1/2 cup honey
1 package (16 oz.) filo pastry sheets
Honey syrup:
1 cup honey
3/4 cup water
1/2 tsp. grated lemon peel
3 whole cloves
1 cinnamon stick, 3 inches long
1 1/2 tsps. lemon juice

Combine walnuts and spices in medium bowl. Reserve 1/2 cup clarified butter for brushing top and bottom layers; stir honey into remaining 1 cup butter. Brush bottom of 13 x 9 x 2 inch baking pan with clarified butter. Cut filo sheets in half crosswise; trim to 13 x 9 inch rectangles. Cover filo with waxed paper and damp towel to keep from drying out.

Line pan with 10 sheets of filo, brushing each with clarified butter; sprinkle with 1/3 cup walnut mixture. Place 2 sheets filo on top of walnut layer, brushing each with honey-butter mixture. Sprinkle with 1/3 cup walnut mixture. Repeat, layering 2 sheets filo, brushing each with honey-walnut mixture and sprinkling with 1/3 cup walnut mixture until all nut mixture is used. Top with remaining filo sheets, brushing each with clarified butter. With sharp knife, cut baklava into diamond-shaped pieces, carefully cutting through all layers.

Bake in preheated 325 degrees F oven 45 minutes. Reduce heat to 275 degrees F and bake 20 minutes more. Remove from oven; while still hot, carefully spoon cool honey syrup over entire surface.

To prepare syrup: Combine honey, water, lemon peel, cloves and cinnamon in small saucepan over medium heat. Bring to a boil. Reduce heat to low and simmer 20 minutes. Add lemon juice; simmer 5 minutes more. Remove from heat; cool. Remove cloves and cinnamon before using.

Tip: Baklava may be wrapped in foil or placed in freezer-safe containers and frozen. To serve, place unwrapped thawed baklava on baking sheet; bake in preheated 325 degrees F oven 12 minutes or until heated and crisp on top. Cool before serving.

Yields: 3 dozen pieces

MONKEY BARS

3 cups miniature marshmallows
1/2 cup honey
1/3 cup butter or margarine
1/4 cup peanut butter
2 tsps. vanilla
1/4 tsp. salt

2 cups quick-cooking rolled oats
4 cups crispy rice cereal
1/2 cup flaked or shredded coconut
1/4 cup peanuts

Combine marshmallows, honey, butter, peanut butter, vanilla and salt in medium saucepan. Melt marshmallow mixture over low heat, stirring constantly. Combine oats, rice cereal, coconut and peanuts in 13 x 9 x 2 inch baking pan. Pour marshmallow mixture over dry ingredients. Mix until thoroughly coated. Pack mixture firmly into pan. Cool and cut into 24 bars.

To microwave: Microwave marshmallows, honey, butter, peanut butter, vanilla and salt in 2 quart microwave safe bowl on high (100%) 2 1/2 to 3 minutes. Continue as above.

Yields: 2 dozen bars

LUSCIOUS COCONUT CAKE

1 package (18.25 oz.) white cake mix without pudding
1 can (3 1/2 oz.) flaked coconut, divided (about 1 1/3 cups)
1 cup water
1/3 cup plus 3 tbs. Amaretto di Amore, divided
2 egg whites
1/2 cup cream of coconut
Tipsy coconut frosting:
2 cups whipping cream
1/2 cup sifted Domino confectioners 10-X sugar
3 tbs. Amaretto di Amore

Combine cake mix, 1 cup coconut, water, 1/3 cup Amaretto di Amore, and egg whites; beat 2

minutes at high speed of an electric mixer. Reduce speed to low, beat 1 minute. Pour batter into 2 greased and floured 8 inch cake pans. Bake at 350 degrees F for 22 to 27 minutes or until wooden pick inserted in center comes out clean.

Cool cake pans on wire racks 10 minutes; remove from pans and place on wire racks. Punch holes in top of each layer with a wooden pick.

Combine cream of coconut and remaining 3 tablespoons Amaretto di Amore; stir well. Drizzle cream of coconut mixture over warm cake. Let cake cool completely on wire racks.

Stack layers, spreading about 1 1/2 cups tipsy coconut frosting between layers. Spread top and sides with remaining tipsy coconut frosting, and sprinkle with remaining coconut. Cover and chill at least 4 hours.

To prepare frosting: Combine all ingredients in a medium bowl, beat at medium speed of an electric mixer until soft peaks form.

Yields: one 2-layer cake

HONEY ICE CREAM

2 cups milk
3/4 cup honey
dash salt
2 eggs, beaten
2 cups heavy cream
1 tbs. vanilla

Heat milk in medium saucepan over medium heat but do not boil; stir in honey and salt. Pour small amount of hot liquid into eggs; return to milk mixture. Cook and stir over medium high heat 5 minutes. Cool thoroughly at room temperature. Stir in cream and vanilla. Refrigerate until cold. Freeze in ice cream maker according to manufacturer's directions.

Honey ice milk: Substitute 4 cups low fat milk for milk and heavy cream in recipe above.

Yields: about 5 cups

TEMPURA

1 cup cold water
1 cup sifted all-purpose flour
1/2 cup cream cornstarch
1 tbs. vegetable oil
1 egg
1/2 tsp. white pepper
1 tsp. salt
1 tsp. baking powder

In a large bowl, combine ingredients and mix until smooth. Let sit for 15 minutes.

Use shrimp—peeled, deveined and butterflied, or thinly sliced pork or chicken. Also great with vegetables including cauliflowerets, eggplant, onion, green pepper and mushrooms. Heat oil in large skillet to 350 degrees F. If items are watery, sprinkle them with a little flour before coating. Dip items in batter and coat thoroughly, allowing excess batter to drip into bowl. Fry a few pieces at a time until golden brown, 2 to 3 minutes. Be sure that meat items are thoroughly cooked. Use 4 ounces of meat per serving. Great as finger foods or for use in oriental dishes. Serve with your favorite cocktail or hot sauce.

Yields: 10 servings

BEAN TUNA LOAF

1 cup dry beans (about 2 1/2 cups, cooked)
1 can (6 1/2 oz.) tuna, flaked
1/2 cup dry bread crumbs
1/2 cup milk
2 tbs. grated onion
1/4 cup chopped sweet pickles
1 tbs. lemon juice
1 tsp. salt
2 eggs, beaten
1 can (8 oz.) tomato sauce

Cook beans as directed below. Drain and mash beans coarsely with fork. Add remaining ingredients, except tomato sauce. Spread into greased 5 x 8 inch loaf pan or 8 inch square pan. Bake at 350 degrees F for 50 to 60 minutes. Slice or cut into squares to serve. Accompany with heated tomato sauce.

To cook beans: Soak beans overnight in cold water, using 3 cups water to each cup of dried beans. For quick soak, cover beans with measured amount of water, bring to boil and boil 2 minutes. Cover and let stand 1 hour. Simmer soaked beans in soaking liquid until tender, 1 to 1 1/2 hours.

Variation with canned beans: Substitute 2 cans (15 ounces) beans (any variety of canned dry beans) for cooked dry beans in recipe for Bean Tuna Loaf. Proceed as directed in recipe above.

Yields: 6 to 8 servings

CATFISH NUGGETS WITH CHAMPAGNE MUSTARD SAUCE

2 lbs. U.S. farm-raised catfish fillets
1/2 cup yellow cornmeal
1/2 tsp. salt
1/2 tsp. dried oregano,
1/3 cup milk
1 egg
vegetable oil
Champagne mustard sauce:
1/2 cup sugar
1/3 cup dry mustard (use fine or very fine mustard for best results)
1/3 cup champagne vinegar or white wine vinegar
2 egg yolks

Cut catfish in 1 inch nuggets. Combine cornmeal, salt and oregano. In another bowl combine milk and egg. Dip catfish nuggets into milk mixture and then into cornmeal mixture, tossing to coat.

Fry a single layer of nuggets in a skillet with hot oil (350 degrees F) until golden brown. Drain on paper towels. Serve immediately.

Champagne mustard sauce: In a small heavy saucepan stir sugar and mustard together. Add vinegar and egg yolks. Cook over medium-low heat 10 minutes or until thickened, stirring constantly with a whisk. Remove from heat. Transfer to a small bowl. Cover and chill. Before serving, let stand at room temperature about 10 minutes.

Yields: 8 servings and 1 cup sauce

CLASSIC FRIED CATFISH

3/4 cup yellow cornmeal
1/4 cup flour
2 tsps. salt
1 tsp. cayenne pepper
1/4 tsp. garlic powder
4 genuine U.S. farm-raised catfish fillets
vegetable oil

Combine cornmeal, flour, salt, cayenne pepper and garlic powder. Coat farm-raised catfish with mixture, shaking off excess. Fill deep pot or 12 inch skillet half full with vegetable oil. Heat to 350 degrees F. Add catfish in single layer and fry until golden brown, about 5 to 6 minutes, depending on size. Remove and drain on paper towels.

Yields: 4 servings

LOBSTER FORESTIERE

2 lbs. fresh lobster
3/4 cup light cream
4 tbs. butter
1/4 cup finely chopped shallots
1 cup chopped mushrooms - buttons & morel's
1 tbs. flour
2 tsps. Dijon mustard
1 tsp. Worcestershire sauce
2 egg yolks
Tabasco, salt and pepper to taste
1 cup buttered bread crumbs
2 tbs. finely chopped parsley

Cook the lobster as directed. Strain and reserve 1/4 cup of liquor.

Warm the cream in a small saucepan.

Melt the butter in another saucepan and sauté the shallots and mushrooms until tender. Stir in the flour and cook until bubbling. Remove from heat and whisk in the warm cream. Return to heat and boil, stirring constantly, until the sauce thickens. Simmer at least 3 minutes. Add the mustard and Worcestershire sauce.

Whisk egg yolk and lobster liquor in a bowl. Whisk in 1/2 cup of the hot sauce, a spoonful at a time. Then slowly beat in the remaining sauce. Add Tabasco and season to taste. Transfer the enriched sauce to the saucepan, and stirring carefully, bring to a simmer over moderate heat.

Arrange the lobsters in their shells on a baking sheet. Distribute the creamed mushroom sauce over lobsters. Top with a mixture of buttered crumbs and parsley.

Yields: 4 servings

SALMON SOUFFLÉ EN SURPRISE

6 eggs, separated
2 tbs. water
1/4 tsp. cayenne
1/4 tsp. red pepper flakes
1 cup lowfat ricotta cheese
1/2 cup Monterey jack cheese
1/4 cup freshly grated parmesan cheese
1 can (7 1/2 oz.) Bumble Bee pink or red salmon (pureed)

Preheat oven to 425 degrees F. With an electric mixer set on high, beat egg whites until stiff.

In a separate bowl, beat the yolks (you can throw one or two away if you're watching your cholesterol) and add the water, spices and cheeses. Mix well. Stir one third of the whites into the yolk mixture. Then gently fold in the remaining whites. Spoon the soufflé mixture into soufflé dishes. Add salmon and top with remaining soufflé mixture.

Set dish into hot oven and bake until puffed and golden, about 15 to 20 minutes. Serve immediately.

Yields: 4 servings

GRILLED CATFISH WITH FRESH SALSA

4 genuine U.S. farm-raised catfish fillets
1/2 tsp. garlic salt
1/2 tsp. pepper
3 med. tomatoes, chopped
1/4 cup chopped onion
2 med. jalapeno peppers, chopped
2 tbs. white wine vinegar
1 tsp. salt

To prepare the catfish: Sprinkle farm-raised catfish fillets with garlic salt and pepper. Place in well oiled grill basket or on well oiled grill rack.

Grill uncovered directly over medium-hot coals about 5 minutes per side or until fish flakes easily.

To prepare the salsa: In a bowl, combine tomatoes, onion, jalapeno peppers, vinegar and salt. Stir well. Let stand at room temperature for about 30 minutes before serving.

Yields: 4 servings and 3 cups salsa

PASTA PRIMAVERA

1 tbs. unsalted butter
1 med. red onion (diced)
2 to 3 cloves garlic (minced or pressed)
1 lb. thin asparagus, cut diagonally in 1/4 inch slices, tips intact
1 cup mushrooms (thinly sliced)
1 cup cauliflower (florets only)
1 zucchini cut into 1/4 inch slices
1 carrot halved lengthwise and cut diagonally into thin slices
1/2 cup vegetable broth or vegetarian chicken broth
1/4 cup dry white wine
2 tbs. chopped fresh basil or 1 tbs. dried basil
1 tbs. each chopped fresh rosemary and oregano or 1 tbs. each dried rosemary and oregano
2 cans (7 1/2 oz.) Bumble Bee Salmon (red or pink)
1 can (12 1/2 oz.) Bumble Bee Tuna (white or light)
1 can (8 oz.) Bumble Bee whole oysters
1 cup frozen peas (thawed)
2 to 3 tbs. minced fresh parsley (optional)
1 lb. any flavor or color linguini or fettucini (cooked and drained)
1/2 cup freshly grated parmesan cheese or romano cheese

Heat wok or large deep skillet over medium-high heat. Add butter, onion and garlic; stirfry until onion is tender, about 2 minutes.

Stir in next 5 ingredients; stirfry 2 minutes.

Increase heat to high. Add liquids and seasonings. Bring to a boil; boil until liquid is slightly reduced, about 3 minutes.

Add all seafood and peas. Heat through, stirring gently for 1 minute. Add pasta and cheese; toss until cheese is evenly distributed and pasta is heated through.

Yields: 6 servings

LOBSTER FRA DIAVLO

4 fresh Maine lobsters (1 to 1 1/2 lb.)
3 ozs. olive oil
1 tbs. minced garlic
1/2 tsp. basil
1/2 tsp. oregano
1/4 tsp. white pepper
1/4 tsp. crushed red pepper
3 to 4 dashes Tabasco sauce
24 ozs. marinara sauce
1/2 cup dry red wine
pasta for 4 servings

Boil Maine lobster, cool, pick all lobster meat out of body and claws. Set aside. In a sauté pan heat oil and garlic at medium heat. Cook just enough to heat garlic slightly (about 30 seconds). Add Maine lobster, and all of the spices. Cook at a medium heat for 1 to 2 minutes.

Add marina sauce and red wine. Bring to a boil, then let simmer 3 to 4 minutes. Taste, adjust seasonings if necessary. Serve over pasta.

Yields: 4 servings

SALMON CROQUETTES

1 can (15 1/2 oz.) Bumble Bee pink salmon
2 cups mashed potatoes
1/2 cup diced celery
1/2 cup minced onion
2 tbs. chopped parsley

1 tbs. vegetable oil
1 egg
2 tsps. Worcestershire sauce
2 tsps. lemon juice
1/2 tsp. salt
dash pepper
1 cup cornflake crumbs, or cornmeal
hot oil for frying
tartar sauce

Drain and flake salmon. Combine salmon and mashed potatoes. Sauté celery, onion and parsley in 1 tablespoon oil. Cool slightly. Stir in salmon mixture along with egg, Worcestershire sauce, lemon juice, salt and pepper. Spread mixture in a greased pan. Chill thoroughly. Shape into about 1 inch diameter balls. Coat with crumbs. Allow to dry on rack in refrigerator 1 hour. Fry in hot oil 2 to 4 minutes until brown on all sides. Serve at once, or hold in 350 degrees F oven to keep warm. Serve with tartar sauce.

Yields: 4 to 6 servings

WALDORF SALAD

1/2 to 1 cup each long grain brown and wild rice
3 cups water
1/2 cup orange juice
1/4 tsp. salt (optional)
1 cup each sliced celery and halved red grapes
1 each tart red and green apple (cored and diced)
1/2 cup coarsely chopped toasted walnuts
1/4 cup coarsely chopped dried apricots
1 can (8 oz.) pineapple chunks in juice
1 can (12 1/2 oz.) Bumble Bee tuna (white or light)
Dressing:
1/4 to 1/2 cup each plain nonfat yogurt and or lowfat pureed ricotta cheese
1 tbs. each grated orange and lemon rind
dash freshly grated nutmeg and cloves
1 tbs. orange juice

1 tsp. fructose (optional)
Garnish:
orange and lemon slices
kiwi fruit slices

Rinse rice thoroughly under cold running water in a strainer. Place rice, water, orange juice and salt in heavy bottomed 3 quart saucepan and bring to a boil. Reduce heat to simmer and cover loosely. Cook 45 to 55 minutes or until rice is done and most of the liquid has been absorbed. Remove from heat and cool quickly.

Make dressing by combining all ingredients. Include pineapple juice for increased flavor profile and thinner viscosity.

When rice is cooked and cooled, add fruits and nuts plus dressing and mix carefully.

Chill and serve with fruit garnish.

Yields: 4 servings

CHEESY CATFISH

2 lbs. genuine U.S. farm-raised catfish fillets
2 tbs. margarine, melted
1/2 cup parmesan cheese, grated
1/4 cup yellow cornmeal
1/4 cup flour
1/2 tsp. pepper
1 tsp. Spanish paprika

Pour melted margarine into baking pan. Combine parmesan cheese, cornmeal, flour, pepper and paprika in a paper bag. Place farm-raised catfish fillets in bag and shake to coat each fillet. Place fish in baking dish, turning once to coat with margarine. Sprinkle remaining cheese/cornmeal mixture over fish. Bake at 400 degrees F until golden brown and fish flakes when tested with a fork (approximately 10 to 15 minutes).

Yields: 8 servings

30

MAINE STOVETOP LOBSTER BAKE

4 lbs. Great Eastern mussels
4 Maine lobsters (1 1/4 lb.)
12 small red potatoes
4 ears sweet corn, shucked
except for innermost leaves
4 to 8 small boiling onions
2 cups water
1 cup butter (2 sticks)
2 lemons, cut into wedges
5 lbs. Rockweed (seaweed)
If unavailable, add 2 tbs.
salt to water and a rack to
lift lobster off the bottom of
the pan.

Rinse mussels in cold water. Pull black threads out of mussels at the hinge of the shells. Parboil onions and potatoes. In a large 12 x 16 inch roasting pan, place a one inch layer of seaweed. Place lobsters on top of the seaweed and arrange corn and onions between the lobsters and the sides of the pan. Place more seaweed over lobster and gently add mussels and potatoes being careful not to keep the top of the Bake level. Cover with remaining seaweed and add water to the pan. Cover tightly with lid or foil and place on the stove or a preheated grill to cook. (If using a grill make sure the coals are very hot.) Start timing the Bake when you first see steam. Cook covered for 15 minutes. Serve with melted butter and lemon wedges on the side.

Yields: 4 servings

SEAFOOD SALAD SANDWICH AND SOUP

1 can (14.75 oz.) Bumble
Bee pink or red salmon
1 can (12.5 oz.) Bumble Bee
white or light tuna
1 can (7.5 oz.) Bumble Bee
shrimp
half basket of fresh berries
of your choice
Seafood salad dressing:
2 tbs. (1 oz.) light cream
cheese

2 tbs. (1 oz.) plain yogurt or
light mayonnaise
1 tbs. minced celery
1 tbs. green onion
1 tsp. lemon juice
1 tbs. fresh dillweed
1 tbs. fresh minded parsley
(optional)
Garnish:
lemon wedges or wheels
romaine lettuce
springs of dill

For seafood salad dressing: Cream first two ingredients completely. Fold in remaining ingredients.

For salad: Top open-faced sandwiches with a lettuce leaf. Divide seafood salad evenly among four slices. Top each of the remaining 4 slices with 2 tomato slices and then with 2 avocado slices.

Arrange 2 melon slices, berries and lemon wheels on plate. Garnish seafood salad sandwich tops with sprigs of dill.

Yields: 4 to 6 servings

SEAFOOD SALAD WITH DILL

Dressing:
1/2 cup plain yogurt
1/2 cup sour half and half
1/4 cup lemon juice
2 tbs. minced celery
2 tbs. green onion
2 tbs. minced fresh dill
2 tbs. parsley
Barley salad:
2 cups barley cooked in 4
cups chicken broth
1 cup red and green pepper,
julienned
1 cup crookneck and zuc-
chini, quartered and sliced
1 cup broccoli (steamed in
microwave 4 minutes)
1 cup cauliflower (steamed
or microwaved 4 minutes)
1 can (14.75 oz.) Bumble
Bee red or pink skinless
boneless salmon
1 can (12.5 oz.) Bumble Bee
white or light tuna in water

Bring rinsed barley to boiling point in chicken broth. Reduce heat and simmer. Cover and cook for 20 minutes.

Combine dressing ingredients and set aside in refrigerator.

Prepare all vegetables and toss in lg. bowl with seafood. Combine with barley and fold in dressing.

Serve main dish salad garnished with lemon wedges and parsley sprigs.

Yields: 4 servings

SALMON FONDUE TOPPED EGGS IN PUFF PASTRY SHELLS

2 tbs. each butter and flour
1/4 tsp. cayenne
1/2 cup each lowfat milk
and evaporated skim milk
1/2 cup dry white wine
1/4 cup freshly grated
parmesan cheese
1 can (6 1/2 oz.) Bumble
Bee skinless boneless
salmon (pink or red)
4 baked puff pastry shells
heat and hold scrambled
eggs
1/4 cup minced parsley
Heat and hold scrambled
eggs:
These eggs will not dry out,
even if kept warm on an
electric warming tray for as
long as an hour.
1 tsp. butter
2 tsps. each butter and flour
3 tbs. each plain yogurt and
kefir or light sour cream
8 to 10 eggs

Melt butter in chafing dish or saucepan over medium-high heat. Tilt pan and stir in flour and seasonings. Blend well.

Add milk slowly, stirring briskly with a wooden spoon or wire whisk. Cook over medium heat, stirring constantly, until mixture boils and thickens. Stir in wine, cheese and seafood; heat through.

Fill pastry shells with eggs. Spoon sauce over. Garnish with minced parsley.

Heat and hold scrambled eggs:

In a small saucepan, melt the 2 teaspoons of butter. Stir in flour and cook until bubbly. Remove from heat and blend in yogurt and kefir or light sour cream.

Return to heat and cook, stirring, until bubbly and smooth; set aside.

Beat eggs lightly. In a wide nonstick frying pan, melt the 1 teaspoon of butter. Pour in eggs and allow to set. Run spatula around edge, lifting to allow uncooked eggs to flow underneath until eggs are softly set.

Remove from heat and gently stir in yogurt mixture. Eggs can be served immediately or held in a serving dish on a warming tray. Assemble the egg-filled shells yourself, or let each guest help themselves.

Yields: 4 servings

CURRIED TUNA SALAD

Salad:
2 tbs. lite mayonnaise
2 tbs. plain yogurt
2 tbs. fresh lemon juice
1 to 2 tsp. curry powder
1 tbs. mango chutney
1 can (12.5 oz.) Bumble Bee white or light, solid or chunk, tuna (drained)
1/2 cup celery, thinly sliced
1/2 cup thinly sliced green onion
1 cup red apple, cored and diced
1 cup green tart apple, cored and diced
1 bunch red or green seedless grapes (halved lengthwise)
Garnish:
sliced almonds toasted
red or green grapes
2 sm. cantaloupe or honeydew melons

Combine mayonnaise, yogurt, lemon juice, curry powder and mango chutney. Gently fold in remaining ingredients. Season to taste and chill. Flute and seed melons. Refrigerate until ready to fill. Fill hollows with mixture and garnish with almonds and grapes.

Yields: 4 servings

SALMON FETTUCINI

1 can (15 1/2 oz.) Bumble Bee pink salmon
1 package (8 oz.) fettucini (or use spaghetti)
boiling salted water
2 cloves garlic, minced
4 cups sliced fresh mushrooms
1 cup diced green onion
1/2 tsp. oregano, crumbled
1/2 tsp. sweet basil, crumbled
1/4 tsp. rosemary, crumbled
1/2 cup butter
1/2 cup olive oil
1/3 cup dry white wine
1 med. zucchini, julienne
chopped parsley
grated parmesan cheese

Drain salmon. Remove skin, if desired. Mash bones. Cook fettucini in water 5 to 7 minutes until just tender. Sauté garlic, mushrooms, onion, oregano, basil and rosemary in butter and olive oil until mushrooms are golden. Stir in wine and zucchini. Simmer 1 minute or until zucchini is tender crisp. Remove from heat. Gently fold in salmon. Toss with cooked fettucini. Top with parsley. Serve with generous amounts of parmesan cheese.

Yields: 4 to 6 servings

CATFISH FILLETS WITH PARSLEY-PECAN SAUCE

2 cups all-purpose flour
1 tbs. cayenne pepper
1 tbs. plus 1 tsp. salt
6 genuine U.S. catfish fillets, about 6 ozs. each
2 tbs. vegetable oil
2 tbs. unsalted butter
2 cups parsley-pecan sauce
Parsley-pecan sauce:
2 cups tightly packed fresh parsley, leaves and tender stems only
1/2 cup olive oil
1/2 cup broken pecan meats
1 lg. clove garlic, chopped
1/2 cup freshly grated parmesan cheese
1/2 cup freshly grated romano cheese
2 tbs. unsalted butter, cut into pieces

Mix flour, cayenne pepper and salt. Spread on large platter and dredge each fillet, shaking off excess. Set aside on sheet of waxed paper. Heat half the oil and butter in a skillet large enough to accommodate 3 fillets. When butter is foaming but not brown, add fillets and sauté on one side for about 4 minutes, until light golden.

Turn fillets and spread the browned side with sauce; continue to sauté until underside is browned, about another 4 minutes. Cover skillet for a few minutes to melt sauce. Remove fish to platter.

Add remaining oil and butter and cook remaining fillets.

To prepare parsley-pecan sauce: Place parsley in food processor and process until coarsely chopped, turning machine off and on and scraping down sides. Add all other ingredients except salt, and process until mixture makes a smooth paste. Store, tightly covered in refrigerator.

Yields: 6 servings and 2 cups sauce

SHRIMP MOSTACCIOLI

1 lb. mostaccioli, ziti or other med. pasta shape, uncooked
5 1/2 cups tangerine or orange juice, divided
1 lg. yellow onion, minced
1 tbs. minced, seeded jalapeno pepper
2 bay leaves
2 tbs. minced garlic, divided
1 tbs. olive or vegetable oil
1 med. red onion, thinly sliced
1 lb. med. shrimp, peeled and deveined

salt and freshly ground
pepper to taste
1 cup diced Brie cheese
(about 4 ozs.)
2 tbs. thinly sliced basil
leaves
1 cup tangerine or orange
segments
1/3 cup slivered almonds,
lightly tossed

Combine 5 cups of the tangerine or orange juice, the yellow onion, jalapeno, bay leaves and 1 tablespoon of garlic in a medium saucepan. Bring to a boil and cook until liquid is reduced by two-thirds. Remove the bay leaves. Allow to cool. Transfer juice mixture to a blender and blend until smooth. Add salt and pepper to taste and set aside.

Prepare pasta according to package directions. While pasta is cooking, add the oil, red onion and shrimp to a medium skillet. Sauté 1 minute. Add the remaining 1/2 cup tangerine or orange juice to the skillet and cook over low heat.

Drain the pasta, return it to the pot and add the reserved orange sauce and the shrimp mixture. Cook over low heat 1 minute. Stir in the Brie and basil. Stir until the Brie is melted. Transfer to a serving bowl. Garnish with orange segments and toasted almonds. Serve immediately.

Yields: 4 to 6 servings

LOBSTER AMERICAN WITH RICE AND HARICOTS VERTS

3/4 pound haricots verts or
thin green beans
1 tsp. unsalted butter
1 1/2 tsp. all-purpose flour
1 tbs. minced fresh tarragon
1 tbs. mined fresh chives
4 cups boiled long-grain
rice, preferably jasmine
Lobster stock:
2 1 1/2 lb. live lobster
1 tbs. olive oil
1 med. onion, coarsely
chopped
1 sm. carrot, coarsely
chopped
1 clove garlic, thinly sliced
1/4 cup cognac
3/4 cup dry white wine
2 large Italian plum tomatoes, finely chopped
3 fresh flat-leaf parsley
sprigs
1 fresh thyme spring or 1/4
tsp. dried
1 bay leaf
salt to taste
freshly ground pepper to
taste

In a medium saucepan of boiling salted water, cook the haricots verts over moderately high heat until tender, about 5 minutes. Drain and keep warm.

In a small bowl, work the butter into the flour to form a paste, then whisk the paste into the hot lobster stock. Bring to a boil over high heat, whisking constantly. Reduce the heat to low, add the lobster meat, tarragon and half of the chives and stir until warmed through.

To serve, arrange the rice in a ring on a platter. Spoon the lobster and sauce in the center. Arrange the haricots verts around the rice and garnish with the remaining chives.

For lobster stock: Bring a large pot of salted water to a boil. Plunge in the lobsters head first, cover and simmer over moderate heat for 17 minutes. Transfer the lobsters to a large bowl and let cool for about 1 hour.

Working over the bowl to catch the liquid, detach the lobster tails from the bodies. Using kitchen shears, snip through the soft underside of the tail shells and remove the meat. Twist off the claws, crack them open and remove the meat. Pull out and discard the intestinal vein that runs down the tail. Cut the lobster meat into 1/2 inch pieces and add to the bowl. Discard the sand sac behind the eyes and chop the shells and head into 1 inch pieces.

Heat the olive oil in a large, heavy, non-reactive saucepan. Add the onion and carrot and cook over moderately high heat, stirring occasionally, until lightly colored, about 3 minutes. Add the lobster shells and garlic and cook until fragrant, about 3 minutes longer. Add the cognac and ignite with a match. Cook until the flame burns out, about 1 minute.

Add the wine, tomatoes, parsley, thyme, bay leaf, 1/4 teaspoon salt and 5 cups of water to the saucepan. Bring to a boil, cover and simmer over moderately low heat, stirring occasionally, for 50 minutes. Pass the stock through a fine strainer into a large clean saucepan and discard the solids. Add any liquid from the lobster meat and boil over high heat until reduced to 1 cup, about 15 minutes. Season the stock with salt and pepper. (This recipe can be prepared to this point up to 4 hours ahead. Cover and let the lobster meat and stock stand separately at room temperature. Re-warm the stock before proceeding.)

Yields: 4 servings

SOLE REMOULADE

4 sole fillets (1 lb.)
Remoulade sauce:
pepper to taste
dill weed
2 tbs. water
2 fresh California nectarines
or peaches, sliced (2 cups)

Prepare remoulade sauce. Roll up sole fillets and fasten with wooden picks. (If fillets are lg., cut in 1/2 lengthwise before rolling.) Stand on end, turban-fashion, in microwave-safe dish. Season with pepper and dill weed. Add water to dish. Cover and microwave on high power 3 to 4 minutes or until fish is done. Add nectarine slices to dish and microwave, covered, 1 minute or until hot. Transfer fish and fruit to serving platter and remove picks. Serve with remoulade sauce.

Yields: 4 servings

ARTICHOKE SCALLOP SALAD

2 lg. California artichokes, prepared and cooked as directed for whole artichokes
12 ozs. bay scallops
1/2 cup lime juice
2 tbs. each chopped cilantro stems and leaves
2 tsps. sugar
1 tsp. cornstarch
3 drops hot pepper sauce
1/2 cup grated Swiss cheese

Cut artichokes in half lengthwise. Remove center petals and fuzzy centers. Place scallops, lime juice and cilantro stems in a microwave-safe container; marinate 10 minutes. Cover with waxed paper; microwave at medium (50%) 5 minutes. Remove scallops from marinade. Strain marinade into microwave-safe container; stir in cilantro leaves, sugar, cornstarch, and hot pepper sauce. Microwave at high (100%) 2 minutes.

Arrange scallops on each artichoke half; drizzle with heated mixture. Garnish with cheese. Microwave at medium 2 minutes or until thoroughly heated.

Yields: 4 servings

MARINATED OYSTER SALAD

1 package Italian salad dressing mix (for approximately 8 ozs. dressing)
1 pint Maryland oysters, standards
1 cup cooked spiral pasta
1 cup cooked spinach noodles

1 cup cooked elbow macaroni
1/2 cup celery, sliced diagonally
1/2 cup carrots, sliced 1/4 inch rounds
1/2 cup radishes, sliced thinly
1/2 cup green or sweet red pepper, sliced
1/2 cup broccoli flowerettes
1/4 cup parsley, chopped

Night before: prepare salad dressing according to package directions. Poach oysters in their own liquor until edges begin to ruffle. Drain oysters and marinate in salad dressing overnight.

Several hours before serving: cook pastas according to package directions; drain and rinse in cold water until pasta is cold. Prepare vegetables. Combine pastas, vegetables and drained oysters; toss gently to mix, adding dressing as needed (about 1/2 cup). Marinate at least 1 hour. Serve on lettuce bed with extra dressing on side.

Yields: 6 to 8 servings

SEAFOOD GRAPEFRUIT SALAD

1/4 cup salad oil
2 lg. cloves garlic, minced
2 cups green beans cut in 1 inch pieces
1 lb. scallops
2 cups grapefruit sections grapefruit juice, drained from sections approximately 1/3 cup
3 tbs. vinegar
3/4 tsp. crushed fennel seeds
1/4 tsp. salt
1/2 cup sliced, pitted black olives

In medium skillet heat oil; cook garlic until golden. Add green beans; stir-fry 2 to 3 minutes until crisp-tender. Remove with slotted spoon to a lg. bowl. In same skillet, stir-fry scallops 2 to 3 minutes until done. Remove with slotted spoon

and add to green beans.

Add grapefruit juice to skillet. Stir in vinegar, fennel seeds and salt. Boil mixture, uncovered, until reduced to 1/3 cup. Return beans and scallops to skillet. Add grapefruit sections and olives; toss lightly. Serve immediately.

Yields: 4 servings

SHRIMP AVOCADO BOAT

6 to 8 ozs. cleaned boiled shrimp
1/4 cup diced green pepper
1/4 cup thinly sliced celery
1/4 cup sliced water chestnuts or toasted almond slivers
2 cups cooked shell macaroni
1 carambola cut into star slices (save 4 slices for garnish)
2 ripe avocados cut in half, pit removed and sprinkled with lime juice to prevent browning
Dressing:
1/2 to 3/4 cup mayonnaise
1 tbs. chopped onion
1 tbs. French dressing
1 tbs. lime juice
1/4 tsp. salt
1/2 tsp. Dijon-style mustard
freshly ground pepper

Prepare dressing and combine it with all salad ingredients except avocado. Chill thoroughly to blend flavors.

To serve, spoon salad into avocado boats. Top each serving with a star slice of carambola.

Yields: 4 servings

SHRIMP PAPAYA SALAD

2 tbs. sugar
2 tbs. fish sauce
juice of 2 lemons
3 cloves of garlic, minced
1 tbs. crushed black pepper (or regular black pepper)
3 fresh sm. chili peppers, chopped

3 cups green papaya, shredded
1 cup cooked shrimp, sliced
2 tbs. roasted peanuts, chopped
2 tbs. mixed fresh herbs, chopped (mint, basil, cilantro in equal parts)
1/2 cup tomato, diced

Combine sugar, fish sauce, lemon juice, garlic, black pepper and chili peppers in a mixing bowl until sugar is dissolved. Toss with remaining ingredients.

Yields: 6 to 8 servings

CRAB SALAD

1 lb. green beans, cut into 2 inch lengths
4 med. boiling potatoes (about 1 1/4 lbs.)
1/3 cup olive oil
1/4 cup white wine vinegar
1 tbs. thinly sliced chives or green onion
1/4 tsp. salt
1/4 tsp. pepper
6 cups torn butter lettuce leaves (1 head)
3/4 to 1 lb. crabmeat
1/4 cup sm. ripe black olives
1 cup cherry tomatoes

Cook potatoes in boiling water 32 minutes or until tender, drain, cool 10 minutes. Cut potatoes in 1 inch chunks and place in a shallow dish. Cook beans in boiling water 10 minutes or until tender; drain and cool 10 minutes. Add to potatoes.

Combine oil, vinegar, chives, salt and pepper in sm. jar with tight fitting lid. Shake well and pour 2/3 over potatoes and beans. Refrigerate, covered, 2 hours or up to 24 hours, stirring occasionally.

To serve arrange lettuce on 4 plates and spoon potato bean mixture on top. Divide crabmeat among the plates and garnish with olives and tomatoes. Drizzle remaining dressing on top.

Yields: 4 servings

CREAMED SALMON IN PASTRY SHELLS

1 can (15 1/2 oz.) Bumble Bee pink salmon
1 cup chopped green onion
3 tbs. butter
2 tbs. flour
1 tbs. Dijon mustard
1 tsp. oregano, crumbled
1 chicken bouillon cube, crumbed
1 cup water
1 cup half and half
1 package (10 oz.) frozen broccolettes
6 baked puff pastry shells (may be purchased in the frozen food section of supermarket), toasted English muffins or toast points

Drain salmon. In medium saucepan, sauté onion in 1 tablespoon butter. Melt remaining 2 tablespoons butter in same saucepan. Stir in flour, mustard, oregano and bouillon cube. Gradually stir in water, then half and half until blended. Simmer 5 minutes. Cook broccoli according to package directions. Drain well. Stir in salmon and broccoli. Serve spooned over pastry shells.

Yields: 6 servings

SALMON FLORENTINE

1 can (15 1/2 oz.) Bumble Bee pink salmon
1 package (8 oz.) medium width egg noodles, cooked
2 cups sliced fresh mushrooms
1/2 cup chopped onion
1/4 cup butter
1/4 cup flour
1 can (14 1/2 oz.) chicken broth
3/4 cup milk
1 package (10 oz.) frozen chopped spinach, thawed, drained
1/4 cup chopped pimento
1 tsp. dillweed, crumbled
1/4 tsp. salt
1/4 tsp. pepper
1 1/2 cups crushed potato chips

Drain salmon. Pour cooked noodles into 2 quart casserole dish. In large saucepan, sauté mushrooms and onion in butter. Stir in flour and cook until bubbly. Gradually stir in chicken broth, then milk. Simmer 2 minutes. Remove from heat. Stir in salmon, spinach, pimento and seasonings. Pour over noodles and mix. Bake in 350 degrees F oven 30 minutes. Sprinkle with potato chips. Bake 10 minutes longer.

Yields: 4 to 6 servings

PASTA WITH CATFISH AND ARTICHOKES

2 genuine U.S. farm-raised catfish fillets
3 tbs. butter or margarine
1 cup sliced artichoke hearts
1 red pepper, cut into julienne strips
1 carrot, cut into julienne strips
1 zucchini, cut into julienne strips
2/3 cup heavy cream or 2/3 cup lowfat milk
1/4 lb. angel hair pasta
1/2 cup grated parmesan cheese
1/4 tsp. ground nutmeg

Cut farm-raised catfish fillets in half crosswise and slice into thin strips. Sauté zucchini. Cook until tender. Stir in heavy cream, keep warm.

Cook pasta according to package directions, drain. Toss well with cream mixture and cheese. Sprinkle with nutmeg.

Yields: 8 servings

6

FRUIT
SIDE DISHES

SPICED APPLES AND GRAPES

Vinegar solution:
2 qts. cold water
1 tbs. coarse salt
1 tbs. white vinegar
4 lbs. red delicious apples, unpeeled
Syrup:
2 cups white vinegar
2 cups water
3 1/2 cups sugar
1 tsp. ground ginger
3 cinnamon sticks, 2 inches long, broken in half
1 tbs. whole cloves
2 cups seedless grapes (1 lb.)

To prepare vinegar solution mix cold water, salt and vinegar in a large bowl. Core apples; cut into quarters or eighths, depending on size. Drop apples in vinegar solution to prevent discoloration. To prepare syrup place vinegar, water, sugar, ginger and cinnamon in a large stainless steel or enamel kettle. Tie cloves in cheesecloth; add to kettle; bring to a boil. Rinse one quarter of the apples well and add to the boiling syrup. Return to a boil; simmer, uncovered, until apples are barely tender, 3 to 5 minutes. With a slotted spoon remove apples to a large bowl, repeat with remaining apples. Add grapes to boiling syrup; simmer, uncovered, until skins break, about 1 minute. Add to the bowl containing apples. Pour syrup over fruits and refrigerate overnight. To process, place fruits and syrup in a large kettle; bring to a boil. Pack fruits and syrup into six 1 pint hot sterilized canning jars, leaving 1/4 inch head space.

Place a cinnamon stick half in each jar. Cover, following manufacturer's directions. Process in boiling water bath for 20 minutes. Cool jars and check seals according to manufacturer's direction.

Yields: six (1 pint) jars

AMBROSIA WITH HONEY LIME CREAM DRESSING

1/4 cup honey
2 tbs. lime juice
3 oranges, peeled and sliced
2 bananas, peeled and sliced
1 each red and green apple, cored and cubed
1 cup shredded coconut
Honey lime cream dressing:
1/2 cup whipping cream
2 tbs. honey
1 tsp. grated lime peel

Combine honey and lime juice in large bowl; toss fruit with honey mixture. Layer fruit alternately with coconut in serving bowl. Top with honey lime cream dressing.

To prepare dressing: Beat whipping cream with electric mixer in large bowl until fluffy. Drizzle in honey and beat until stiff. Fold in lime peel.

Yields: 4 servings

HONEY BERRY PUREE

2 cups fresh blackberries or raspberries
1/4 cup honey
2 tbs. fruit-flavored or regular brandy (optional)

Place berries in blender or food processor; process until pureed. Or, mash berries with fork in medium bowl. Press through strainer to remove seeds, if desired. Stir in honey and brandy, if desired, until blended.

Tip: Serve honey berry puree over fruits, flan, pudding or ice cream.

Yields: 1 1/4 cups

ICED RASPBERRY SOUP

2 cups fresh raspberries
1 cup orange juice
3/4 cup white grape juice
2 tbs. red currant jelly
2 tsps. cornstarch
honey to taste

Puree raspberries and orange juice in blender or food processor. Rub through fine strainer and transfer to medium saucepan. Add white grape juice or China tea. In separate bowl, mix jelly and arrowroot or cornstarch. Add to soup mixture. Stir over low heat until mixture boils. Add light honey to taste. Reduce heat very low and simmer 10 minutes. Chill thoroughly. Serve in individual bowls embedded in crushed ice. Garnish with 1/2 cup heavy cream, whipped. Sprinkle with 1 tbs. grated orange rind.

Yields: 4 to 6 servings

BERRY DELIGHTFUL

2 cups fresh blueberries
1 cup seedless grapes
2 bananas, sliced
1 cup almonds, slivered or chopped
1/2 cup flaked coconut
1 cup plain yogurt

Mix all ingredients in a large bowl and garnish with coconut.

Yields: 6 to 8 servings

CRUNCHY BACON AND FRUIT SALAD

1 package (12 ozs.) lower-salt bacon, cut into 1 inch pieces or 8 ozs. sliced ham, cut into 1 inch pieces
1/2 cup fat-free mayonnaise
1 tbs. milk
1/2 tsp. curry powder
2 med. red apples, cut into 1/2 inch pieces or 2 oranges, peeled and cut into 1/2 inch pieces
1/2 cup sliced celery
1 sm. cantaloupe
1/4 cup chopped pecans, toasted

Cook bacon in large skillet over medium heat until crisp; drain on paper towels. Set aside. (Omit this step if using ham.)

Meanwhile slowly combine mayonnaise, milk and curry powder in medium bowl. Add bacon or ham, apples and celery; toss lightly until coated.

Cut ends off cantaloupe and cut four 1 inch thick crosswise slices. Cut off rind and remove seeds. Place a cantaloupe slice on each of 4 individual plates; spoon an equal amount of salad into center. Sprinkle with pecans.

Yields: 4 servings

SESAME SAUTÉ

1/4 cup flour
3 tbs. sesame seeds
1/8 tsp. salt
1/4 tsp. paprika
4 to 6 Chiquita bananas
1/3 cup (approximately) light cream or evaporated milk
1/4 cup butter or margarine
Berkshire sauce:
1/2 cup red currant jelly
1/2 tsp. prepared hot mustard
1/2 cup dry white wine (Chablis or Dry Sauterne)
2 tsps. cornstarch
1 tsp. finely sliced orange peel

Mix flour with sesame seeds, salt and paprika. Peel bananas and cut in half crosswise. Put cream in a flat pan. Dip bananas in cream and then roll in flour mixture to coat all sides.

Heat butter in a large skillet and sauté bananas slowly, 5 to 8 minutes, turning to brown on all sides. Bananas are done when easily pierced with a fork. Serve plain or with Berkshire sauce.

To prepare Berkshire sauce: In a small skillet, blend jelly and mustard. Place over low heat and stir with wire whisk or fork until jelly is melted. Combine wine and cornstarch and stir into jelly. Continue to cook and stir until mixture boils and is thickened. Add orange peel. Serve hot over sautéed bananas.

Suggestion: This is an eye catching and deliciously provocative vegetable to serve with baked ham, poultry or cold sliced meats of any variety.

Yields: 4 servings

FRUIT SOUP

5 fresh California nectarines, diced
1 cup plain low-fat yogurt
1/2 cup low-fat milk
1 tbs. sugar

1 tsp. almond extract
1/4 tsp. curry powder
1/2 cup strawberries, diced
mint leaves (optional)

Reserve 1/2 cup nectarines. Put remaining nectarines, yogurt, milk, sugar, almond extract and curry in blender; blend until smooth. Stir in reserved nectarines and strawberries. Chill; garnish with mint.

Yields: 6 servings

HONEY STRAWBERRY PRESERVES

6 cups sliced fresh strawberries
2 boxes (1 3/4 ozs. each) powdered pectin
1 3/4 cups honey
2 tbs. fresh lemon juice

Combine strawberries and pectin in 5 quart saucepan; crush berries to blend completely. Bring mixture to a full rolling boil over medium heat. Boil hard for 1 minute, stirring constantly. Stir in honey and lemon juice; return to a full rolling boil. Boil hard 5 minutes, stirring constantly. Remove from heat. Skim off foam. Ladle into clean hot canning jars to within 1/4 inch of tops. Seal according to manufacturer's directions.

Place jars on rack in canner. Process 10 minutes in boiling water bath with boiling water two inches above jar tops. Remove jars from canner. Place on thick cloth or wire rack; cool away from drafts. After 12 hours test lids for proper seal; remove rings from sealed jars.

Yields: 3 pints

7

LUNCH & LIGHT MEALS

PASTRAMI AND GREENS WITH WARM CHUTNEY DRESSING

8 ozs. thinly sliced beef pastrami or corned beef
6 cups torn mixed salad greens (curly endive, romaine, leaf lettuce)
Warm chutney dressing:
2 slices bacon, cut lengthwise into 1/2 inch pieces
1 sm. onion, cut into thin wedges
1/2 cup water
1/3 cup Major Grey mango chutney, chopped
1/4 cup red wine vinegar
1 tsp. Dijon-style mustard

In medium skillet, cook bacon over medium heat until crisp. Remove and drain bacon.

In same skillet, add onion to bacon drippings; cook and stir 2 minutes. Increase heat to high. Add remaining dressing ingredients; cook and stir 2 minutes.

In large bowl, combine salad greens and half of hot dressing; toss to coat. Place greens on serving platter; arrange beef pastrami over greens. Spoon remaining dressing over beef pastrami; sprinkle with reserved bacon. Serve immediately.

Yields: 4 servings

PORK BURGERS ON SANDWICH BUNS

1 lb. lean ground pork
seasoned pepper
4 lg. soft sandwich buns

Divide pork into 4 portions and shape into patties about 3/4 inch thick, handling meat as little as possible. Sprinkle both sides of patties with seasoned pepper.

Grill over direct heat over medium hot fire 5 minutes per side, turning once. Serve immediately on buns with favorite condiments.

Yields: 4 servings

PORK PICCATA SANDWICHES

4 pork cutlets, (3 to 4 ozs. each, 1/4 inch thick)
lemon pepper
2 tsps. butter
4 lg. sandwich buns, split
lemon wedges

Coat cutlets well with lemon pepper to taste. In a large non-stick skillet, heat butter to sizzling. Add cutlets (do not crowd) to hot pan; cook quickly to brown both sides, turning once. Place cutlets on buns; serve with wedge of lemon.

Yields: 4 servings

PORK SALAD A LA GRECQUE

12 ozs. (about 1 1/2 cups) roasted pork loin, cut into
1 sm. head Boston or bibb lettuce
1 pint cherry tomatoes
1/4 lb. firm feta cheese
2 tbs. olive oil
4 tbs. lemon juice
1 tsp. dried rosemary, crushed
1 tsp. dried tarragon, crumbled
1 tsp. dried thyme
1/4 lb. Nicoise olives, or 1 jar (6 oz.) oil-packed black olives

Wash lettuce and dry with paper towels. Arrange lettuce in shallow serving bowl. Wash and dry tomatoes and remove stems.

Cut feta cheese into small cubes. Combine olive oil, lemon juice, rosemary, tarragon and thyme. Add tomatoes and olives, and toss until evenly coated. Add cheese, olives and pork, and toss gently.

Yields: 4 servings

PORK TENDERLOIN AU JUS SANDWICH

1/2 tsp. beef bouillon granules
1/2 tsp. paprika
1/8 tsp. salt
1/2 lb. pork tenderloin, sliced 1/4 inch thick
6 to 8 mushrooms, thinly sliced
2 green onions
1/2 tsp. butter
2 crusty rolls or toasted whole wheat bread

Stir together bouillon granules, paprika and salt in microwave-safe 9 inch pie plate. Add pork tenderloin slices, turning to coat both sides evenly with paprika mixture. Cover with plastic wrap; vent 1 corner.

Microwave on medium-low (30% power, about 200 watts) 4 minutes; turn slices over, rearranging so least-cooked parts are to outside edges of dish. Re-cover and continue microwaving on medium-low 3 to 5 minutes. Let stand, covered, 3 to 5 minutes.

Meanwhile, place mushrooms and chopped white part of onions in microwave-safe measure; top with butter and cover with plastic wrap. Microwave (High) 45 to 60 seconds or until mushrooms are tender. Arrange tenderloin slices on tops and bottoms of rolls; spoon mushrooms over tenderloin; sprinkle with finely chopped green part of onions. Spoon meat and mushroom juices over sandwiches or combine juices and pass to serve.

Yields: 2 servings

PERFECT GRILLED BURGERS

1 1/2 lbs. lean ground beef
salt and pepper (optional)
6 hamburger buns, split
Basil marinated tomatoes:
6 tomato slices, 1/4 inch thick
6 thin red onion slices
1 tbs. thinly sliced fresh basil
1 tbs. olive oil
2 tsps. red wine vinegar
1/2 tsp. sugar
Mango salsa:
2 lbs. fresh mangoes, peeled, seeded
2 tbs. chopped green onion
1 tbs. fresh lime juice
1 tbs. chopped fresh cilantro
1 serrano or jalapeno pepper, seeded, finely chopped

Shape ground beef into six 1/2 inch thick patties.

Place patties on grll over medium coals. Grill 7 to 9 minutes or until no longer pink and juices run clear, turning once. Season with salt and pepper, if desired, after turning.

Serve grilled burgers on buns with basil marinated tomatoes, mango salsa or crisp and spicy cabbage relish, if desired.

Basil marinated tomatoes: Place tomato slices in shallow dish; top each with one onion slice.

Combine remaining ingredients, mixing until well blended. Pour over tomato and onion. Cover and refrigerate up to 1 hour. Serve with perfect grilled burgers.

Mango salsa: Coarsely chop mangoes to make 1 1/2 cups. In medium bowl, combine mangoes with remaining ingredients; mix lightly. Cover and refrigerate. Serve with perfect grilled burgers.
Yields: 1 1/2 cups

Yields: 6 servings

PITA BURGERS WITH CUCUMBER-YOGURT SAUCE

1 lb. lean ground beef
1/2 cup plain low-fat yogurt
1/3 cup chopped cucumber
2 tsps. Pepper-Herb Mix, divided
1/4 tsp. salt
2 pita pocket breads, halved and warmed
1 med. tomato, cut into 8 thin slices
Pepper-herb mix:
2 tbs. dried basil leaves
1 tbs. each lemon-pepper and onion powder
1 1/2 tsps. rubbed sage

Combine yogurt, cucumber, 1/2 teaspoon herb mix and salt in a small bowl; reserve.

Shape ground beef into four 1/2 inch thick patties. Sprinkle remaining 1 1/2 teaspoons herb mix over both sides of patties.

Meanwhile heat large nonstick skillet over medium heat 5 minutes. Place patties in skillet and cook 6 to 8 minutes, turning once. Season with salt, if desired.

To serve, place a burger in each pita half; add 2 tomato slices and yogurt sauce as desired.

Pepper-herb mix: Combine all ingredients. Store, covered, in airtight container. Shake before using to blend. yields about 1/3 cup.

Serving suggestion: Serve with fresh fruit.

Yields: 4 servings

HARVEST-THYME BEEF SANDWICHES

1 lb. boneless beef top sirloin steak, cut 3/4 inch thick
1/4 tsp. salt
1/4 tsp. pepper
8 lg. oval slices rye or sour-dough bread, toasted
lettuce
Relish:
1 cup shredded carrot
1 cup shredded turnip
3 tbs. sliced green onions
2 tbs. prepared fat-free Italian dressing
1/4 tsp. dried thyme leaves

Heat large nonstick skillet over medium heat until hot. Place beef steak in skillet; cook 10 to 13 minutes for rare to medium doneness, turning once. Season with salt and pepper.

Meanwhile in medium bowl, combine relish ingredients; mix well.

Line 4 slices of toasted bread with lettuce; spoon equal amount of relish over lettuce. Trim fat from steak. Carve steak crosswise into thin slices. Arrange beef over relish; close sandwiches with remaining toasted bread.

Yields: 4 servings

PHILADELPHIA STEAK SANDWICHES

8 ozs. beef tip steaks, cut 1/8 to 1/4 inch thick
2 French-style rolls, split lengthwise
2 tbs. vegetable oil
1 med. onion, coarsely chopped
1 sm. green bell pepper, coarsely chopped
1/4 tsp. salt
1/8 tsp. black pepper
1/4 cup pasteurized process cheese spread, warmed

Cut beef tip steaks into 1/2 inch strips; reserve. Wrap rolls in aluminum foil; heat in 350 degrees F oven 5 to 7 minutes or until warm.

Meanwhile, heat oil in large nonstick skillet over medium-high heat. Add onion and green pepper; stir-fry 4 minutes. Add beef strips; stir-fry 2 minutes. Sprinkle with salt and black pepper. Place an equal amount of beef mixture on bottom half of each roll; top with an equal amount of cheese. Cover with top half of roll. Serve with celery sticks.

Yields: 2 servings

SALSA TOPPED BURGERS

4 hamburger rolls, toasted
1 cup thinly sliced lettuce
Grilled burgers:
1 lb. ground beef (80 percent lean)
salt and pepper, as desired
Salsa:
1 med. tomato, seeded and coarsely chopped
1 tbs. thinly sliced green onion
1 1/2 tsps. chopped cilantro (fresh coriander) or parsley
1 1/2 tsps. red wine vinegar
1 sm. clove garlic, minced
1/8 tsp. each salt and coarse grind black pepper
1/2 to 1 jalapeno pepper, seeded and minced

For salsa topping, combine tomato, onion, cilantro, vinegar, garlic, salt, pepper and jalapeno pepper; cover and set aside.

Grilled burgers: Shape ground beef into four 1/2 inch thick patties. Place patties on grid over medium coals . Grill 10 minutes for medium (160 degrees F), or to desired doneness, turning once. Season with salt and pepper.

Place grilled burgers on roll bottoms; top each with an equal amount of salsa and lettuce. Cover with roll tops.

Yields: 4 servings

SAUSAGE AND PEPERONATA SANDWICHES

1 lb. fully-cooked bratwurst (8 sausages), grilled or broiled
2 yellow bell peppers, each cut in half
2 red bell peppers, each cut in half
1 tbs. olive oil
1 lg. red onion, thinly sliced and separated into rings
2 lg. cloves garlic, crushed
8 pieces French baguette (each 6 inches long), split horizontally

Cut peppers lengthwise into thin strips. Heat oil in skillet. Add peppers, onion and garlic; cook over medium-high heat 5 minutes, stirring frequently. Reduce heat to medium-low, cover tightly and continue cooking 40 to 45 minutes or until mixture is very soft and almost creamy, stirring occasionally. (If mixture becomes too dry, add 1 to 2 tablespoons water.)

Toast cut sides of bread under broiler. Place grilled bratwurst in French bread pieces. Top each with equal amounts of Peperonata. Serve immediately

Yields: 8 servings

SAVORY BEEF BURGERS

1 lb. extra lean ground beef (85 percent lean)
2 tbs. minced onion
1 tbs. Dijon-style mustard
3/4 tsp. dried Italian seasoning
1/4 tsp. each ground cumin, cracked black pepper and salt
8 to 12 bibb lettuce leaves
8 med. tomato slices cut 1/4 inch thick
8 thin red onion rings

Combine ground beef, minced onion, mustard, Italian seasoning, cumin, pepper and salt, mixing lightly but thoroughly. Divide beef mixture into 4 equal portions; shape into patties 4 inches in diameter.

Place patties on rack in broiler pan so surface of meat is 3 to 4 inches from heat source. Broil to desired doneness, 8 to 10 minutes, turning once.

Place 2 or 3 lettuce leaves on each of 4 individual plates; top with 2 tomato slices, 2 onion rings and a burger. Garnish as desired.

Yields: 4 servings

SHORTCUT ITALIAN BEEF SANDWICHES

1 lb. beef round tip steaks, cut 1/4 inch thick
1 cup ready-to-serve beef broth
1/4 tsp. dried oregano leaves
1 tbs. vegetable oil
2 sm. green bell peppers, cut into thin strips
1 med. onion, sliced
2 cloves garlic, crushed
1/4 tsp. dried oregano
4 Italian rolls, split

In small saucepan, combine broth and 1/4 teaspoon oregano; simmer 10 to 15 minutes.

Meanwhile in large nonstick skillet, heat oil over medium-high heat until hot. Add bell peppers, onion, garlic and 1/4 teaspoon oregano; cook and stir 3 to 4 minutes or until tender. Remove from skillet; keep warm.

In same skillet, cook steaks (1/2 at a time) 1 to 1 1/2 minutes or until outside surface is no longer pink, turning once.

Dip cut surface of bottom half of each roll in broth; top with steak and equal amounts of vegetables. Dip cut surface of top half of each roll in broth; close sandwiches.

Yields: 4 servings

SIRLOIN CITRUS SALAD

1 lb. boneless beef top sirloin , cut 1 inch thick

1 tbs. olive oil
4 cups torn romaine lettuce
2 oranges, peeled and separated into segments
1/4 cup walnuts, toasted
sliced strawberries, optional
Citrus vinaigrette:
2 tbs. each orange juice and red wine vinegar
1 tbs. olive oil
2 tsps. honey
1 1/4 tsps. Dijon-style mustard

To prepare citrus vinaigrette: Thoroughly combine above ingredients.

Prepare citrus vinaigrette; reserve. Cut beef steak into 1/8 inch thick strips; cut each strip in half.

Heat oil in a large nonstick skillet over medium-high heat. Stir-fry beef (1/2 at a time) 1 to 2 minutes. Remove with slotted spoon; season with salt, if desired.

Toss lettuce, beef and oranges in large bowl. Sprinkle with walnuts. Drizzle with citrus vinaigrette. Garnish with strawberries, if desired. Serve immediately.

Recipe may also be prepared using beef top round steak cut 1 inch thick or flank steak.

Serving suggestion: Serve with sesame bread sticks.

Yields: 4 servings

SWEET AND SOUR WIENERS 'N' BEANS

1 cup dried Idaho red or pink beans (about 3 cups cooked)
3 cups water
1 tsp. salt
1 lb. wieners
2 tbs. butter or margarine
1 sm. onion, sliced
1 green pepper, cut in strips
2 tbs. flour
1 can (13 1/4 oz.) pineapple chunks
1/2 cup water
1 can (8 oz.) tomato sauce
1 beef bouillon cube
1/4 tsp. salt

2 tbs. sugar
2 tbs. lemon juice
1 tbs. soy sauce

Soak beans in water overnight. Cook beans in soaking water with the addition of 1 teaspoon salt until tender, about 2 hours. Drain. Score wieners, making shallow (1/4 inch) diagonal cuts, 1 inch apart. Brown slightly in butter and remove. Sauté onion and green pepper in remaining butter. Blend in flour. Drain pineapple, reserving syrup. Add pineapple syrup, water, tomato sauce and bouillon cube in skillet. Cook, stirring, until bouillon cube is dissolved and sauce is smooth. Add beans, salt, sugar, lemon juice and soy sauce. Cover and simmer 10 minutes. Add pineapple and wieners and simmer just until heated through.

Yields: 6 servings

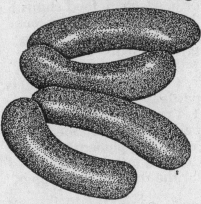

SOUTHWESTERN FRANKFURTERS

1 lb. beef frankfurters (8 to 10)
1/2 cup chopped cucumber
1 can (4 oz.) chopped green chilies, undrained
1 med. tomato, chopped
1/2 tsp. ground cumin
8 to 10 taco shells
1/2 avocado, peeled, seeded and cut into 8 to 10 slices

Place frankfurters on grid over medium coals. Grill 8 to 10 minutes, turning occasionally.

Meanwhile, combine cucumber, chilies, tomato and cumin. Place 1 tablespoon cucumber relish in each taco shell; top with a grilled

frankfurter. Place avocado slice on 1 side of each frankfurter; top with an additional tablespoon of relish.

Yields: 8 to 10 servings

SUPER BOWL DELI SUB

1/2 lb. thinly sliced ham
1/4 lb. thinly sliced hard salami
1/4 lb. sliced bologna
1 loaf Italian or Vienna bread, unsliced (approximately 1 lb.)
3 cups sliced romaine lettuce, 1/2 inch thick
3/4 cup thin red onion wedges
1 jar (7 oz.) roasted red peppers, rinsed, drained, cut into strips
1/4 cup prepared Italian dressing
4 slices Monterey jack cheese with jalapeno pepper (approximately 4 ozs.)
1 tbs. prepared Italian dressing

Cut bread lengthwise in half. Remove part of soft center from top and bottom halves; reserve crumbs for another use.

In large bowl, combine lettuce, onion, red peppers and 1/4 cup dressing; mix lightly. Fill bottom half of loaf with lettuce mixture.

Layer ham, salami and bologna over lettuce mixture; top with cheese.

Brush remaining 1 tablespoon dressing on inside of top half of loaf. Close sandwich with top half of loaf; cut crosswise into 8 portions.

Yields: 8 servings

THREE PEPPER BURGERS

1/2 cup short thin green bell pepper strips
1/2 cup short thin red or yellow bell pepper strips
1 sm. garlic clove, minced
1/4 tsp. dried oregano leaves

1 1/2 tsps. olive oil
1/8 tsp. salt
4 onion rolls, toasted
4 slices mozzarella or provolone cheese (1 oz. each)
Grilled burgers:
1 lb. ground beef (80 percent lean)
salt and pepper, as desired

Cook peppers, garlic and oregano in hot oil in small nonstick frying pan over medium-high heat, stirring frequently, until crisp-tender, about 3 minutes. Remove from heat; stir in salt.

Shape ground beef into four 1/2 inch thick patties. Place patties on grid over medium coals. Grill 10 minutes for medium (160 degrees F), or to desired doneness, turning once.

Season with salt and pepper, as desired, after turning.

Place grilled burgers on roll bottoms; top each with a cheese slice and an equal amount of pepper mixture. Cover with roll tops.

Yields: 4 servings

VEAL KNOCKWURST

4 fully cooked veal
knockwurst or bratwurst
links (approximately 12
ozs.)
1/2 cup chopped onion
1/2 cup chopped red bell
pepper
2 tsps. vegetable oil
1 cup (8 ozs.) sauerkraut,
drained
2 tbs. honey mustard
1 tbs. water
4 French rolls, split,
warmed

In large nonstick skillet, brown knockwurst over medium heat 4 to 6 minutes, turning occasionally. Push knockwurst to one side of skillet. Add onion, bell pepper and oil; cook and stir 1 minute.

Stir in sauerkraut, mustard and water; reduce heat to low. Cover tightly; cook 10 minutes.

Place knockwurst in rolls; top

each with equal amount of sauerkraut mixture.

Yields: 4 servings

WARM BEEF 'N GREENS SALAD

8 to 12 ozs. boneless beef
chuck top blade steak (stir-
fry section)
1 clove garlic, minced
1/2 tsp. salt
2 tbs. vegetable oil
1/2 tsp. dried thyme leaves
1/4 tsp. freshly ground
black pepper
3 tbs. balsamic vinegar,
divided (Balsamic vinegar is
an Italian aged vinegar with
a distinctive flavor. It is
available in the imported
section of the supermarket
or in specialty food shops.)
3 cups mixed salad greens
(spinach, leaf lettuce, mustard greens)
1/2 cup slivered red onion
1/3 cup frozen corn kernels,
partially thawed
1/4 cup canned roasted red
pepper strips, drained (One
jar, (2 oz.) pimientos,
drained, may be substituted
for the roasted red pepper.

Slice beef chuck top blade steak into strips, 1/2 inch wide and 1/4 inch thick. Mash garlic; combine with salt to form a paste. Combine paste with oil, thyme, black pepper and 1 tablespoon of the vinegar in medium bowl. Add beef strips; stir to coat. Marinate 20 minutes.

Arrange mixed greens on 2 salad plates. Remove beef from marinade; drain well. Combine marinade with remaining 2 tbs. vinegar.

Heat large skillet over high heat. Add beef strips; stir-fry 2 minutes. Add onion, corn and red pepper; continue cooking 30 seconds. Spoon steak mixture over greens. Heat marinade mixture to a boil. Spoon over salad.

Yields: 2 servings

BEEF AND BLACK-EYED PEA SALAD

1 1/2 lbs. boneless beef top
sirloin steak, cut 1 1/2
inches thick
1 bag (16 oz.) frozen black-
eyed peas
lime-chili vinaigrette, divided
1/4 cup red wine vinegar
1 cup jicama cut into 1/4
inch cubes (one can (8 oz.)
water chestnuts, drained
and diced, may be substi-
tuted for the jicama)
1 red or green bell pepper,
cut into 1 inch strips
1 can (4 oz.) diced green
chilies, drained
1/2 cup each sliced green
onions and sliced pitted ripe
olives
1/4 cup chopped fresh
cilantro or parsley
8 romaine lettuce leaves
Lime-chili vinaigrette:
1/2 cup each fresh lime
juice and vegetable oil
1 tsp. each ground cumin,
chili powder, salt and sugar
1/2 tsp. minced garlic

Cook black-eyed peas according to package directions; drain and reserve.

Meanwhile, trim excess fat from beef top sirloin steak. Prepare lime-chili vinaigrette.

Combine 1/4 cup of the vinaigrette and the vinegar. Place steak in plastic bag; add vinegar mixture, turning to coat steak. Close bag securely; marinate in refrigerator 30 minutes to 1 hour, turning at least once.

Remove steak from marinade; discard marinade. Place steak on rack in broiler pan so surface of meat is 3 inches from heat source. Broil 12 to 15 minutes or to desired doneness, turning once.

Meanwhile, combine remaining vinaigrette, the cooked black-eyed peas, jicama, pepper, chilies, green onions and olives in large skillet.

Cover; simmer over medium-low heat 5 minutes or until heated through. Add cilantro.

Line serving dish with lettuce leaves. Spoon pea mixture onto lettuce leaves; make depression in center. Carve steak diagonally into thin slices; arrange in center of pea mixture. Garnish with cherry tomatoes and cilantro sprigs, if desired.

Lime-chili vinaigrette: Whisk together lime juice and vegetable oil, cumin, chili powder, salt and pepper and minced garlic.

Yields: 6 servings

HERB SALAD AND WARM BEEF

1 lb. beef flank steak (recipe may also be prepared using beef top sirloin or top round steak cut 1 inch thick)
1/2 cup red wine vinegar
2 cloves garlic, crushed
2 tsps. dried basil leaves
1 tsp. sugar
1/2 tsp. salt
6 cups torn mixed salad greens
1 tbs. olive oil
1 med. onion, cut into thin wedges
1 med. red bell pepper, cut into strips

Cut beef steak lengthwise into 3 strips; slice across the grain into 1/8 inch thick strips. Combine vinegar, garlic, basil, sugar and salt; reserve. Place salad greens in serving bowl.

Heat oil in large nonstick skillet over medium-high heat. Stir-fry beef strips (1/2 at a time) 1 to 2 minutes. Remove with slotted spoon; keep warm.

Add onion and bell pepper to same skillet; stir-fry 2 to 3 minutes or until crisp-tender. Return beef to skillet with reserved dressing; heat through.

Spoon beef mixture and hot dressing over salad greens. Toss and serve immediately. Season with pepper, if desired.

Serving suggestion: Serve with warm dinner rolls.

Yields: 4 servings

REUBEN BEAN SANDWICHES

1 cup sauerkraut, drained (8 oz. can)
2 cups cooked or canned California light or dark red kidney or pink beans home-cooked or canned corned beef
4 slices cheddar, Jack or Swiss cheese
8 thin slices rye or other bread
oil or butter

In a saucepan, mix kraut, drained beans and corned beef. Heat till bubbly. Lay a slice of cheese on each of 4 slices of bread and top with 1/2 cup of bean-beef-kraut mixture. Press a second bread slice firmly on top to make a sandwich. Brown both sides quickly on an oiled griddle or skillet. Serve hot with cold drinks.

Yields: 4 sandwiches

SPICY MEATBALL SANDWICHES

12 cooked (1/2 recipe) large savory meatballs
2 tbs. water
1/2 green bell pepper, cut into thin strips
1/2 onion, cut into thin strips
1 1/4 cups prepared low-fat spaghetti sauce
1/2 tsp. dried basil leaves
4 hoagie rolls (each 5 inches long), split
1/4 cup shredded part-skim mozzarella cheese (optional)
Savory meatballs:
2 lbs. lean ground beef
1 cup soft bread crumbs
2 eggs
1/4 cup finely chopped onion
2 cloves garlic, crushed
1 tsp. salt
1/4 tsp. pepper

In large nonstick skillet, heat water over medium heat until hot.

Add bell pepper and onion; cook and stir 4 minutes or until water is evaporated and vegetables are tender. Reduce heat to medium-low; add meatballs, sauce and basil. Cover and cook 5 to 6 minutes or until heated through, stirring occasionally.

Spoon equal amounts of meatball mixture on bottom half of each roll; top with 1 tablespoon cheese, if desired. Close with top half of roll.

Heat oven to 350 degrees F. In large bowl, combine all ingredients, mixing lightly but thoroughly.

For 24 large meatballs: Shape beef mixture into 24 meatballs; place on rack in broiler pan.

Bake in 350 degrees F oven 25 to 30 minutes or until no longer pink and juices run clear.

Yields: 4 servings

ZESTY BASIL BURGERS

1 lb. lean ground beef
3 tbs. finely chopped onion
1 clove garlic, crushed
3/4 tsp. salt
1/4 tsp. pepper
4 crusty rolls, split
1 cup packed spinach leaves
4 tomato slices
Basil mayonnaise:
3 tbs. reduced-calorie mayonnaise
1 tbs. chopped fresh basil or
1 tsp. dried basil leaves
1 tsp. Dijon-style mustard

In medium bowl, combine ground beef, onion, garlic, salt and pepper, mixing lightly but thoroughly. Shape into four oval 1/2 inch thick patties.

Heat large nonstick skillet over medium heat until hot. Place patties in skillet; cook 7 to 8 minutes or until no longer pink and juices run clear, turning once.

Meanwhile in small bowl, combine basil mayonnaise ingredients; mix well.

Line bottom half of each roll with spinach and tomato. Place burger on tomato; top with 1 tablespoon mayonnaise mixture. Close with top half of roll.

Yields: 4 servings

CABBAGE, APPLE AND BEEF SAUSAGE SALAD

1/2 lb. reduced-fat fully-cooked smoked beef sausage link, cut into 1/2 inch thick slices
2 tsps. vegetable oil
1 sm. onion, cut into thin wedges
2 med. red apples, each cut into 12 wedges
6 1/2 cups (3/4 lbs.) packaged coleslaw mix
1/2 tsp. salt (optional)
Dressing:
1/4 cup apple jelly
2 tbs. cider vinegar
1 tbs. Dijon-style mustard
1/4 tsp. pepper

In large nonstick skillet, heat oil over medium heat until hot. Add onion and apples; cover and cook 5 minutes. Stir in coleslaw mix; continue cooking, covered, 2 to 4 minutes or until cabbage is crisp-tender. Season with salt, if desired. Remove to serving platter; keep warm.

In same skillet, add beef sausage; cook and stir over medium-high heat 2 minutes. Stir in combined dressing ingredients; cook 2 minutes or until sauce is reduced and slightly thickened. Spoon over cabbage mixture. Serve immediately.

Cook's Tip: The shredded cabbage in the packaged coleslaw mix may vary in thickness. Watch cooking time carefully; do not overcook. Thinly sliced green cabbage may be substituted for packaged coleslaw mix.

Yields: 6 servings

TURKEY HAM SALAD IN PINEAPPLE BOATS

1 package (3 oz.) chicken-flavored instant Oriental noodle soup, cooked accord-ing to package directions and cooled
1 1/3 cups turkey ham, cut into 2x1/4 inch strips
1/3 cup green onion, thinly sliced
1/4 cup water chestnuts, sliced
1/3 cup mango chutney, chopped
1/4 tsp. cayenne pepper
2 sm. pineapples
2 tbs. almonds, toasted

In medium-size bowl combine noodles, turkey ham, green onions, water chestnuts, chutney and cayenne pepper. Cover and refrigerate overnight.

Just before serving, cut pineapples in 1/2 lengthwise. With a grapefruit knife remove pineapple meat from skin; reserve skins for serving. Cut pineapple meat into 1/2 inch cubes. Add 3 cups pineapple cubes to turkey mixture.

To serve, spoon turkey mixture into reserved pineapple skins; top with almonds.

Yields: 4 servings

B.L.T. TART

1 1/4 lbs. Florida tomatoes (about 3 med.)
1 (9 inch) frozen deep dish pie crust
8 ozs. bacon (about 6 slices)
2 tbs. butter or margarine
2 1/2 cups sliced leeks (white and green portions)
4 eggs
1 1/2 cups heavy (whipping) cream
1/2 tsp. salt
1/4 tsp. ground black pepper
1/8 tsp. ground nutmeg

Use tomatoes held at room temperature until fully ripe; core and slice 1/4 inch thick; set aside.

Preheat oven to 425 degrees F. Pierce bottom and sides of pie crust with fork tines. Bake 5 minutes. Remove to a wire rack. Reduce heat to 350 degrees F.

In a large skillet cook bacon until crisp, about 4 minutes, turning occasionally; drain. Pour drippings out of skillet; wipe skillet with paper towel.

In skillet heat butter until melted; add leeks; cook and stir until crisp-tender, about 3 minutes. Crumble or cut bacon into small pieces; sprinkle over crust. Scatter leek mixture over bacon.

In a medium bowl lightly beat eggs; add cream, salt, black pepper and nutmeg; pour into crust. Bake until almost set, about 35 minutes. Arrange tomatoes on filling. Bake until filling is firm, about 10 minutes. Cool 10 minutes before serving.

Yields: 6 servings

ARM-CHAIR QUARTERBACK TURKEY DAGWOOD

16 slices low-calorie whole wheat bread
2 tomatoes, sliced
8 cups iceberg lettuce, shredded
2 packages (6 oz.) smoked turkey breast slices
8 slices (1 oz. each) reduced fat cheddar cheese
8 tbs. sweet hot mustard
Mock guacamole:
2 lg. cloves garlic
2 cups frozen peas, cooked according to package directions and drained
1/2 cup fresh cilantro leaves
1/4 cup onion, chopped
1 tbs. lemon juice
1/4 tsp. pepper
1/8 tsp. hot pepper sauce

To prepare mock guacamole; in food processor bowl, fitted with metal blade and motor running, drop garlic cloves through food tube; process 10 seconds.

Through feed tube, add peas, cilantro, onion, lemon juice, pepper and hot pepper sauce; process until smooth. Chill at least 1 hour.

Spread 3 tablespoons mock guacamole on 8 slices of bread.

Arrange in a layer 2 tomato slices, 1 cup lettuce, 2 slices turkey and 1 slice of cheese over top of guacamole on each bread slice.

Spread 1 tablespoon mustard over each remaining slice of bread and place on top of each sandwich. To serve, slice each sandwich in 1/2.

Yields: 8 servings

EASY ANTIPASTO SANDWICH

12 ozs. thinly sliced cooked lean roast beef
1/2 cup Italian dressing, divided
1 loaf Vienna bread, unsliced (8 ozs.)
2 tbs. chopped ripe olives
6 Boston lettuce leaves
6 thin tomato slices
6 very thin onion slices
6 thin bell pepper rings
6 thin slices provolone cheese

Place beef in plastic bag. Add 1/3 cup of the dressing, turning to coat beef. Close bag securely; marinate in refrigerator 1 to 2 hours.

Cut bread lengthwise in 1/2. Combine remaining dressing and olives; spoon over bottom 1/2 of bread.

To assemble, place lettuce, tomato, onion, green pepper and cheese in layers on bottom 1/2 of bread. Remove beef from marinade; arrange over cheese. Cover with top 1/2 of bread.

To serve, cut into slices.

Yields: 6 servings

MAINE SARDINE COLE SLAW

3 cans (3 3/4 to 4 ozs. each) Maine sardines
4 cups shredded cabbage
1/4 cup chopped onion
1/4 cup chopped parsley
2 hard cooked eggs, chopped
salad greens

paprika
Cole slaw dressing:
1/2 cup salad oil
3 tbs. vinegar
1 tbs. chopped green pepper
1 tbs. chopped pimiento
1 tbs. chopped sweet pickle
1 tsp. salt
1/4 tsp. paprika
dash cayenne pepper

Drain sardines and cut into large pieces. Combine cabbage, onion, parsley, eggs, and dressing. Arrange on salad greens. Top with sardines and sprinkle with paprika.

Cole slaw dressing: Combine all ingredients and mix thoroughly.

Yields: 6 servings

ROASTED SWISS ONION SANDWICH

1 med. red onion
2 ozs. Swiss cheese, grated
2 tsp. sour cream
shot of Tabasco sauce
pinch salt and freshly ground black pepper
2 slices seeded rye bread, lightly toasted
1 sm. dill pickle, sliced thinly, for garnish

Preheat broiler. Place whole onion, unpeeled, on small foil-covered baking pan. Cook, turning every 5 to 10 minutes, about 45 minutes or until charred on outside and soft throughout. Set aside to cool.

Peel and discard outer charred skin. Chop onion and mix in small bowl with Swiss cheese, sour cream, Tabasco sauce, salt and pepper. Spread evenly on 2 slices of toasted rye bread. Broil until warmed throughout and cheese is melted. Top with dill pickle.

Yields: 1 serving

POTATO-TOMATO LUNCHEON SALAD

2 Washington russet potatoes (8 to 10 ozs. each)

1/2 to 3/4 cup bottled reduced calorie Italian dressing, divided
1 can (6 1/4 or 6 1/2 oz.) light tuna, packed in water
2 tbs. each chopped parsley and celery
1 tbs. minced onion
salt and pepper to taste
3 med. tomatoes, sliced 1/2 inch thick
4 parsley sprigs
4 lemon wedges

Pierce potatoes several times with fork and microwave at high (100% power) 7 to 9 minutes or until tender. Turn potatoes and rotate 1/4 turn halfway through cooking time. Let stand, cover, 5 minutes.

Peel and dice potatoes. Pour 1/4 cup dressing over potatoes; toss gently and refrigerate until cold. Add remaining ingredients except tomatoes, lettuce and garnish. Add 1/4 to 1/2 cup remaining dressing; toss gently. Arrange 2 slices tomatoes on each lettuce-lined salad plate. Mound potato salad on tomatoes. Garnish with parsley and lemon wedges.

Yields: 4 servings

SALAD FLORIDA

2 cups water
1/2 cup frozen concentrated orange juice, thawed, undiluted
1 tsp. dried rosemary
1/2 tsp. whole coriander seeds
2 whole chicken breasts, skinned, boned and split
1 lb. raw shrimp, peeled and deveined
1/2 cup dry sherry (optional)
1 head red leaf lettuce
2 lg. grapefruit, peeled and sliced
2 oranges, peeled and sliced
2 tsps. ground anise seed
Orange sauce:
1/2 cup sour cream
1/4 cup frozen concentrated orange, thawed, undiluted

1/4 tsp. horseradish
2 ozs. Grand Marnier or orange liqueur (optional)

In a medium saucepan bring water to boiling. Add concentrated orange juice, rosemary and coriander. Reduce heat. Add chicken breast; simmer 25 minutes or until chicken is almost done. Add shrimp. Cover.

Remove saucepan from heat. (Shrimp will cook through in the hot liquid.) Add sherry, if desired. Allow mixture to cool to room temperature. Chill overnight.

To serve, line platter with red lettuce leaves. Arrange grapefruit and orange slices around edge of platter; sprinkle lightly with ground anise seed. Cut chicken in cubes.

Arrange shrimp and chicken in center or platter. Spoon orange sauce over salad before serving.

Orange sauce: in a small bowl combine all ingredients.

Yields: 4 servings

SUNNY VEGETARIAN SANDWICH

3/4 cup (2 oz.) low-fat cottage cheese
1/2 tsp. lemon juice
1 sm. clove garlic, minced
3 to 4 drops Tabasco (hot pepper) sauce, or to taste
salt and pepper, if desired
4 slices whole wheat bread
1/4 cup (1 oz.) chopped California walnuts
1 sm. zucchini, very thinly sliced
1 carrot, very thinly sliced
1/2 cup (about 1/2 oz.) sprouts, such as alfalfa or onion sprouts
4 slices tomato

In a small bowl, combine the cottage cheese, lemon juice and garlic, and blend until smooth. Season with Tabasco, and salt and pepper, if desired. Spread each slice of bread 1/4 of the mixture.

Divide the walnuts, zucchini and carrot slices equally between 2 of the slices, then top the same slices with half of the sprouts and 2 slices of tomato each. Top with the other slices of bread. Press gently on the sandwiches, then cut in 1/2 diagonally. Serve with a pear or apple.

Yields: 2 servings

CHEESEBURGER BABIES

1 lb. lean ground beef
8 dinner rolls or sm. buns (2 1/2 inch diameter)
assorted cheeses and condiments

Divide ground beef into 8 equal portions; shape into patties 3 inches in diameter. Place patties on grid over medium coals. Grill 6 to 7 minutes for medium doneness, turning once. Or, arrange patties on rack of broiler pan so meat is 3 to 4 inches from heat. Broil 4 to 6 minutes for medium doneness, turning once. Place burger on bottom 1/2 of roll; top with American cheese slice and if desired, dill pickle slice. Cover with roll top.

For sail burger babies, arrange lettuce leaf and small tomato slice on roll bottom; top with burger, cheese slice and roll top. Cut 1 ounce slice of cheese diagonally to form 4 triangles. Thread thin pretzel stick along 1 side of each triangle to form sail. Carefully push bottom of pretzel stick through roll top.

For inside-out burger babies, divide ground beef into 16 equal portions; shape each into patties 3 inches in diameter. Top 1 patty with 1/2 of a 1 ounce slice of Mozzarella or American cheese folded in 1/2; top with second patty sealing edges gently with fingers. Repeat with remaining meat and cheese. Grill or broil as directed above. Serve on rolls with catsup and pickles.

Yields: 8 small burgers

GRINDER SANDWICH

1 green pepper, seeded and cut into rings

1 clove garlic, peeled and minced
2 tbs. olive oil
1/2 tsp. dried minced onion
1/2 lb. ham, thinly sliced
1 med. tomato, thinly sliced
1 loaf (14 ozs.) French bread, split lengthwise
4 ozs. thinly sliced Provolone

In a medium skillet over medium-high heat, sauté green pepper and garlic in oil until pepper is crisp-tender. Toss with dried onion. Remove green pepper, reserving oil mixture.

Layer ham, tomatoes and green pepper on bottom 1/2 of French bread. Drizzle oil mixture over top, sprinkle with oregano; top with cheese slices. Cover with top of bread.

Wrap loaf in foil; bake at 350 degrees F for 25 minutes.

Yields: 4 servings

GYRO-STYLE PORK SANDWICH

1 lb. boneless pork loin
4 tbs. olive oil
1 tbs. prepared mustard
1/2 cup lemon juice
2 cloves garlic, minced
1 tsp. oregano, dried
1 cup plain yogurt
1 cucumber, peeled and chopped
1/2 tsp. garlic, crushed
1/2 tsp. dill
2 pita loaves, halved
1 sm. red onion, peeled and thinly sliced

Cut pork crosswise into thin slices. Slice then into strips 5x 1/2 inch. Combine olive oil, mustard, lemon juice, garlic and oregano. Pour over pork slices. Cover and refrigerate for 1 to 8 hours. Meanwhile, in small bowl stir together yogurt, cucumber, garlic and dill. Cover and refrigerate.

Preheat oven to 450 degrees F. Drain marinade from pork slices and place pork in single layer in shallow pan. Roast until crisp, about 10 minutes. Open each pita 1/2 to form a pocket. Distribute pork among each 1/2. Top each sandwich with some chilled yogurt mixture and sliced onions.

Yields: 4 servings

PORK AU JUS SANDWICHES

1 lb. boneless pork roast
1 envelope (from a 2 1/2 oz. box) onion soup mix
16 mushrooms, thinly sliced
1 tsp. butter
4 crusty French rolls, split

Preheat oven to 350 degrees F. Coat pork roast with the soup mix, place in a shallow pan and roast for 45 minutes, until meat thermometer inserted registers 155 degrees F. Remove roast from oven and let rest for 5 minutes.

Scrape any pan drippings into a microwave-safe measuring cup; add water to measure 1/3 cup. Cover and microwave on high for 20 to 30 seconds, until boiling. Place mushrooms in microwave-safe container, top with butter and cover with plastic wrap. Microwave on high for 45 to 60 seconds until mushrooms are tender. Slice roast and place in rolls; spoon over mushrooms and some of the pan juices. Serve immediately.

Yields: 4 servings

OPEN FACE SARDINE SANDWICH

3 cans (3 3/4 or 4 ozs. each) Maine sardines
1 med. onion, thinly sliced
3 tomatoes, thinly sliced
6 lg. slices buttered rye bread
3/4 cup Thousand Island dressing

Drain sardines and split in half lengthwise. Separate onion slices into rings. Place sardines on bread. Cover with tomato slices and onion rings. Top each sandwich with dressing.

Yields: 6 servings

HAM SALAD WITH HOT PEANUT DRESSING

3/4 lb. boneless ham
2 tbs. vegetable oil
1/4 cup peanut butter
3 tbs. fresh lime juice
1 tbs. soy sauce
1 tsp. ground ginger
1 clove garlic, minced
1 tbs. sugar
1 med. cucumber, seeded and thinly sliced
1/2 red onion, thinly sliced
6 cups romaine or curly endive, torn
1 head radiccio or Boston lettuce

Thinly slice ham and heat briefly in microwave or in skillet over medium heat. Set aside and keep warm.

Combine salad oil, peanut butter, lime juice, soy sauce, ginger, garlic and sugar in a blender or food processor; blend well. Heat dressing in a microwave in glass measuring cup or on stovetop in a small saucepan.

Toss cucumber, red onion, romaine and endive together. Arrange salads on individual salad plates as follows: line plates with radiccio, top with tossed vegetables, arrange ham slices atop and spoon over hot dressing.

Yields: 6 servings

HONEY-LIME TENDERLOIN SANDWICHES

2 pork tenderloins (about 2 lbs.)
1/2 cup fresh lime juice
1/4 cup honey
1/4 cup water
2 cloves garlic, minced
8 hard rolls, split

Combine lime juice, honey, water and garlic. Place pork tenderloins in plastic bag or utility dish; add marinade, turning pork to coat. Tie bag securely or cover dish and marinate in refrigerator 6 hours or overnight, turning pork once.

Drain, reserving marinade. Place pork on a rack in open roasting pan. Roast at 375 degrees F for 20 to 30 minutes.

Place reserved marinade in a small saucepan, cover and cook 5 minutes; keep warm. Carve pork into thin slices; place in shallow serving dish. Pour warm marinade over pork, serve in rolls.

Yields: 8 servings

HOT PORK PEAR SALAD

1 lb. pork cutlets
2 lg. firm pears
2 tbs. vegetable oil, divided
1/4 cup cider vinegar
2 tbs. sugar
1/2 tsp. salt
1/4 cup raisins
1/2 cup walnuts, toasted
5 to 6 cups salad greens

Cut pork into 3x1/4 inch strips; set aside. Pare and core pears; cut into 12 slices.

Heat 1 tablespoon oil in a heavy frypan; sauté the pears until tender but firm. Remove from pan and set aside. Stir-fry pork strips, adding the additional tablespoon of oil if necessary, until done, about 3 minutes. Remove meat from pan, pour off excess fat.

Add vinegar, sugar and salt to pan juices; heat until sugar dissolves. Add pears, pork and raisins; stir to heat and mix. Put salad greens in a large salad bowl; spoon over pork mixture, toss. Sprinkle with walnuts.

Yields: 6 servings

ITALIAN PORK SANDWICHES

1 lb. boneless pork, cut into 3/4 inch cubes
1 bottle (8 oz.) low-calorie Italian dressing (purchased)
4 French-style rolls, split and toasted

In self-sealing plastic bag, marinate pork cubes in dressing, refrigerated, overnight (6 to 24 hours). Discard dressing and thread pork cubes onto barbecue skewers.

(Note: If using wooden skewers, soak skewers in water for an hour before using to prevent burning.) Grill or broil, about 4 inches from heat, for 8 to 10 minutes, turning to brown all sides. Place cubes inside rolls and serve.

Yields: 4 servings

LENTIL AND RICE SALAD

1 2/3 cups cooked rice (cooked in fat-free chicken broth), cooled
1 cup cooked lentils, cooled
1/2 cup chopped fresh tomatoes
1/4 cup sliced green onions, including tops
1 tbs. snipped fresh parsley
1 clove garlic, minced
1/4 tsp. ground black pepper
1/4 cup Italian dressing
lettuce leaves

Combine all ingredients except lettuce in medium bowl. Serve on lettuce leaves.

Yields: 4 servings

MARINATED BEAN AND HAM SALAD

4 cups cooked Idaho sm. red, great northern or pink beans (or combinations)
1/4 cup diced green pepper
3/4 cup thinly sliced celery
1/2 cup thinly sliced onion
2 tbs. chopped parsley

2/3 cup vegetable oil
1/2 cup wine vinegar
1 1/2 tsps. sugar
3/4 tsp. salt
1/2 tsp. garlic powder
freshly ground pepper to taste
1 1/2 cups slivered ham
tomato wedges and green pepper rings (optional)

Toss beans with green pepper, celery, onion and parsley. Combine oil, vinegar, sugar, salt, garlic powder and pepper. Pour over beans; toss to combine. Cover and refrigerate several hours. Add ham at serving time. Garnish with tomato wedges and green pepper rings, if desired.

Yields: 6 to 8 servings

MONTE CRISTO SANDWICHES

8 ozs. thinly sliced fully-cooked ham
4 ozs. Swiss cheese, sliced
8 1/2 inch thick slices French or Vienna bread
4 eggs
1/3 cup milk
3 tbs. butter or margarine

For each sandwich, place 2 ounces ham and 1 oz. Swiss cheese between 2 slices of bread. In a mixing bowl beat together eggs and milk. Dip sandwiches in the egg mixture, turning carefully, until all of the mixture is absorbed. Melt butter in a large skillet or on griddle. Place sandwiches in skillet and cook slowly 8 to 10 minutes; turn and continue cooking until cheese is melted and both sides are golden.

Yields: 4 servings

MARINATED BLACK BEAN SALAD

1 1/2 cups cooked black beans or 1 (15 oz.) can; rinsed and drained (may substitute red kidney or garbanzo for black beans)

3 cups cooked brown rice
1/2 cup chopped onions
1 cup chopped broccoli
Dressing:
4 tbs. corn or safflower oil
4 tbs. red wine vinegar
1 tsp. salt
2 tsps. thyme
1/2 tsp. pepper
1/4 tsp. garlic powder
2 tbs. parsley flakes

If using dry beans, soak overnight and cook according to package directions. Drain well. Mix dressing ingredients together and toss gently with beans, rice, onions and broccoli. Marinate for a few hours to allow flavor to develop. Serve chilled.

Yields: 12 servings

MARINATED PORK SALAD

1 lb. pork tenderloin
1/4 cup bottled or home-made Italian dressing
6 cups romaine, washed and torn
6 tbs. mayonnaise
1 tbs. lemon juice
2 tsps. Worcestershire sauce
4 drops Tabasco
3/4 cup croutons
2 tbs. shredded parmesan cheese
freshly ground pepper

Slice pork into 1/4 inch thick slices. Put pork into a non-metal bowl; pour dressing over and marinate at least 1 hour, turning once or twice.

Combine mayonnaise, lemon juice, Worcestershire sauce and Tabasco. Broil or sauté pork, 2 minutes on each side or until done. Cut into 1/2 inch strips. Toss pork, romaine, croutons, parmesan cheese and ground pepper together. Serve topped with a spoonful of dressing.

Note: cooked pork may be used. Marinate 2 cups cut-up lean pork in Italian dressing for 1 hour.

Yields: 6 servings

MEATS
BEEF-LAMB-PORK-VEAL

8

TANGY EYE ROUND STEAK

1 beef eye round steak, cut
1 inch thick (about 8 ozs.)
juice of 1 lime
1/2 tsp. each garlic salt,
ground coriander and cumin
1/4 tsp. freshly ground
black pepper
1/2 tsp. vegetable oil

Combine lime juice, garlic salt, coriander, cumin and pepper. Place beef eye round steak in plastic bag; add lime juice mixture, turning to coat steak. Close bag securely; marinate in refrigerator 30 minutes, turning once. Remove steak from marinade; discard marinade.

Heat small nonstick skillet over medium heat. Brush pan lightly with oil. Add steak; pan-broil 8 minutes, turning once. Carve into thin slices. Serve with rice, if desired.

Yields: 2 servings

TANGY BEEF BARBECUE

1 lb. beef top round steak,
cut 3/4 inch thick
1 med. onion, thinly sliced
and separated into rings
1/3 cup catsup
2 tbs. packed brown sugar
1 tbs. cider vinegar
1 tsp. each cornstarch, dry
mustard and hot pepper
sauce
1/2 tsp. salt
4 corn muffins, quartered

Cut beef top round steak into 1/8 inch strips. Place onions in single layer over bottom of 11 3/4 x 7 1/2 inch microwave-safe dish. Cover with waxed paper; microwave at high 2 minutes. Arrange beef strips over onions. Microwave, covered, at medium (50% power) 5 minutes. Pour off drippings.

Meanwhile, combine catsup, brown sugar, vinegar, cornstarch, dry mustard, hot pepper sauce and salt, mixing thoroughly. Stir into beef mixture; microwave, covered, at medium 8 minutes, stirring after 4 minutes. (If using a full-size oven, microwave at medium 6 to 7 minutes, stirring after 3 1/2 minutes.)

Arrange muffins on 4 individual plates. Stir beef mixture; spoon an equal portion over each muffin.

Yields: 4 servings

TENDERLOIN STEAKS IN MINUTES

2 beef tenderloin steaks, cut
1 inch thick (about 4 ozs.
each)
1/4 tsp. each coarse ground
black pepper and minced
garlic
1 tsp. vegetable oil
2 tbs. ready-to-serve beef
broth
1 1/2 tsps. red wine vinegar
1/4 tsp. cornstarch
1 tsp. butter

Preheat microwave browning dish at high 6 minutes. Combine pepper and garlic; press into both sides of beef tenderloin steaks.

Lightly brush hot browning dish with oil; add steaks.

Microwave at high 2 minutes, turning after 1 minute. (If using a full-size 650 watt oven, microwave steaks at high 2 minutes and 45 seconds, turning after 1 1/2 minutes; microwave sauce at high 1 1/2 minutes, stirring after 45 seconds. If using a full-size 700 watt oven, microwave steaks at high 1 minute and 45 seconds, turning after 1 minute; microwave sauce at high 1 1/2 minutes, stirring after 45 seconds.) Remove steaks; keep warm.

Combine broth, vinegar and cornstarch. Deglaze dish by adding broth mixture and stirring until meat juices attached to dish are dissolved. Microwave at high 2 minutes, stirring after 1 minute. Stir in butter; spoon sauce over steaks.

Yields: 2 servings

TENDERLOIN STEAKS WITH SHIITAKE MUSHROOMS

4 beef tenderloin steaks, cut
1 inch thick (about 4 ozs.
each)
3 to 4 ozs. fresh shiitake
mushrooms
olive oil
stir-fried noodles and vegetables
2 tbs. chopped shallots or
onions
1/4 cup ready-to-serve beef
broth
2 tbs. brandy
1 tsp. Worcestershire sauce
Stir-fried noodles and

vegetables:
2 tsps. vegetable oil
1 clove garlic, minced
1 dried red chile pepper
1/2 cup diagonally sliced carrot
1 red bell pepper, cut into thin strips
1/4 lb. fresh pea pods
1/2 cup cooked Chinese noodles

Wipe mushrooms with damp paper towel; remove stems and discard. Cut mushrooms into 1/4 inch strips; reserve.

Heat large nonstick skillet over medium-high heat. Brush pan lightly with oil. Add beef tenderloin steaks; pan-broil to desired doneness, 6 to 8 minutes, turning once.

Meanwhile, prepare stir-fried noodles and vegetables. Remove steaks to platter; keep warm. Reduce heat to medium. Brush same pan lightly with oil. Add reserved mushrooms and shallots; cook and stir 1 to 2 minutes or until tender. Add broth, brandy and Worcestershire sauce; continue cooking 1 to 2 minutes or until liquid is slightly reduced. Spoon mushrooms and sauce over steaks. Serve with stir-fried noodles and vegetables.

Stir-fried noodles and vegetables: Heat wok or large heavy skillet over medium-high heat. Add oil, garlic, dried red pepper, carrot and red bell pepper; stir-fry 3 minutes. Add pea pods; continue to stir-fry 2 minutes. Add noodles; cook and stir until hot. Discard dried red pepper.

Yields: 4 servings

TERIYAKI-MARINATED STEAK

1 well-trimmed beef top round steak, cut 1 1/2 inches thick (approximately 2 lbs.)
Marinade:
3/4 cup prepared teriyaki sauce

2 tbs. dry sherry
1 tbs. finely chopped fresh ginger

In small bowl, combine marinade ingredients; mix well. Place steak and marinade in plastic bag, turning to coat. Close bag securely and marinate in refrigerator 6 to 8 hours (or overnight, if desired), turning occasionally.

Remove steak from marinade; discard marinade. Cook steak over medium ash-covered coals. (To maintain consistent temperature of coals while cooking, add 8 new briquettes around outer edge of ash-covered coals before cooking steak.) Place steak on grid; grill uncovered 27 to 29 minutes for medium rare doneness, turning occasionally. Carve steak crosswise into thin slices.

Yields: 8 servings

TEXAS BARBECUE BEEF BRISKET

1 boneless beef brisket (6 to 8 lbs.)
2 tsps. paprika
1 tsp. freshly ground black pepper, divided
1 tbs. butter
1 med. onion, grated
1 1/2 cups catsup
1 tbs. each fresh lemon juice and Worcestershire sauce
1 tsp. hot pepper sauce

Trim external fat on beef brisket to 1/4 inch. Combine paprika and 1/2 teaspoon of the black pepper; rub evenly over surface of beef brisket. Place brisket, fat side down, in 11 1/2 x 9 inch disposable foil pan. Add 1 cup water. Cover pan tightly with aluminum foil. Place in center of grid over very low coals (use a single layer of coals with space in between each); cover cooker. Cook 5 hours, turning brisket over every 1 1/2 hours; use baster to remove fat from pan as it accumulates. Add 1/2 cup water, if needed, to pan during cooking.

(Add just enough briquettes during cooking to keep coals at a very low temperature.) Remove brisket from pan; place on grid, fat side down, directly over very low coals. Reserve pan drippings. Cover; continue cooking 30 minutes.

Meanwhile, skim fat from pan drippings; reserve 1 cup drippings. Melt butter in medium saucepan over medium heat. Add onion; cook until tender-crisp. Add reserved pan drippings, remaining 1/2 teaspoon black pepper, the catsup, the lemon juice, Worcestershire sauce and hot pepper sauce; simmer 15 minutes. Carve brisket into thin slices across the grain; serve with sauce. Garnish with fresh peppers and lemon and lime slices.

Note: For a smoky flavor, soak oak, pecan, mesquite or hickory chips in water 30 minutes and add to very low coals.

Yields: 18 to 24 servings

THREE EASY MEATBALL MEALS

1 lb. lean ground beef
1/2 cup soft or 1/4 cup dry bread crumbs
1 egg
2 tbs. finely chopped onion
1 clove garlic, crushed
1/2 tsp. salt
1/8 tsp. pepper

Basic meatballs that cook in less than 15 minutes are one of the most versatile recipes around. These simple meatballs can be used to make hearty sandwiches, savory soup or a stew in 40 minutes or less.

Heat oven to 400 degrees F. In large bowl, combine all ingredients, mixing lightly but thoroughly. Pinch off approximately 1 1/2 inch pieces of beef mixture to make 20 meatballs; place in ungreased 15 x 10 inch jelly-roll pan.

Bake 10 to 13 minutes or until no longer pink and juices run clear. Use meatballs in one of the recipes below, proceeding as directed.

Cook's Tip: To make soft bread crumbs, place 1 slice torn bread in food processor, fitted with steel blade, or blender container. Cover; process 30 seconds, pulsing on and off until fine crumbs. Yields: approximately 2/3 cup

Spicy Beef 'n Zucchini Soup: In large saucepan, combine 2 cups diced zucchini, 1 can (14 ounces) ready-to-serve beef broth, 1 cup prepared chunky salsa and 1 cup water; bring to a boil. Reduce heat; simmer 3 to 5 minutes or until zucchini is crisp-tender. Stir in meatballs and 1 tablespoon chopped fresh cilantro; heat through. Top with corn chips, if desired, immediately before serving. Yields: 4 servings

Italian meatball sandwiches: Heat 1 teaspoon vegetable oil in large skillet over medium heat. Cook and stir 3/4 cup thin bell pepper strips and 3/4 cup thin onion wedges 3 to 4 minutes or until tender. Reduce heat to medium-low; add meatballs and 1 jar (14 ounces) prepared spaghetti sauce. Cover; cook 5 to 6 minutes to heat through, stirring occasionally. Spoon equal amounts into 4 split hoagie rolls; sprinkle with shredded mozzarella cheese, if desired. Yields: 4 sandwiches

Easy meatball stew: In large saucepan, combine 1 jar (12 ounces) brown beef gravy, 1 small can (8 ounces) stewed tomatoes (undrained), 3/4 cup water, 3/4 teaspoon dried thyme leaves and 1/8 teaspoon pepper; bring to a boil. Stir in 1 package (16 ounces) frozen vegetable (with potato) mixture. Reduce heat; simmer 10 to 15 minutes or until vegetables are tender. Stir in meatballs; heat through.

Yields: 4 servings

THREE-PEPPER BEEF KABOBS

1 lb. boneless beef sirloin steak, cut 1 inch thick

**2 tbs. vegetable oil
1 tbs. each fresh lemon juice and water
2 tsps. Dijon-style mustard
1 tsp. honey
1/2 tsp. dried oregano leaves
1/4 tsp. pepper
1 med. green, red or yellow bell pepper, cut into 1 inch pieces
8 lg. mushrooms**

Cut beef steak into 1 inch pieces. Whisk together oil, lemon juice, water, mustard, honey, oregano and pepper in large bowl; add beef, bell pepper and mushrooms, stirring to coat.

Alternately thread pieces of beef, bell pepper and mushrooms on each of four 12 inch skewers. Place kabobs on rack in broiler pan so surface of meat is 3 to 4 inches from heat.

Broil 9 to 12 minutes for rare to medium, turning occasionally. Season with salt, if desired.

Note: Beef kabobs may also be grilled. Place on grid over medium coals. Grill 8 to 11 minutes.

Yields: 4 servings

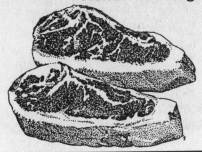

TOP LOIN STEAKS WITH EGGPLANT RELISH

**2 beef top loin steaks, cut 1 inch thick (approximately 1 lb.)
1 Japanese eggplant (approximately 1/4 lb.)
1 med. red bell pepper
1 sm. clove garlic, minced
1 tbs. chopped cilantro
2 tsps. balsamic vinegar (two tsps. red wine vinegar and 1/4 teaspoon sugar may be substituted for balsamic vinegar)**

1/4 teaspoon lemon pepper

Place eggplant and red pepper on rack in broiler pan 2 to 3 inches from the heat. Broil 8 to 10 minutes or until skin blisters, turning occasionally.

Place vegetables in paper bag; close and let stand until cool. Remove skins.

Finely chop eggplant. Remove seeds and veins from pepper; finely chop. Combine eggplant, pepper, garlic, cilantro, vinegar and lemon pepper.

Preheat 10 inch nonstick or heavy skillet over medium heat 5 minutes. Pan-broil steaks 9 to 11 minutes for rare (140 degrees F) to medium (160 degrees F), turning once.

Carve steak into thin slices. Spoon eggplant relish over steak slices.

Yields: 4 servings

TOP ROUND AROMATICA

**2 lb. beef top round steak, cut 1 inch thick
1 to 2 tbs. black peppercorns, crushed
1 tbs. butter
1/4 tsp. garlic powder
1 tbs. vegetable oil
1/4 cup dry red wine
2 tbs. cognac
1/2 cup whipping cream
2 tbs. chopped fresh parsley
parsley sprigs**

Combine crushed peppercorns, butter and garlic powder; spread evenly on both sides of beef steak.

Heat oil in heavy frying pan over medium heat. Add steak and panfry 8 to 10 minutes for rare to medium, turning once. Place steak on serving platter; keep warm.

Deglaze pan with wine and cognac over high heat; cook 1 minute. Reduce heat to medium; stir in cream and chopped parsley. Continue cooking 1 to 2 minutes. Season with salt to taste.

Carve steak diagonally across the

grain into thin slices. Pour sauce over steak; garnish with parsley.

Yields: 8 servings

TROPICAL GRILLED FLANK STEAK WITH FRESH FRUIT SALSA

1 1/2 lb. beef flank steak
1/4 cup fresh orange juice
2 tbs. each chili sauce, soy sauce and vegetable oil
1 tsp. each sugar and grated orange peel
2 cloves garlic, minced
1/2 tsp. salt
1/8 tsp. hot pepper sauce
1 med. orange, thinly sliced
fresh fruit salsa
orange wedges
fresh cilantro
Fresh fruit salsa:
1/2 cup each diced pineapple, mango, papaya and green apple
1/4 cup each diced red and green bell pepper
2 tbs. rice vinegar or white wine vinegar
1 tbs. minced fresh cilantro
4 tsps. sugar
1/4 tsp. crushed red pepper pods

Combine orange juice, chili sauce, soy sauce, oil, sugar, orange peel, garlic, salt and hot pepper sauce. Place beef steak in plastic bag; add marinade, turning to coat. Place orange slices on top of steak. Close bag securely and marinate in refrigerator 3 hours (or overnight, if desired), turning occasionally. Pour off marinade and orange slices; discard. Place steak on grid over medium coals. (Test about 4 inches above coals for medium with 4-second hand count.) Grill 10 to 14 minutes, turning once.

Meanwhile prepare fresh fruit salsa. Carve steak into thin slices. Serve steak with salsa. Garnish with orange wedges and cilantro.

Fresh fruit salsa: Combine pineapple, mango, papaya, apple, red and green pepper, vinegar, cilantro, sugar and red pepper. (May be prepared one day in advance, if desired.) Yields: about 2 1/2 cups

Yields: 4 servings

BEEF AND MUSHROOM GRAVY

2 1/2 lbs. boneless beef chuck arm pot roast
3/4 tsp. dried marjoram leaves
3/4 tsp. pepper
vegetable cooking spray
1 can (13 3/4 to 14 1/2 oz.) ready-to-serve beef broth
1 cup Burgundy wine
2 cloves garlic, crushed
1 bag (1 lb.) baby carrots
1/2 lb. sm. mushrooms
1 lg. onion, cut into 1 inch pieces
2 to 2 1/2 tbs. cornstarch, dissolved in 1/4 cup water

Trim fat from beef. Cut beef into 1 inch pieces. Combine marjoram and pepper; sprinkle over beef. Spray Dutch oven with cooking spray; heat over medium heat until hot. Add beef (1/2 at a time) and brown evenly, stirring occasionally. Pour off drippings.

Stir in broth, wine and garlic. Bring to a boil; reduce heat to low. Cover tightly and simmer 1 1/2 hours. Add carrots, mushrooms and onion. Cover and continue cooking 30 minutes or until beef and vegetables are tender.

Stir in cornstarch mixture. Bring to a boil; cook and stir 1 minute or until thickened.

Yields: 8 servings

BEEF STROGANOFF

1 lb. beef tenderloin tips
1 1/2 cups uncooked farfalle (bow tie) pasta
1/2 lb. mushrooms, cut into 1/2 inch slices
1/3 cup coarsely chopped onion
2 tsps. vegetable oil
1 to 2 tbs. all-purpose flour
3/4 cup ready-to-serve beef broth
1 tbs. sliced green onion
1/4 cup dairy sour half and half

Cook pasta according to package directions. Keep warm.

Meanwhile trim fat from beef; cut into 1 x 1/2 inch pieces. Spray large nonstick skillet with vegetable cooking spray. Heat skillet over medium-high heat until hot. Add beef (1/2 at a time) and stir-fry 1 to 2 minutes or until outside surface is no longer pink. Remove from skillet; keep warm. Season with salt and pepper, if desired.

In same skillet, cook mushrooms and onion in oil 2 minutes or until tender; stir in flour. Gradually add broth, stirring until blended. Bring to a boil; cook and stir 2 minutes. Return beef to skillet; heat through.

Serve beef mixture over pasta. Sprinkle with green onion; pass sour half and half to dollop on top.

Yields: 4 servings

CORNED BEEF, POTATO AND PEPPER HASH

12 ozs. cooked corned beef, cut into 1/2 inch cubes
1 tsp. salt
1 lb. russet potatoes, cut into 1/2 inch cubes
2 tbs. butter, divided
1 med. onion, coarsely chopped
1/3 cup each chopped red, yellow and green bell pepper
3 tbs. chopped parsley
1/4 cup half and half
3 tbs. dry white wine
1/2 tsp. dry mustard
1/8 tsp. pepper

Bring water to a boil in large saucepan; add salt and potatoes. Return to a boil. Cook 5 minutes; drain well.

Melt 1 tablespoon of the butter in cast-iron or large heavy skillet

52

over medium-high heat; add onion and peppers. Cook and stir 2 minutes or until tender-crisp; remove from pan. Add corned beef, potatoes and parsley to onion mixture; mix lightly.

Combine half and half, wine, mustard and pepper; add to corned beef mixture and mix well. Wipe out cast-iron skillet with paper towel; place over medium heat until hot. Add remaining 1 tablespoon butter. Add corned beef mixture, pressing down firmly. Cook hash 15 minutes or until browned, turning with flat spatula several times.

Yields: 4 servings

NECTARINE BEEF SAUTÉ

8 ozs. sirloin steak, thinly sliced
pepper
flour
2 tbs. low-sodium soy sauce
1 tbs. honey
1 red onion, cut in 1/2, sliced 1/4 inch thick
1 tsp. vegetable oil
1 clove garlic, finely chopped
2 fresh California nectarines, sliced 1/4 inch thick
1 pinch cayenne pepper

Season steak strips with pepper; lightly dredge meat in flour; reserve. Combine soy sauce and honey; reserve. Sauté onion in hot oil until tender crisp. Add garlic and steak; sauté until browned.

Add nectarine slices, reserved soy mixture and cayenne pepper. Cook, stirring constantly, until nectarine slices are warmed and liquid is reduced to glaze, about 1 minute.

Yields: 3 servings

GLAZED FLANK STEAK

1 flank steak, about 1 1/2 lbs. or 1 1/2 lbs. London broil, about 1 1/2 inches thick

1/3 cup soy sauce
2 tbs. worcestershire sauce
3 tbs. honey
1/2 cup white wine
2 scallions, minced
3 lg. garlic cloves, minced
1/3 cup olive oil

With a sharp knife, score both sides of the steak in a criss-cross pattern about 1/8 inch deep.

To make marinade, mix together soy sauce, worcestershire sauce, honey, white wine, scallions and garlic. Whisk in olive oil. Place steak in a glass of ceramic baking dish and pour in marinade; turn to coat both side of meat. Marinate in refrigerator for several hours or overnight.

When ready to grill, remove steak, reserving as much marinade as possible. Place steak on an oiled grill set 4 to 6 inches from coals. Grill, turning and brushing with marinade several times, until outside is well browned and inside is still pink and juicy, about 10 to 12 minutes for flank steak, 20 to 26 minutes for London broil. Transfer to a cutting board and let rest about 5 minutes before carving diagonal into thin slices.

Yields: 4 to 6 servings

CHEF'S PRIME WITH CHINESE SPICES

2 to 4 lb. boneless pork rib-end roast
1 tbs. coarse salt
1 tbs. five-spice powder
4 tsps. ground black pepper
1 tbs. grated orange peel
1 tsp. ground cumin

Mix together seasoning ingredients and rub over surface or pork. Cover and refrigerate overnight. Roast pork in shallow pan in preheated 325 degrees F oven until meat thermometer registers 155 degrees F, about 45 minutes to 1 1/2 hours. Let roast rest 5 to 10 minutes before carving.

Yields: 8 servings

PEPPER BEEF STEAK AND POTATO WEDGES

1 1/2 lb. boneless beef top sirloin steak, cut 1 1/4 inches thick
Steak seasoning:
3 lg. clove garlic, crushed
2 tsps. dried oregano leaves
1/2 tsp. lemon pepper
Potato wedges:
1 tbs. olive oil
1/2 tsp. lemon pepper
3 all-purpose potatoes, each cut into 6 wedges

Combine steak seasoning ingredients; press into both sides of beef steak.

In medium bowl, combine oil and 1/2 tsp. lemon pepper. Add potatoes; toss to coat.

Place steak on one side of rack in broiler pan so surface of meat is 3 to 4 inches from heat; arrange potatoes on the other side. Broil 18 to 20 minutes until steak is rare to medium doneness and potatoes are tender, turning steak and potato wedges once.

Trim fat from steak. Carve steak crosswise into slices and serve with potatoes.

Yields: 6 servings

BASIL BEEF POT ROAST

1 boneless beef chuck shoulder pot roast (3 to 3 1/2 lbs.)
2 cloves garlic, minced
1 1/2 tsps. dried basil leaves, divided
1 tsp. salt
1/2 tsp. coarse ground black pepper
1 tbs. vegetable oil
1 cup water
2 onions, quartered
1 strip lemon peel (1 1/2 x 1/2 inch)
5 med. carrots, cut into 1 inch pieces
2 med. zucchini
1 tbs. each cornstarch and fresh lemon juice

Mash garlic; combine with 1 tsp. of the basil, the salt and pepper to form a paste. Rub surface of beef chuck shoulder pot roast with garlic mixture.

Heat oil in Dutch oven over medium-high heat. Add pot roast; cook until evenly browned. Pour off drippings. Add water, onions and lemon peel. Cover tightly; reduce heat and simmer 2 hours. Add carrots; continue cooking, covered, 30 minutes.

Meanwhile, cut zucchini in half lengthwise; cut each half into 1 inch pieces. Add zucchini; cook, covered, 7 to 10 minutes or until zucchini is tender. Remove beef and vegetables to warm platter.

Strain cooking liquid; skim and discard fat. Combine cornstarch, lemon juice and remaining 1/2 tsp. basil; stir into 2 cups cooking liquid. Bring to a boil; boil 1 minute, stirring constantly. Serve pot roast and vegetables with gravy.

Yields: 9 to 10 servings

LEMON-HERB GRILLED VEAL CHOPS

4 veal rib or loin chops, cut 1 inch thick
4 slices firm, ripe tomato, approximately 1 inch thick
salt (optional)
Marinade:
3 tbs. fresh lemon juice
3 tbs. olive oil
3 cloves garlic, quartered
2 tsps. dried oregano leaves, crushed
1 tsp. freshly ground black pepper

In bowl or food processor, place marinade ingredients; process to blend. Reserve 1 tbs..

Place veal chops in shallow dish; spread remaining marinade on both sides of chops. Cover; marinate in refrigerator up to 2 hours. Spread reserved marinade on one side of each tomato slice.

Place veal on grid over medium coals. Grill 12 to 14 minutes,

uncovered (10 to 12 minutes covered), for medium or to desired doneness; turn once. Place tomato slices on grid during last 6 minutes of grilling time. Grill until heated through; turn once. Season veal and tomatoes with salt after grilling, as desired.

Yields: 4 servings

BEEF AND BARLEY WITH SUGAR SNAP PEAS

1 lb. lean ground beef
1/2 lb. mushrooms, sliced
1 med. onion, chopped
1 lg. carrot, thinly sliced
1 clove garlic, crushed
1 can (13 3/4 to 14 1/2 oz.) ready-to-serve beef broth
1/2 cup quick-cooking barley
1/2 tsp. salt
1/4 tsp. pepper
1 package (8 oz.) frozen sugar snap peas, defrosted
1/4 cup chopped fresh parsley
1 tsp. grated lemon peel

In large nonstick skillet, cook and stir ground beef, mushrooms, onion, carrot and garlic over medium heat 8 to 10 minutes or until beef is no longer pink, breaking up into 3/4 inch crumbles. Pour off drippings.

Stir in broth, barley, salt and pepper. Bring to a boil; reduce heat to medium-low. Cover tightly and simmer 10 minutes.

Add peas; continue cooking 2 to 5 minutes or until barley is tender. Stir in parsley and lemon peel.

Yields: 4 servings

BEEF WITH PAN-GRILLED ZUCCHINI

1 boneless beef top sirloin steak, cut 1/2 inch thick (about 1 1/4 lbs.)
1 clove garlic, minced
1 tsp. dried rosemary leaves, crushed

3/4 tsp. salt, divided
1/4 tsp. coarse ground black pepper, divided
1 tbs. plus 2 tsps. olive oil
4 sm. zucchini, cut in half lengthwise
2 tbs. fresh lemon juice, divided

Cut boneless beef top sirloin into 4 serving size pieces. Place each piece on flat surface; cover with waxed paper and flatten with bottom of heavy saucepan, mallet or side of cleaver to 1/4 inch thickness.

Mash garlic; combine with rosemary, 1/2 tsp. of the salt and 1/8 tsp. of the pepper. Combine with 1 tbs. oil; rub both sides of steaks with garlic mixture. Score cut side of each zucchini in a diamond pattern, 1 inch apart and 1/8 inch deep. Pat zucchini dry.

Heat heavy nonstick skillet over medium-high heat 3 minutes. Add remaining 2 tsps. oil and the zucchini. Cook 3 minutes; turn and continue cooking 3 minutes or until tender. Remove zucchini to platter; season with remaining 1/4 tsp. salt, 1/8 tsp. pepper and 1 tbs. of the lemon juice; keep warm.

Heat same skillet over medium-high heat. Quickly cook steaks, 2 at a time, 1 minute or to desired doneness, turning once. Add remaining 1 tbs. lemon juice to pan, turning steaks to glaze. Serve steaks with zucchini.

Yields: 4 servings

LEMONY BEEF, VEGETABLES AND BARLEY

1 lb. lean ground beef
8 ozs. mushrooms, sliced
1 med. onion, chopped
1 clove garlic, crushed
1 can (14 oz.) ready-to-serve beef broth
1/2 cup quick cooking barley
1/2 tsp. salt
1/4 tsp. pepper

1 package (10 oz.) frozen peas and carrots, defrosted
1 tsp. grated lemon peel

In large nonstick skillet, cook and stir ground beef, mushrooms, onion and garlic over medium heat 8 to 10 minutes or until beef is no longer pink, breaking up into 3/4 inch crumbles. Pour off drippings.

Stir in broth, barley, salt and pepper. Bring to a boil; reduce heat to medium-low. Cover tightly; simmer 10 minutes.

Add peas and carrots; continue cooking 2 to 5 minutes or until barley is tender. Stir in lemon peel.

Yields: 4 servings

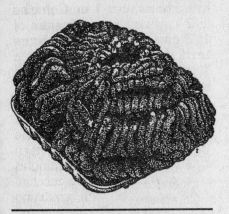

MINI BEEF LOAVES

8 ozs. ground beef (80 percent lean)
2 tbs. dry bread crumbs
1/2 sm. onion, minced
1 tbs. milk
1 egg, slightly beaten
1 1/2 tsps. prepared horse-radish
1/4 tsp. each dill weed and salt
paprika
Yogurt-dill sauce:
1/4 cup each chopped seeded cucumber and plain yogurt
1 tsp. minced onion
1/8 tsp. each dill weed and garlic powder

Prepare yogurt-dill sauce. Combine ground beef, bread crumbs, onion, milk, egg, horseradish, dill weed and salt, mixing lightly but thoroughly.

Divide beef mixture into 2 equal portions; shape into sm. loaves. Arrange loaves in microwave-safe dish. Sprinkle each loaf lightly with paprika. Cover with waxed paper; microwave at high 4 to 4 1/2 minutes, rotating dish 1/2 turn after 2 minutes. Let stand 5 minutes. Top with yogurt-dill sauce. Serve with assorted vegetables, if desired.

Yogurt-dill sauce: Combine all ingredients. Season with salt, if desired. Cover; refrigerate.

Yields: 2 servings

RACK OF LAMB

2 well-trimmed 6-rib lamb rib roasts (approximately 1 1/2 lbs. each)
1/4 cup coarse-grain Dijon-style mustard
1/2 cup seasoned dry bread crumbs
2 tbs. dried thyme leaves

Generously spread all sides of lamb roasts with mustard. In sm. bowl, combine bread crumbs and thyme; pat mixture over mustard.

Place roasts, fat side down, on grid over medium coals. Cover grill; grill 10 minutes. Turn over; grill, covered, an additional 18 to 20 minutes for rare to medium doneness or until thermometer registers 140 degrees F for rare, 160 degrees F for medium. Remove roasts and let stand 10 minutes before carving.

Carve roasts between ribs into slices.

Yields: 6 servings

THAI LAMB KABOBS

1 to 1 1/2 lbs. well-trimmed boneless lamb leg, cut into 1 1/2 inch pieces
cilantro sprigs (optional)
Marinade:
1/3 cup unsweetened coconut milk
3 tbs. coarsely chopped fresh cilantro

3 tbs. fresh lime juice
2 tbs. vegetable oil
1 tsps. ground cumin

Combine marinade ingredients. Cover and refrigerate 1/3 cup marinade for brushing on kabobs during grilling. Place lamb in plastic bag; add remaining marinade, turning to coat. Close bag securely and marinate in refrigerator 6 to 8 hours (or overnight, if desired), turning occasionally.

Remove lamb from marinade; discard marinade. Thread lamb onto four to six 12 inch metal skewers. Place kabobs on grid over medium coals. Grill 15 to 20 minutes for medium doneness, turning occasionally. Brush all sides of kabobs with reserved marinade during last 5 minutes of grilling. Garnish with cilantro, if desired.

Yields: 4 to 6 servings

ORANGE PEPPERED GLAZED SPICY LAMB CHOPS

8 well-trimmed lamb loin or rib chops, cut 1 inch thick
Glaze:
1/3 cup orange marmalade
1 tbs. balsamic vinegar
1 tsp. Dijon-style mustard
Seasoning:
1/2 tsp. garlic salt
1/2 tsp. coarse grind black pepper
1/2 tsp. dried rosemary leaves, crushed

In small bowl, combine glaze ingredients; set aside.

Combine seasoning ingredients; press into both sides of lamb chops.

Place chops on grid over medium coals. Grill chops 9 to 11 minutes for rare to medium doneness, turning once. Brush both sides of chops with glaze during last 3 to 4 minutes of grilling.

Yields: 4 servings

SANTA FE LAMB CHOPS

4 well trimmed lamb shoulder arm or blade chops, cut 3/4 inch thick
lime wedges (optional)
Marinade:
2 tbs. fresh lime juice
2 tbs. Dijon-style mustard
1 tbs. finely chopped pickled jalapeno pepper
2 tsps. dried oregano leaves
1 tsp. ground cumin
1/4 tsp. salt

Combine marinade ingredients. Place lamb chops in plastic bag; add marinade, turning to coat. Close bag securely and marinate in refrigerator 6 to 8 hours (or overnight, if desired), turning occasionally.

Remove chops from marinade; discard marinade. Place chops on grid over medium coals. Grill 12 to 14 minutes for rare to medium doneness, turning once. Garnish lamb with lime, if desired.

Yields: 4 servings

MOROCCAN LAMB WITH CURRIED CARROT SPINACH SALAD

1 1/2 to 2 lb. boneless lamb loin (double) roast, tied
1 cup plain yogurt, divided
1/4 cup thinly sliced onion
2 tbs. each chopped cilantro and fresh orange juice
2 cloves garlic
1/2 tsp. each ground cardamom and cumin
1/4 tsp. coarsely ground black pepper
8 cups thinly sliced mixed greens, such as spinach and romaine
3 cups diagonally sliced carrots
cilantro and orange slices, optional
Curry vinaigrette:
2 tbs. olive oil
1 tbs. fresh orange juice
1 tsp. minced fresh ginger
1/4 tsp. each sugar and curry powder
salt and pepper

Combine 2/3 cup yogurt, onion, cilantro, orange juice, garlic and spices in blender container; process until smooth. Add salt to taste.

Combine 1/2 cup yogurt mixture with remaining plain yogurt for sauce; refrigerate until serving.

Place lamb in plastic bag; pour remaining yogurt mixture from blender over roast, turning to coat. Close bag securely and marinate in refrigerator 2 hours; turn occasionally.

Remove lamb from marinade and place on grid over medium coals. Grill about 20 minutes for rare (140 degrees F), turning 1/4 turn every 5 minutes. Let stand 10 minutes.

Meanwhile, prepare curry vinaigrette. Whisk together olive oil, orange juice, minced fresh ginger, sugar and curry powder. Season with salt and pepper.

Toss greens and carrots with vinaigrette; place on large serving platter. Carve roast into slices and arrange over salad. Garnish as desired. Serve with reserved sauce.

Yields: 6 to 8 servings

GRILLED LAMB RIBLETS DIJON

4 racks lamb breast spareribs (approximately 5 lbs.)
2 lemons, halved
1 tbs. each ground coriander and ground cumin
2 tsps. ground black pepper
4 lg. cloves garlic, crushed
3/4 cup Dijon-style mustard

Rub lamb racks with cut sides of lemons. Combine coriander, cumin and pepper; sprinkle equal amounts on both sides of lamb. Place seasoned lamb in plastic bags. Close bags securely and refrigerate 1 hour.

Combine garlic with mustard.

Brush both sides of lamb with 1/2 cup of mustard mixture. Place lamb on grid over medium coals. Grill 16 minutes, turning once.

Cover grill; continue grilling 25 minutes or until lamb is tender, turning occasionally. Remove cover, brush both sides of lamb with remaining mustard mixture. Continue grilling 8 minutes, turning once.

Yields: 6 to 8 servings

CHAMPAGNE SPICED LAMB CHOPS

8 well trimmed lamb rib or loin chops, cut 1 inch thick
1/2 cup rice wine vinegar
1/2 cup champagne mustard
1 tsp. each minced fresh rosemary and thyme leaves (or 1/2 tsp. dried)

Place lamb chops in plastic bag; add vinegar, turning to coat. Close bag securely and marinate in refrigerator 2 to 4 hours.

Combine mustard, rosemary and thyme. Remove lamb from marinade. Spread mustard mixture evenly over both sides of chops. Place chops on grid over medium coals.

Grill 9 to 10 minutes for medium (160 degrees F), turning once.

Yields: 4 servings

GREEK LAMB A LA LEEK

1 1/2 lbs. well trimmed boneless lamb leg, cut into 1 1/2 inch pieces
1 cup plain yogurt
1 envelope (1.8 oz.) leek soup mix
juice of 1 lime
1 tbs. white wine Worcestershire sauce
1 tsp. crushed red pepper pods
1 each red and yellow bell pepper, cut into 1 in. pieces
6 pita bread rounds
fresh spinach leaves

Combine yogurt, soup mix, lime juice, Worcestershire sauce and red pepper pods. Place lamb pieces in plastic bag; add marinade, turning to coat. Close bag securely and marinate in refrigerator 3 hours or overnight, if desired; turn occasionally.

Alternately thread lamb and pepper pieces on each of six 12 inch skewers. Place on grid over medium coals. Grill 15 to 20 minutes, turning occasionally.

Place 6 pita rounds on platter and top with spinach leaves. Remove lamb and peppers from skewers onto spinach leaves. Fold pita around lamb to serve.

Yields: 6 servings

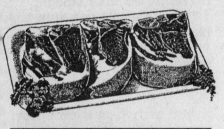

JALAPENO MARINATED LAMB CHOPS

**8 well trimmed lamb loin or rib chops, cut 1 inch thick
1/4 jalapeno pepper, seeded
1 lg. clove garlic, halved
1 sm. onion, quartered
1 piece fresh ginger, peeled (about 1 inch)
2 tbs. each honey, orange juice, peanut oil, and soy sauce
1/8 tsp. coarsely ground black pepper
orange slices and cilantro, optional**

Combine jalapeno pepper, garlic, onion and ginger in blender container; process until finely chopped. Add honey, orange juice, oil, soy sauce and black pepper; process until blended.

Place lamb in plastic bag; add marinade, turning to coat. Close bag securely and marinate in refrigerator 15 to 30 minutes; turn occasionally.

Place chops on grid over

medium coals. Grill 9 to 10 minutes for medium (160 degrees F), turning once.

Garnish as desired.

Yields: 4 servings

BARBARA'S GRILLED LEG OF LAMB

**4 to 5 lb. well trimmed butterflied lamb leg
2 tsps. Szechwan peppercorns
2 med. onions, each cut into 8 pieces
2 jalapeno peppers, seeded
6 cloves garlic
1 piece fresh ginger, peeled (about 2 inches)
2 tsps. Dijon-style mustard
1/2 cup each honey and soy sauce
1/4 cup vegetable oil
Italian parsley, optional**

Place peppercorns in food processor or blender; process 1 minute. Add onions, jalapeno peppers, garlic, ginger and mustard; puree. Add honey, soy sauce and oil; process until well blended. Reserve 1 cup.

Place lamb in plastic bag; add remaining marinade, turning to coat. Close bag securely and marinate in refrigerator 6 to 8 hours or overnight, if desired; turn occasionally.

Remove lamb from marinade. Thread 2 long metal skewers through lamb to secure and facilitate turning roast. Place lamb on grid over medium coals.

Grill 40 to 60 minutes or until desired degree of doneness; 140 degrees F for rare, 150 degrees F for medium rare and 160 degrees F for medium.

Turn lamb several times during cooking, brushing with reserved marinade during last 10 minutes of cooking time. Let stand 10 minutes. Remove skewers and carve into thin slices.

Garnish with parsley, if desired.

Yields: 4 servings

LEMONY LAMB KEBOBS

**2 lbs. well trimmed boneless lamb leg, cut into 1 1/2 inch pieces
1/2 cup vegetable oil
2/3 cup chopped onion
3 tbs. each cider vinegar and lemon juice
2 cloves garlic, quartered
1 1/2 tsps. salt
1/2 tsp. dry mustard
1/8 tsp. pepper
1 bay leaf
2 lemons, each cut into 6 wedges
12 med. mushrooms
lemon slices and mushrooms, optional**

Combine oil, onion, vinegar, lemon juice, garlic and seasonings. Reserve 1/2 cup marinade. Place lamb in plastic bag; add remaining marinade, turning to coat. Close bag securely and marinate in refrigerator 6 to 8 hours or overnight, if desired; turn occasionally.

Alternately thread 4 lamb pieces, 2 lemon wedges and 2 mushrooms on each of six 12 inch skewers. Place on grid over medium coals.

Grill 15 to 20 minutes or to desired degree of doneness, turning and brushing with reserved marinade.

Garnish as desired.

Yields: 6 servings

BARBECUED PORK STEAKS

**4 pork blade steaks, cut 1 to 1 1/4 inches thick
1/2 cup bottled barbecue sauce
1/3 cup honey
1 tbs. Worcestershire sauce
1 tsp. garlic salt
1/2 tsp. prepared mustard**

Pound steaks with meat mallet. For sauce, in a small bowl, combine the remaining ingredients; mix well.

Place steaks on grill about 4 inches above medium-slow coals. Cook about 8 minutes on each side. Brush steaks with sauce and continue cooking 5 minutes more, turning and brushing with sauce.

Yields: 4 servings

PEACH-GLAZED COUNTRY HAM

1 country-style ham (10 to 14 lb.)
2/3 cup peach preserves
pecan halves

Using a stiff brush, thoroughly scrub the country-style ham. Place ham in a large pot; cover with water and soak for 12 to 24 hours, changing water several times. Drain. Cover ham with fresh water and bring to boiling. Reduce heat and simmer for 20 to 25 minutes per pound. Ham is done when flat (pelvic) bone moves easily.

Lift the ham from the pan. When ham is cool enough to handle, remove the rind with a sharp knife, leaving 1/4 inch thick layer of fat. Score the ham at 1 inch intervals. Spread with peach preserves and dot with pecan halves. Bake ham in a 400 degrees F oven for about 20 minutes or until the glaze browns.

Transfer ham to a serving platter and cool to room temperature. To serve, cut ham into paper-thin slices.

Yields: 50 servings

PORK AND BROCCOLI STIR-FRY

1 lb. boneless pork loin
1 bunch fresh broccoli
1 red or green bell pepper
3/4 cup chicken broth
1 tbs. cornstarch
2 tbs. oyster-flavored sauce
1 tbs. soy sauce
1/8 tsp. ground ginger
1 tbs. vegetable oil
1 clove garlic, minced

1/2 cup fresh mushrooms, sliced
1/4 cup green onions, sliced
hot cooked rice (optional)

Partially freeze pork; slice across grain into 1/4 inch slices. Clean broccoli, slice stalks into 1/4 inch slices; cut off the flowerettes. Remove stem and seeds from pepper and cut into thin strips. Set aside.

Combine chicken broth, cornstarch, oyster-flavored sauce, soy sauce, and ginger; set aside. Pour oil around top of preheated wok to cover sides. Heat oil over medium-high heat. Add pork, broccoli stalks, pepper and garlic; stir-fry 4 minutes or until pork is browned. Add broccoli flowerettes, mushrooms and onion; stir-fry 2 minutes.

Stir chicken broth mixture; gradually add to wok, mix well. Cook 3 minutes or until thickened and bubbly, stirring constantly. Serve over hot cooked rice, if desired.

Yields: 6 servings

PORK TENDERLOIN WITH BERNAISE SAUCE

1 lb. pork tenderloin
1 tbs. vegetable oil
1 tbs. butter or margarine
freshly ground pepper
1/4 cup water
1/4 cup red wine
1/4 cup white wine vinegar with tarragon
2 tbs. white wine
1 green onion, sliced
1/4 tsp. dried tarragon leaves
1/4 tsp. parsley flakes
3 egg yolks
1/2 tsp. dry mustard
1/2 cup butter or margarine, melted
2 tbs. capers, drained
fresh basil (optional)

Combine oil and 1 tablespoon butter in a heavy skillet over medium heat; stirring to mix as

butter melts. Add tenderloin and cook until brown on all sides, turning occasionally. Sprinkle with freshly ground pepper.

Add water and red wine to skillet. Cover tightly and cook over low heat for 12 to 15 minutes or until done. Set aside and keep warm.

Meanwhile, combine vinegar, white wine, green onion, dried tarragon and parsley flakes in a small saucepan. Cook over medium-high heat for 10 to 15 minutes or until reduced by 1/2.

Place egg yolks, mustard and vinegar mixture in blender container. With motor running, gradually add melted butter in a slow steady stream. Blend until thickened. Stir in capers.

Pour sauce onto heated serving platter. Place whole tenderloin on top. Garnish with fresh basil, if desired.

Yields: 4 servings

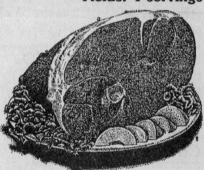

MUSTARD-GLAZED HAM

1 fully-cooked ham (5 lb.)
3 tbs. Dijon-style mustard
2 tbs. brown sugar
2 tsps. dry white wine

Place ham on rack in a shallow roasting pan. Insert meat thermometer in the thickest part of ham. Bake, uncovered, in a 325 degrees F oven for 1 3/4 to 2 1/4 hours or until meat thermometer registers 140 degrees F.

Meanwhile, for glaze, in a small bowl combine the mustard, brown sugar and white wine; mix well. Brush ham 2 or 3 times with the glaze during the last 20 minutes of cooking time.

Yields: 20 servings

RIO GRANDE PORK ROAST

3 to 4 lb. boneless pork loin
garlic pepper
1/2 cup barbecue sauce
1/2 cup apple or grape jelly
1 tsp. chili powder

Rub surfaces of roast well with garlic pepper. Place roast in a shallow pan and place in a preheated 350 degrees F oven; roast for 30 minutes.

To make basting sauce, combine remaining ingredients in a small bowl, stir to mix well. Pour basting sauce over roast and continue to roast, basting occasionally, until meat thermometer inserted registers 155 degrees F, about 20 to 30 more minutes. Remove roast from pan and let rest 10 minutes before slicing to serve.

Remove pan drippings to a small saucepan, add enough water to make 1 cup and bring to a boil; boil for 3 to 4 minutes. Serve sauce on side with roast.

Yields: 12 servings

PORK TENDERLOIN EN CROUTE

1 lb. pork tenderloin
1/2 cup dry red wine
1/8 tsp. dried tarragon
1 clove garlic, minced
2 tbs. butter or margarine
1 1/2 cups all-purpose flour
1/2 tsp. salt
1/2 cup shortening or lard
1 egg white
1 tbs. water
2 tsps. cornstarch

For marinade, in a heavy plastic bag combine wine, tarragon, and garlic; hold open end securely and turn bag to mix. Place tenderloin in bag; tie securely. Marinate in refrigerator 2 to 4 hours, turning occasionally.

Remove tenderloin, reserving marinade. Melt butter in a large, heavy skillet. Add tenderloin and brown on all sides. Add marinade; cover and simmer 10 minutes. Remove tenderloin, reserving marinade in skillet. Place tenderloin on a cookie sheet and place in freezer for 30 minutes.

In a mixing bowl, stir together flour and salt. Cut in lard with a pastry blender till crumbs are the size of peas. Add cold water, 1 tablespoon at a time, mixing with a fork after each addition. Form dough into a ball; turn onto a lightly floured surface. Flatten dough and roll into a rectangle about 2 inches longer than tenderloin and 1/8 inch thick. Remove tenderloin from freezer and place on pastry. Trim edges and sides. Fold in ends of pastry and wrap pastry around tenderloin, trimming to leave about 1/2 inch overlap. Seal edge with cold water.

Beat egg white until foamy; add 1 tablespoon water and mix well. Brush pastry with egg white wash. Bake in a 350 degree F oven for 20 to 25 minutes, or till golden brown.

Meanwhile, for sauce, measure the reserved marinade and add wine or cold water to equal 1 cup, if necessary. Stir in cornstarch, mixing well. Cook over medium heat till slightly thickened and bubbly.

Slice tenderloin with sharp bread knife. Serve with sauce.

Yields: 4 servings

PORK MEDALLIONS WITH CREAMY CAPER SAUCE

2 pork tenderloins (about 1 1/2 lbs. total)
2 tbs. butter or margarine
1/4 tsp. salt
2/3 cup dry white wine
2/3 cup light cream
1 clove garlic, minced
1/8 tsp. white pepper
2 tbs. capers, drained

Cut each tenderloin crosswise into 6 1 inch thick slices. With a meat mallet or cleaver, pound each slice to 1/2 inch thickness.

In a large skillet cook pork medallions in hot butter over medium heat about 3 to 4 minutes on each side. Remove pork to a warm platter; season with salt.

For the sauce, add wine to skillet drippings. Bring to boiling, scraping up any browned bits in skillet. Add cream, garlic and pepper. Cook and stir 3 minutes or until thickened. Remove from heat, stir in capers. To serve, pour sauce over pork.

Yields: 6 servings

PORK TENDERLOIN FLAMBE´

1 lb. pork tenderloin
1 tsp. butter or margarine
1 tsp. olive oil
1/2 cup beef broth
1/2 cup sliced green onion
1 tsp. Worcestershire sauce
1/2 tsp. dried thyme, crushed
1 cup sliced fresh mushrooms
3 tbs. brandy

Cut pork into eight 1 1/2 inch slices. Using fingers, press each slice to a 1 inch thickness. Heat butter and olive oil in a large skillet until butter melts. Add pork, cook over medium heat about 5 minutes on each side or until done. Remove pork, reserving drippings in skillet. Cover to keep warm.

Add the broth, the onion, Worcestershire, thyme and mushrooms to skillet. Bring mixture to boiling; reduce heat and simmer for 2 to 3 minutes or until vegetables are very tender, scraping brown bits from bottom of skillet. Return pork to skillet.

Heat brandy over high heat in a small saucepan until simmering. Pour heated brandy over pork; ignite with a long match. Gently stir pork until flames subside. Remove pork to a serving platter and spoon on sauce.

Yields: 4 servings

CHEESY HAM-FILLED BRIOCHE

1 1/2 cups fully-cooked ham, cubed
2 tbs. butter or margarine
1/4 fresh green pepper, chopped
1/4 cup fresh mushrooms, sliced
1 tbs. all-purpose flour
1/4 tsp. dry mustard
1/8 tsp. pepper
1 1/4 cups milk
1 cup shredded cheddar cheese (4 ozs.)
4 brioche or rich dinner rolls

In a medium skillet melt butter, add green pepper and sauté 3 minutes. Add mushrooms and cook over medium heat till tender. Remove mushrooms and green pepper, reserving drippings in skillet. Add flour, dry mustard, and pepper to pan drippings, stirring until smooth. Slowly stir in milk; cook over medium heat until thickened and bubbly, stirring constantly. Reduce heat to low and add cheese, stirring until smooth. Gently stir in ham, mushrooms and green pepper; heat through. Cut tops from brioche. Spoon ham mixture over brioche; replace tops.

Yields: 4 servings

PORK TENDERLOIN IN WINE SAUCE

1 lb. whole pork tenderloin
freshly ground black pepper
1 tbs. butter or margarine
1 tbs. vegetable oil
1/4 cup dry red wine
1/4 cup water
1/8 tsp. basil leaves, crushed
1/2 cup dry red wine
1 tbs. cornstarch
3 tbs. water

Rub the pork tenderloin with pepper. Melt butter in a large skillet with cooking oil. Add tenderloin and quickly brown on all sides. Remove from heat and carefully add 1/4 cup wine, 1/4 cup water, and basil. Cover and simmer for 15 to 20 minutes or till pork is done. Remove tenderloin and keep warm. Drain the pan drippings, reserving 1/3 cup.

For sauce, in a small saucepan combine 1/2 cup wine, cornstarch and 3 tablespoons water; mix with a wire whisk till cornstarch is dissolved. Stir in the reserved drippings; cook over medium heat till thickened and bubbly, stirring constantly. Slice the tenderloin and serve with sauce.

Yields: 4 servings

CORIANDER CHOPS

1/4 cup coriander seeds
2 tsps. cracked black pepper
1 cup diced onions
1/2 cup diced celery
1/2 cup diced carrot
1 lg. clove garlic, minced
2 sprigs fresh or 1/2 tsp. dry rosemary
2 bay leaves
4 butterfly pork chops, about 1 inch thick
1 tbs. vegetable oil
1/4 cup white wine
1 cup chicken or pork broth
2 tsps. cornstarch
2 tsps. white wine
fresh cilantro or parsley (optional)

Brown coriander seeds in frypan over medium heat. Cool. Crush or grind; mix with pepper and set aside. Combine vegetables, rosemary and bay leaves, set aside. Sprinkle both sides of chops with crushed coriander and pepper. Heat oil in heavy frypan, add chops and brown on both sides. Add vegetables, wine and broth to frypan; cover and simmer 12 to 15 minutes. Remove chops and keep warm. Thicken sauce with 2 teaspoons cornstarch mixed with 2 teaspoons white wine. Serve sauce with chops. Sprinkle with fresh cilantro or parsley, if desired.

Yields: 4 servings

LEMONY PORK CHOPS

4 pork loin chops, 1 1/4 inches thick
1/4 cup lemon juice
2 tbs. vegetable oil
2 tbs. water
2 tbs. snipped parsley
2 tsps. chopped chives
1 tsp. salt
1 tsp. dried tarragon, crushed
1 tsp. grated lemon peel
1/2 tsp. dried savory, crushed

For marinade, in a small saucepan combine lemon juice, oil, water, parsley, chives, salt, tarragon, lemon peel, and savory; simmer 3 to 4 minutes, stirring occasionally. Cool.

Place pork chops in a plastic bag; set in a shallow baking dish. Pour marinade over chops, close bag and tie securely. Marinate in the refrigerator 6 to 8 hours or overnight, turning occasionally to distribute marinade.

Drain chops, reserving marinade. Grill chops over medium coals about 8 minutes. Turn and grill about 8 minutes more, brushing occasionally with the reserved marinade.

Yields: 4 servings

PORK CHOPS FLAMBE'

6 pork loin chops, butterflied, 1/2 inch thick
1 tsps. olive oil
1/4 cup sliced green onion
1 tbs. orange peel
1/2 cup orange liqueur
1/4 cup orange juice
1/4 tsp. dried basil

Heat oil in a non-stick skillet. Add green onion and orange peel; sauté 3 to 4 minutes or till onion is almost tender. Remove onion and orange peel; set aside. Add pork chops and brown on both sides over medium heat; add onion and orange peel.

Add 1/2 of the orange liqueur, the orange juice and basil. Cover and simmer 8 to 10 minutes or till chops are done. Transfer the pork chops to a chafing dish, if desired. In a small saucepan gently heat the remaining orange liqueur. (Do not boil). Ignite with a long match and pour over chops.

Yields: 6 servings

DEVILISH PORK CUTLETS

1 lb. boneless pork loin, cut into 6 equal pieces
1/2 cup flour, seasoned with
1/2 tsp. seasoned salt
1 tsp. butter
1 tsp. vegetable oil
2 tbs. vinegar
3/4 cup chicken broth
1 cup sour cream
2 tbs. Dijon-style mustard
2 tbs. green peppercorns

Place each loin slice between 2 pieces of plastic wrap, flatten to 1/8 inch thickness. Dredge cutlets in seasoned flour. Heat butter and oil in large skillet over medium-high heat. Brown cutlets quickly, about 2 to 3 minutes on each side. Remove from pan and keep warm. Add vinegar and broth to skillet, bring to boil and stir until reduced to about 1/2 cup. Lower heat, stir in sour cream and mustard and whisk until smooth. Add peppercorns, simmer and stir gently until sauce thickens slightly. Pour sauce over cutlets. Garnish with sweet gherkins, if desired.

Yields: 6 servings

PORK TENDERLOIN DIANE

1 lb. pork tenderloin, cut into 8 crosswise pieces
2 tsps. lemon pepper
1 tbs. butter

1 tbs. lemon juice
1 tbs. Worcestershire sauce
1 tsp. Dijon-style mustard
1 tbs. minced parsley or chives

Place each piece of tenderloin between 2 pieces of plastic wrap. Flatten slightly with heel of hand. Sprinkle surfaces of medallions with lemon pepper. Heat butter in heavy skillet, cook tenderloin medallions 3 to 4 minutes on each side. Remove medallions to serving platter, keep warm. Add lemon juice, Worcestershire sauce, and mustard to skillet. Cook, stirring with pan juices, until heated through. Pour sauce over medallions, sprinkle with parsley and serve.

Yields: 4 servings

PORK EN PAPILLOTE

2 tbs. vegetable oil
4 slices boneless loin, 1/2 inch thick
2 tbs. orange juice
2 tbs. teriyaki sauce
1 tbs. sesame oil
1/2 tsp. ground ginger
2 med. carrots, cut into thin julienne strips
2 tsps. sesame seed

Cut 4 15x12 inch pieces of parchment paper or aluminum foil; fold in 1/2 lengthwise, trim each into a large crescent shape. Place crescents on baking sheets. Brush 1 side of each crescent with vegetable oil, leaving edges ungreased.

Pound pork to 1/4 inch thickness. Combine orange juice, teriyaki sauce, sesame oil and ginger in a shallow dish; add pork

and marinate for 30 minutes. Drain pork, reserving marinade; place pork on greased 1/2 of each parchment crescent. Arrange carrots over pork, spoon reserved marinade over carrots and sprinkle with sesame seed. Fold over remaining 1/2 of crescents. Pleat and crimp edges together to seal well, twist ends tightly to seal. Bake at 350 degrees F for 20 minutes or until bags are puffed and lightly browned.

Yields: 4 servings

PORK AU VIN

1 lb. boneless loin, cut into 3/4 inch slices
1 tsp. vegetable oil
8 sm. boiling onions, peeled
1/2 lb. mushrooms, halved
1/2 cup beef broth
1 cup dry red wine
1 tbs. Dijon-style mustard
2 tbs. chopped parsley
1 tsp. cornstarch stirred together with 1 tsp. water

Brown pork in non-stick pan in oil over medium-high heat. Remove pork from pan, add onion and cook, stirring, until onions are browned. Remove onions from pan, add mushrooms and cook, stirring, until lightly browned. Return pork and onions to pan, add broth, wine and mustard; bring to boil, reduce heat, cover and simmer on low heat 8 to 10 minutes. Stir in parsley. Remove pork and vegetables to serving dish. Stir cornstarch-water mixture into cooking juices; bring to a boil, stirring; pour over pork.

Yields: 4 servings

PORK AMANDINE

1 lb. pork tenderloin, cut into 8 equal pieces
2 tsps. butter
1/4 cup slivered almonds
1/4 cup flour
salt and pepper, to taste
1 tbs. lemon juice

Place each tenderloin piece between 2 pieces of plastic wrap and gently press to 1/8 inch thickness. Set aside.

In hot skillet, toast almonds until golden, stirring constantly. Remove almonds and reserve. Lightly coat tenderloin cutlets with flour and sauté over medium heat in butter until golden brown on both sides. Remove cutlets to platter. Add lemon juice and almonds to pan, heat and pour over cutlets.

Yields: 4 servings

PARMESAN PORK TENDERLOIN

1 lb. pork tenderloin
3 tbs. seasoned bread crumbs
1 tbs. grated parmesan cheese
1 tsp. salt
1/8 tsp. pepper
2 tsps. vegetable oil
1 sm. onion, chopped
1 clove garlic, minced

Cut tenderloin crosswise into 8 slices, approximately 1 inch thick. Place each slice on its cut surface and flatten with heel of hand to 1/2 inch thickness. Combine crumbs, parmesan cheese, salt and pepper; dredge pork slices to coat. Panfry slowly, with onion and garlic, in oil in large frying pan 10 minutes.

Yields: 4 servings

PORK KIEV

4 boneless pork loin chops, (4 ozs. each), butterflied
4 tsps. butter, chilled
2 cloves crushed garlic
2 tsps. chopped parsley
2 tsps. chopped chives
1/2 tsp. ground pepper
1/2 cup flour
1 egg beaten w/1 tsp. water
1/2 cup fine, dry bread crumbs
2 tbs. vegetable oil

Between 2 pieces of plastic wrap, pound each butterflied chop to 1/8 inch thickness. In the center of each, place 1 tsp. cold butter and sprinkle with seasonings, distributing evenly over chops. Fold in 2 opposite sides and roll up. Dredge each roll in flour, dip in egg wash, and roll in bread crumbs. Cover and chill 2 to 12 hours. Heat oil in heavy skillet, cook pork rolls 12 to 15 minutes, turning carefully to brown all sides.

Yields: 4 servings

PORK DIVAN

4 boneless center loin pork chops, 1 inch thick
1 tsp. vegetable oil
2 tbs. butter
2 tbs. flour
1 1/2 cups milk
1/2 cup grated parmesan cheese, divided
1/2 tsp. ground nutmeg
1 tbs. dry sherry
1/2 tsp. Worcestershire sauce
1 lg. bunch broccoli

In a heavy saucepan melt butter, add the flour and stir to blend. Add milk, cook and stir until sauce is thickened and smooth. Stir in 6 tablespoons parmesan cheese, the nutmeg, the sherry, and the Worcestershire sauce. Set aside and keep warm.

Heat oil in non-stick pan over medium-high heat. Brown chops on 1 side, about 3 to 4 minutes; turn to brown other side. Chop broccoli; cook in salted water until tender; drain. Arrange chopped broccoli on serving platter. Pour 1 cup sauce over, top with chops and garnish with additional sauce. Sprinkle with reserved parmesan cheese.

Yields: 4 servings

PORK AU POIVRE

4 boneless pork loin chops, 4 ozs. each

1 cup dry red wine
1/2 cup cognac or other brandy
1 tbs. vegetable oil
1 clove garlic, minced
1/4 cup coarsely ground peppercorns

For marinade, combine wine, Cognac, cooking oil and garlic in a 13x9x2 inch baking dish. Add chops, turning to coat. Cover and refrigerate 4 hours or overnight.

Drain chops, reserve marinade. Press peppercorns onto both sides of chops. Place on rack of broiler pan. Broil 4 to 5 inches from heat for 5 minutes on each side or till done, brushing occasionally with marinade.

Yields: 4 servings

MINI HAM AND MUSHROOM SOUFFLÉS

6 tbs. butter or margarine
1 cup sliced fresh mushrooms
6 tbs. all-purpose flour
1/4 tsp. salt
1/8 tsp. pepper
1 1/2 cups milk
1 cup shredded cheddar cheese (4 ozs.)
1 cup diced fully-cooked ham
6 eggs, separated
3/4 tsp. cream of tartar

In a medium saucepan melt butter. Add mushrooms and sauté till tender. Remove mushrooms, reserving drippings in pan. Stir flour, salt and pepper into drippings till smooth. Gradually stir in milk; cook over medium-high heat till thickened and bubbly, stirring constantly. Remove from heat; add cheese, stirring till melted. Stir in mushrooms and ham.

Beat egg whites and cream of tartar at high speed of electric mixer until stiff peaks form. Using clean beaters, beat egg yolks till thickened and lemon-colored, about 5 minutes. Fold ham mixture into yolks. Pour the yolk mixture over beaten egg whites; fold gently. Spoon mixture into 6 ungreased 1 1/2 cup soufflé dishes. Bake in a 300 degree oven for 45 to 50 minutes or till a knife inserted near center comes out clean. Serve immediately.

TO MAKE ONE LARGE SOUFFLÉ: Spoon mixture into an ungreased 2 quart soufflé dish. Bake in a 300 degree oven for 50 to 60 minutes.

Yields: 6 servings

STACKED SAUSAGE TORTE

1 cup fully-cooked ham, cubed
1 cup salami, cubed
1 package (8 oz.) brown-and-serve sausage links
1 lb. fresh spinach or 1 10 oz. package frozen spinach
5 eggs
1 tsp. water
2 tbs. butter
1 red bell pepper, cut into strips
1 package (8 oz.) mozzarella or Swiss cheese
1 package (17 oz.) frozen puff pastry, defrosted

Steam or cook spinach, drain in strainer, pressing to remove excess moisture. Beat 4 eggs and 1 egg white together. Beat remaining egg yolk with water; set aside. Heat 1 tablespoon butter in an 8 inch omelet pan. When hot, pour in 1/2 the beaten eggs and cook until set, turning if needed to cook top. Remove from pan but do not fold. Repeat with remaining butter and eggs.

Open pastry sheets carefully, pinching to close any holes. Roll 1 sheet into a 12 inch square. Carefully lift and fit into an 8 inch springform pan. Trim second pastry into an 8 inch circle. Make pastry cutouts from scraps.

To assemble: place 1 omelet on pastry in bottom of springform pan. Spoon drained spinach over

this. Layer 1/2 the mozzarella cheese over spinach. Top with ham and red peppers. Add second omelet and arrange sausage links over this. Sprinkle over salami. Top with remaining cheese. Adjust circle over all, cut pastry as needed and pinch edge. Brush pastry with beaten egg yolk and water. Arrange pastry cut-outs atop. Bake in a 375 degree F oven for 70 to 75 minutes. Cool for 10 minutes before cutting. May be served warm or cold.

Yields: 12 servings

ROAST PORK TENDERLOIN WITH GREEN PEPPERCORN SAUCE

2 lbs. pork tenderloin
4 slices bacon
1/2 fresh pineapple or 1 can (8 1/4 oz.) sliced pineapple
1 tbs. butter or margarine
1/4 cup sugar
1/4 cup white wine vinegar
1 1/2 cups chicken broth
1 tsp. green peppercorns in vinegar, drained
1 tbs. cornstarch
1 lb. spinach

Place tenderloin in open roasting pan; criss-cross 2 bacon slices over each. Bake in a 400 degree F oven for 20 minutes or till meat thermometer reads 155 degrees F.

Pare fresh pineapple and slice into 1/2 inch slices.

In a 10 inch skillet melt butter. Sauté pineapple; remove. Add sugar to skillet and cook over medium heat till caramelized, about 5 minutes. Add vinegar and chicken broth; bring to boiling and cook till sugar dissolves. (If using canned pineapple, drain and add juice to chicken broth.) Add peppercorns and boil rapidly to reduce to about 1 cup.

Combine cornstarch and cold water; stir into hot mixture. Cook and stir till thickened and bubbly. Season with salt, if desired. Steam spinach and keep warm.

To serve, slice tenderloin and serve with pineapple and spinach. Spoon peppercorn sauce atop.

Yields: 6 servings

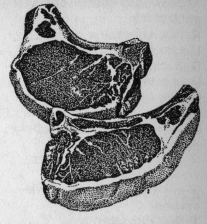

PORK SMITTANE

2 butterfly pork chops, cut 1/2 inch thick
3 tbs. all-purpose flour
1/4 tsp. pepper
2 tsps. butter or margarine
1 tbs. finely chopped green onion
1/3 cup dry white wine
1 tsp. Dijon-style mustard
1/4 cup cold water
1 1/2 tsps. all-purpose flour

Pound pork with a meat mallet to 1/4 inch thickness. Combine 3 tablespoons flour and pepper; dredge chops lightly in flour mixture. In a medium skillet melt butter; add chops and brown on both sides. Remove chops and set aside.

Add green onion to drippings; cook over medium heat till crisp-tender. Stir in wine and mustard. Return chops to skillet. Cover and reduce heat to medium-low. Simmer for 15 to 18 minutes or till done. Remove chops and set aside.

Combine water and 1 1/2 teaspoons flour, mixing to dissolve flour. Add flour mixture to drippings. Cook over medium-high heat till thickened and bubbly, stirring constantly. Return chops to skillet. Cover and cook for 2 to 3 minutes or till heated through.

Yields: 2 servings

PORK CHOPS A LA CAPERS

6 pork loin chops, cut 3/4 inch thick
1 tsp. vegetable oil
1 cup chicken broth
1/2 cup fresh lemon juice
1 cup sliced leeks
1 tbs. minced fresh thyme leaves
1/2 tsp. grated lemon peel
1/4 tsp. salt
1 1/2 cups baby carrots, cooked, drained
2 cups sliced fresh mushrooms
2 tbs. cornstarch
1 cup whipping cream
2 tsps. capers

Brown pork chops in oil in non-stick frypan. Stir in chicken broth, lemon juice, leeks, thyme, lemon peel and salt. Bring to a boil; reduce heat. Cover; simmer 15 to 20 minutes or until pork chops are tender. Place pork chops on serving platter; keep warm.

Add carrots and mushrooms to skillet; simmer 5 minutes. Gradually stir combined cornstarch and whipping cream into pan liquid. Cook and stir until thickened. Stir in capers. Serve sauce over pork chops.

Yields: 6 servings

ROSEMARY PORK MEDALLIONS

4 pork tenderloin medallions (4 ozs. each)
flour for dredging
2 tsps. olive oil
salt and pepper, to taste
1/2 tsp. dried rosemary, crumbled
1/2 cup beef broth
2 tbs. brandy
fresh parsley sprigs
lemon wedges

Preheat oven to 400 degrees F. Dredge pork lightly with flour, shaking off excess. Heat oil in heavy skillet. Add pork and brown about 3 to 4 minutes per side. Season with salt and pepper. Pour off fat from skillet. Press rosemary onto both sides of each medallion. Transfer to baking dish and roast for 8 to 10 minutes.

Meanwhile, deglaze skillet with stock and brandy over medium heat, stirring up brown bits, reducing to 1/2 cup. Pour sauce over pork, garnish with lemon and parsley and serve immediately.

Yields: 4 servings

PORK SCALOPPINI

1 lb. pork tenderloin
1 tsp. each butter and olive oil
1/2 cup flour
salt and pepper to taste

Cut tenderloin crosswise into eight equal pieces. Place each tenderloin piece between 2 pieces of plastic wrap. Using heel of hand, gently press tenderloin pieces to a thickness of 1/8 inch. Coat each piece lightly with flour, shake off excess.

Heat butter and oil in a non-stick frypan over high heat, add pork and brown quickly on both sides, about 4 to 5 minutes total. Remove pork to serving platter, season with salt and pepper and serve immediately.

Yields: 4 servings

PORK TENDERLOIN MEDALLIONS WITH FRESH ASPARAGUS

1 1/2 lbs. pork tenderloin, cut into 3/4 inch slices
1 tbs. butter or margarine
1 cup dry white wine
2 tsps. lemon juice
1/2 tsp. marjoram leaves
1/4 tsp. salt
dash pepper
1 tbs. minced shallots
1 lb. fresh asparagus, cut into 3 inch pieces
2 tbs. all-purpose flour
1 cup half and half
1/2 cup shredded Swiss cheese

Pound pork tenderloin pieces to 1/2 inch thickness. Melt butter in large skillet. Brown pork over medium heat. Stir in wine, lemon juice, marjoram, salt, pepper and shallots. Bring to a boil; reduce heat. Simmer 15 to 20 minutes or until pork is tender. Stir in asparagus. Simmer 5 minutes. Remove pork and asparagus from skillet; keep warm.

Combine flour and half and half; beat until smooth. Gradually stir into boiling liquid in skillet. Cook and stir until thickened. Stir in cheese, pork and asparagus. Cook over low heat until thoroughly heated.

Yields: 6 servings

GRILLED CHEF'S PRIME CRUSTED WITH MUSTARD SEED

3 lb. boneless pork rib-end roast
1 to 2 tsps. coarse-ground pepper
4 to 6 tbs. mustard seed
Dijon mustard

Sprinkle surface of roast evenly with pepper. Put mustard seed in a pan longer than roast; roll meat in seed until heavily coated. Grill over indirect heat on covered grill until meat thermometer registers 155 to 160 degrees F, about 45 minutes to 1 hour. Transfer to a carving board. Slice to serve; serve with mustard.

Yields: 12 servings

PORK MEDALLIONS WITH DIJON-DILL SAUCE

8 ozs. pork tenderloin
1/2 tsp. garlic salt
1/8 tsp. pepper
1/4 cup plain yogurt

2 tsps. Dijon-style mustard
1/4 tsp. each dill weed and
sugar

Cut pork crosswise into 4 pieces. To make medallions, place each piece of pork, cut side down, on flat surface; cover with waxed paper and flatten gently with heel of hand to 1/4 inch thickness. Pan-broil pork in non-stick frying pan over medium heat 3 to 4 minutes per side. Remove medallions to warm platter; season with garlic salt and pepper .

Meanwhile combine yogurt, mustard, dillweed and sugar. Serve sauce with pork medallions.

Note: to serve sauce warm, place mixture in heat-proof measure and warm in hot (not boiling) water 2 to 3 minutes. Do not cook or let curdle.

Yields: 2 servings

PORK CORDON BLEU

**4 boneless pork chops, each
about 4 ozs.
2 ozs. proscuitto or wafer-
thin ham
2 ozs. Swiss cheese, cut into
2x1/4 inch rectangles
1 tsp. dried thyme leaves
1/2 cup flour
1 egg, beaten with 1 tsp.
water
1/2 cup fine dry bread
crumbs
2 tsps. butter**

Slice each chop lengthwise almost in 1/2 to butterfly. Between 2 pieces of plastic wrap, pound each butterflied chop to 1/8 inch thickness. On 1/2 of each chop, place 1 ounce proscuitto and 1 piece of cheese. Sprinkle with 1/4 teaspoon thyme. Roll chops to enclose filling. Coat with flour, dip in egg wash and roll in bread crumbs.

In large frying pan, melt butter. Add pork and cook 10 to 12 minutes, turning frequently to brown all sides.

Yields: 4 servings

PORK A LA KING

**2 cups roast pork loin,
cubed
2 tbs. butter
2 tbs. flour
2 cups milk
3 tbs. green pepper, diced
1 jar (3 oz.) button mushrooms, drained
1 jar (2 oz.) pimiento, diced,
drained
1 cup frozen peas, thawed
1/4 tsp. thyme, crushed
1/2 tsp. seasoned salt
1/4 tsp. pepper
toast, biscuits, corn bread
or waffles (optional)**

In large heavy saucepan, melt butter; blend in flour, whisk in milk and cook, stirring constantly, until thickened. Stir in vegetables and seasonings; gently stir in pork and warm through, stirring gently. Serve over toast, if desired.

Yields: 4 servings

PORK AND ONIONS WITH WILD RICE

**6 green onions
1 lb. boneless pork loin, cut
into 1/2 inch cubes
1 tsp. kitchen browning
sauce
1 package (6 1/2 oz.) fast-
cooking long grain and wild
rice
1 3/4 cups water
1/4 tsp. ground cumin**

Cut white part of green onions in 1 inch lengths; thinly slice green tops and set aside. Combine white onion with pork cubes, browning sauce and about 1/2 of rice seasoning packet in microwave-safe 1 quart casserole. Marinate 10 to 15 minutes at room temp.

Combine remaining rice seasoning packet, rice, water and cumin in microwave-safe 2 quart casserole; cover with lid or plastic wrap. Microwave (High) 4 to 5 minutes or until rice is hot and slightly cooked. Let stand covered about 5 minutes to finish cooking.

Microwave pork mixture, covered with waxed paper, on (High) 5 to 6 minutes, stirring after each 2 minutes, until pork is done. Stir in green onion tops. Fluff rice with a fork and push towards edges of casserole. Spoon pork into center of rice.

Yields: 6 servings

MICROWAVED HERBED PORK ROAST

**3 lb. boneless double-loin
pork roast (rolled and tied)
3 tbs. snipped fresh parsley
1/2 tsp. snipped fresh
oregano
1/4 tsp. snipped fresh
tarragon
1/4 tsp. snipped fresh
thyme
1/4 tsp. snipped fresh dill
1/4 tsp. snipped fresh
chervil
additional fresh herbs (optional)
lemon slices (optional)**

Sprinkle roast lightly with paprika; rub into surface. Combine parsley, oregano, tarragon, thyme, dill and chervil; rub mixture over surface of roast.

Place roast in a 10x16 inch oven cooking bag in a microwave-safe dish; tie bag loosely. Cook 35 to 40 minutes at medium-low (30% power), invert roast and rotate dish 1/2 turn. Cook 30 to 35 minutes more at medium-low. Cover roast in cooking bag with foil and let stand 10 minutes.

Remove roast from bag and place on serving platter. Garnish with herbs and lemon slices; if desired.

Yields: 10 servings

PORK CHOPS WITH PESTO STUFFING

4 pork rib chops, cut 1 1/4 inches thick
1/2 cup firmly packed fresh basil leaves
1/4 cup snipped fresh parsley
1/4 cup grated parmesan cheese
2 tbs. pine nuts
1 clove garlic, peeled and minced
3 tbs. olive oil
3 to 4 slices white bread, lightly toasted and torn into 1/4 inch
2 tbs. water
salt and pepper to taste

With a sharp knife cut opening in the rib side of each chop. Insert knife in each opening and cut a pocket without cutting through to other side of chop. Set chops aside.

Place basil, parsley, parmesan cheese, pine nuts and garlic in blender container or food processor bowl. Blend or process about 30 seconds or until finely chopped. With blender or food processor running, add 1 tbs. olive oil. Transfer mixture to a small bowl; stir in bread pieces. Sprinkle water over bread mixture, tossing lightly to combine.

Spoon about 1/2 cup stuffing mixture into each chop. In a large skillet, brown chops on each side in the remaining hot oil. Place chops in a large baking dish; sprinkle with salt and pepper. Bake, uncovered, in a 350 degrees F oven for 45 minutes to 1 hour or until tender.

Yields: 4 servings

PORK STEAKS WITH GREEN BEANS

2 pork blade steaks, cut 1 inch thick (about 1 lb.)
2 sm. cloves garlic, minced
2 tbs. finely chopped onion
2 tbs. lemon juice
2 tbs. soy sauce
1 tbs. honey
1 package (9 oz.) frozen French-style green beans, thawed

Place steaks in plastic bag or shallow baking dish. Combine garlic, onion, lemon juice, soy sauce and honey; mix well. Pour marinade over pork steaks. Tie bag securely or cover tightly and marinate in refrigerator 2 hours, turning once.

Drain pork steaks, reserving marinade. Place steaks on rack in broiler pan. Broil 4 to 5 inches from heat for 7 to 8 minutes per side. Pour marinade into small saucepan; bring to a boil. Reduce heat; cover tightly and simmer 5 minutes. Add green beans; cover and cook 5 to 8 minutes or until beans are tender. Serve green beans with broiled steaks.

Yields: 4 servings

PORK-STUFFED PEPPERS

3 lg. green peppers
1/4 cup raisins
1 lb. ground pork
1/2 cup chopped onion
1/2 cup chopped carrot
1/2 cup chopped celery
1/4 tsp. salt
1 cup cooked brown rice
2 tbs. sunflower kernels
1/2 cup plain yogurt

Remove tops, seeds, and membranes from peppers. Cut in 1/2 lengthwise. Cook in boiling salted water for 5 minutes; drain. Soak raisins in water 10 to 15 minutes; drain and set aside. Combine pork, onion, carrot, celery and salt in a medium skillet. Cook over low heat until pork is done and vegetables are tender, stirring occasionally. Drain thoroughly. Add rice, sunflower kernels, yogurt and raisins; mix well. Spoon mixture into peppers. Place in a 12x8x2 inch baking dish. Bake at 350 degrees F for 30 to 35 minutes .

Yields: 6 servings

PORK BALLS IN CURRY SAUCE

1 1/2 lbs. lean ground pork
3/4 cup soft bread crumbs
1 egg, lightly beaten
3/4 cup finely chopped onion
1 tsp. salt
1 tbs. vegetable oil
1 to 2 tbs. crushed dried red peppers
1 tbs. curry powder
1 tsp. ground ginger
3 cups chopped onion
2 cloves garlic, minced
2/3 cup cider vinegar
1 cup tomato sauce
1 cup chicken broth
3/4 cup sour cream

Combine ground pork, bread crumbs, egg, onion and salt. Shape into 1 1/2 inch balls .

Heat oil in a fry pan. Add 1/2 pork balls and cook, shaking pan to brown all sides. Remove browned balls from pan and repeat with remainder.

Remove browned balls from pan; pour off fat, measure and return 2 tablespoons to pan. Add red peppers, curry powder and ginger; cook and stir about 1 minute. Add onions, garlic, vinegar, tomato sauce and chicken broth; stir to blend and bring to a boil. Add pork balls; cover; reduce heat and simmer for 45 minutes. Push balls to 1 side and stir in sour cream; carefully mix sauce and balls.

Yields: 8 servings

MEXICAN
SIDE DISHES & ENTREES

9

20 MINUTE TACOS

1 lb. ground beef
1 envelope (1 1/4 oz.) Old
El Paso taco seasoning mix
3/4 cup water
1 box (12 count) Old El
Paso taco shells
Suggested toppers:
shredded or leaf lettuce
shredded cheese
diced tomatoes (or cherry
tomato wedges)
Old El Paso taco sauce

In medium skillet, brown ground beef; drain. Stir in taco seasoning mix and water. Cook and stir on medium heat 10 to 15 minutes.

Heat and crisp taco shells according to package directions.

Spoon 2 tablespoons beef mixture into each taco shell. Garnish with desired toppers.

Yields: 12 tacos

APPLE CINNAMON TOSTADAS A LA MODE

1 box (12 count) Old El
Paso tostada shells
1 tbs. butter, melted
2 tbs. cinnamon sugar (or 2
tbs. sugar and 1/4 tsp.
cinnamon)
2 cans (21 ozs. each) apple
pie filling
vanilla ice cream

Preheat oven to 350 degrees F. Brush tostadas with melted butter. Sprinkle each with 1/2 teaspoon cinnamon sugar and place on two baking sheets.

Top each tostada with 1/3 cup pie filling. Bake 5 minutes.

Let cool slightly and top with a small scoop of vanilla ice cream. Serve immediately.

Yields: 12 tostadas

BANANAS DIEGO

4 Chiquita bananas
2 tbs. catsup
2 tbs. soy sauce
2 tbs. honey
dash garlic powder
4 tbs. coconut

Split peeled bananas lengthwise. Mix catsup with soy sauce, honey, and garlic powder. Brush one cut half with mixture and put halves back together. Place on foil rectangle. Brush outside of banana with remaining catsup mixture and sprinkle with coconut. Close foil around banana to make a package. Chill until ready to cook.

When ready to cook, place on grill approximately 3 inches from coals and cook 6 to 8 minutes. Eat right from package with fork or spoon. Cooking can be adjusted up or down depending on intensity of heat coming from coals and distance of grill from heat. If bananas have been thoroughly chilled, additional time may be needed.

Yields: 4 servings

BANANAS WITH MEXICAN CHOCOLATE SAUCE

1/2 cup light cream
1/2 tsp. instant coffee (dry
granules)
2 bars (4 ozs. each) sweet
cooking chocolate
1/2 cup coffee liqueur
chilled Chiquita bananas
pound cake squares

Heat cream in dessert size fondue pot over medium to low heat. Dissolve coffee in cream. Break chocolate into squares and heat and stir in cream until melted and blended. Stir in coffee liqueur. Continue to keep hot over low heat.

Cut peeled bananas into 1 inch slices. Spear on fondue fork and dip into sauce. Spear cake squares on fork and dip into sauce.

Note: Sauce adheres better to cold bananas than those at room temperature. Place fruit in refrigerator at least an hour before peeling and serving.

Yields: 2 cups sauce

BUSY DAY BURRITOS

1 can (16 oz.) Old El Paso
fat free refried beans
1 jar (16 oz.) Old El Paso
thick 'n chunky salsa, divided usage
1 can (4.5 oz.) Old El Paso
chopped green chilies
1 box (8 count) Old El Paso
flour tortillas
2 cups (8 ozs.) shredded
cheddar cheese

In medium saucepan, combine refried beans, 1/4 cup salsa and green chilies. Cook over medium heat until heated through, stirring constantly.

Heat tortillas according to package directions.

Spoon 1/4 cup bean mixture down center of each tortilla; top with 1/4 cup cheese. Fold bottom edge of each tortilla up to center, covering one half of the filling. Fold in sides of tortilla, overlapping in center, to cover filling. Serve topped with remaining salsa.

Yields: 8 burritos

CHICKEN CHOLUTECA

**3 double broiler-fryer chicken breasts
2 tbs. lime juice
1/2 tsp. salt
dash freshly ground pepper
2 slices bacon, cut up
1/8 tsp. Tabasco sauce
1/4 tsp. basil
1/2 tsp. thyme
2 green onions, cut up (about 1/2 cup)
3/4 cup dry sherry
1 cup coconut milk
1 cup mashed Chiquita banana (2 large bananas)
1/4 cup chopped salted peanuts
hot cooked rice, lightly buttered
parsley sprigs**

Split chicken breasts in half and rub with lime juice, salt and pepper. In a large skillet, cook bacon until crisp. Remove bacon and reserve. Brown chicken breasts in bacon fat. As browned, place in a flat casserole. Stir seasonings in skillet with onion, sherry, coconut milk and mashed banana. Cook and stir from bottom of pan until heated through then pour over chicken in casserole. Bake, covered, in 350 degrees F oven 20 minutes. Uncover and bake 10 minutes longer. If the gravy seems too thick, thin with a bit of wine. Sprinkle chicken with bacon and peanuts and serve with gravy and hot cooked rice. Garnish with parsley.

Note: To make coconut milk: Combine 1 can (3 1/2 ounce) flaked coconut with 1 cup milk. Bring to a boil over high heat, reduce heat and cook below the boiling point 15 minutes, stirring occasionally. Strain milk from coconut, pressing coconut so as to get all the flavor. Discard coconut. Measure coconut milk and, add milk to make 1 cup.

Yields: 6 servings

CHILI BURRITOS

**2 lbs. beef rump roast
1 med. onion, sliced
1/2 tsp. salt
1/4 tsp. pepper
1 lg. onion, chopped
1 tbs. vegetable oil
1 can (16 oz.) pinto or kidney beans, drained
1 can (16 oz.) tomatoes
1 can (4 oz.) chopped green chilies
1 tbs. chili powder
8 (8 inch) tortillas
dairy sour cream, if desired
guacamole, if desired**

To prepare beef rump roast, place roast, sliced onion, salt and pepper in a Dutch oven. Add half an inch of water to the pan; cover tightly and cook over low heat on top of range or in a slow (300 degrees F) oven for 2 to 2 1/2 hours. Let cool slightly in juices. Pour off juices; reserving 1 cup, and skim off fat. Shred beef.

In same Dutch oven, sauté chopped onion in oil over medium heat until tender. Add reserved shredded beef and juices, beans, tomatoes, tomato paste, chilies and chili powder. Bring to a boil; reduce heat and simmer 1 hour or until thickened, stirring occasionally.

Spoon an equal amount of beef mixture into warm tortillas. Roll up for serving. Serve with sour cream and guacamole, if desired.

Yields: 8 servings

FAST FAJITAS

**1 lb. boneless, skinless chicken breast halves, cut into thin strips
1 jar (16 oz.) Old El Paso Homestyle chunky salsa, divided usage
2 tbs. lime juice
1 tbs. olive oil
1 tsp. Worcestershire sauce
1 clove garlic, minced
1 green bell pepper, cut into thin strips
1 medium onion, cut into thin strips
1 can (4.5 oz.) Old El Paso chopped green chilies
1 box (8 count) Old El Paso flour tortillas, heated according to package directions
cilantro leaves, optional**

Combine 1 cup salsa, lime juice, oil, Worcestershire sauce, and garlic; pour over chicken. Cover and refrigerate 20 to 30 minutes.

Place chicken and marinade in medium skillet. Cook over medium-high heat until chicken is done, about 10 minutes. Add pepper, onion and chilies; cook 2 minutes or until liquid has evaporated.

Heat tortillas according to package directions. Top with chicken mixture, adding salsa and cilantro leaves, if desired.

Yields: 8 fajitas

FIESTA BEANS WITH CHEESE

**1 can (16 oz.) Old El Paso refried beans, any variety
1/2 cup Old El Paso thick 'n chunky salsa or picante
1/4 cup (1 oz.) shredded cheddar or Monterey jack cheese
1 tbs. chopped red onion**

In small saucepan, combine refried beans and salsa. Cook over medium heat, stirring occasionally, until heated through.

Top with cheese and onion before serving.

Yields: 4 servings

MEXICAN PIZZA

1 can (16 oz.) Old El Paso refried beans
1/2 cup Old El Paso thick 'n chunky salsa or picante
8 Old El Paso tostada shells
1 can (4.5 oz.) Old El Paso chopped green chilies
1/2 cup diced tomatoes
1/2 cup green bell pepper slices
1 1/2 cups (6 ozs.) shredded Monterey jack/colby cheese

Preheat oven to 350 degrees F. In small bowl, combine refried beans and salsa.

Spread 1/4 cup bean mixture on each tostada shell. Top with 1 tablespoon each chilies, tomatoes and bell peppers. Sprinkle with cheese.

Bake 5 minutes until cheese is melted.

Yields: 8 pizzas

MEXICAN BEEF SALAD

1/2 lb. boneless beef round or sirloin steak
1 tbs. vegetable oil
1 red bell pepper, in thin strips
1 sm. onion, in thin wedges
2 cloves garlic, finely chopped
3/4 tsp. ground cumin
3/4 tsp. dried oregano
1/2 tsp. hot red pepper flakes
1/4 tsp. salt
1/4 tsp. pepper
2 cups shredded romaine lettuce, cut 1/4 inch
1 jalapeno pepper (optional)

Cut beef across grain into thin strips. Heat 1/2 tablespoons oil in nonstick skillet. Stirfry red pepper, onion and garlic 2 to 3 minutes. Remove and reserve. Add remaining oil to skillet. Stirfry beef 2 to 3 minutes. Stir in spices and vegetables. Cook until heated through. Serve mixture over lettuce, garnish with jalapeno pepper.

Yields: 2 servings

MEXICAN BEAN BAKE

2 cups Idaho red beans
1 med. onion, chopped
1 green pepper, chopped
1 clove garlic, minced
3 tbs. butter or margarine
1 lb. ground beef
1 tbs. salt
4 tsps. chili powder
1 can (16 oz.) tomatoes
1/2 cup catsup
1/2 cup shredded Monterey jack or Swiss cheese
corn chips

Soak beans overnight in 6 cups water. Or, quick soak method, add beans to 6 cups boiling water, boil 2 minutes and let stand for 1 hour. Simmer beans in soaking water until tender, about 2 hours. Drain. Sauté onion, green pepper and garlic in butter or margarine until tender. Add ground beef and brown quickly, breaking into small pieces with fork. Stir in salt, chili powder, tomatoes and catsup. Simmer until thick. Mix in drained beans. Place in shallow baking dish. Sprinkle shredded cheese over top and place corn chips around edge. Bake at 350 degrees F for 30 minutes.

Yields: 8 servings

BEAN TAMALE PIE

3 cups cooked pinto beans or 2 cans (15 oz.) pinto beans
1 lg. onion, chopped
2 tbs. vegetable oil
1 lb. ground beef
1 tsp. salt
2 tbs. chili powder
1/2 tsp. oregano
1/2 tsp. basil
2 tbs. sugar
1 can (29 oz.) tomatoes
1 can (6 oz.) tomato paste
1/2 cup sliced ripe olives
1 cup cornmeal
4 cups water
1 tsp. salt
1/4 cup grated parmesan cheese

Drain beans. Sauté onion in oil until tender. Add ground beef and cook until brown, breaking apart with fork. Add salt, chili powder, oregano, basil, sugar, tomatoes, tomato paste, olives and beans. Simmer 1 hour. Combine cornmeal with 1/2 cup water. Bring remaining 3 1/2 cups water to boil. Add salt and cornmeal. Cook 10 minutes. Spread half of cornmeal in bottom of deep casserole. Add bean mixture. Spread remaining cornmeal on top. Sprinkle with parmesan cheese. Bake at 350 degrees F for 25 to 30 minutes.

To cook dry beans: Soak beans overnight in water, using 3 cups water per 1 cup beans. Or, for quick soak method, add measured amount of water to beans. Bring to boil; boil for 2 minutes. Cover and let stand 1 hour. Add 1 teaspoon salt per cup of beans. Cover and simmer until tender, about 1 1/2 ours. One cup dry beans yields about 2 1/2 cups when cooked.

Yields: 6 to 8 servings

FESTIVE BEAN TOSTADAS

1 lb. lean ground beef
1 cup chopped onion
2 cloves garlic, minced
2 cans (8 ozs. each) tomato sauce
1 tsp. dried oregano, crushed
2 to 3 tbs. chili powder
1/8 tsp. ground cumin
2 cans (15 oz.) kidney beans, drained
1 can (2 1/4 oz.) sliced ripe olives, drained
6 to 8 flour tortillas (8 inch) fried until crisp and puffy
shredded iceberg lettuce

shredded cheddar cheese
chopped onion
1 can (7 oz.) green chili
salsa or about 1 cup bottled
red Mexican cooking sauce

Brown ground beef, onion and garlic in skillet over medium heat, breaking up meat with fork. Drain off excess fat. Stir in tomato sauce, oregano, chili powder, cumin, beans and olives. Pour into a 1 1/2 to 2 quart baking dish. Bake at 350 degrees F about 30 minutes, until hot and bubbly. To serve, arrange tortillas on individual plates; spoon a generous amount of hot bean mixture over each tortilla. Pass lettuce, cheese, onion and salsa in separate dishes as condiments to be sprinkled over tostadas.

Cooked Western dry bean variation: Substitute about 3 1/3 cups cooked and drained dark or light red kidney beans for canned beans.

Yields: 6 to 8 servings

CHILIES RELLENO WITH REFRIED BEANS

2 tbs. chopped onion
1 tbs. oil
2 tsps. tomato paste
1/2 tsp. oregano
2 cups refried beans
3 dashes Tabasco
salt, pepper to taste
6 canned Poblano chilies
flour
egg batter
1/2 cup dairy sour cream
1 cup grated cheddar cheese

Sauté onion in oil. Stir in tomato paste, oregano, beans, Tabasco, salt and pepper. Fill chilies with bean mixture. Dip in flour and roll in egg batter. Deep fry until golden. Drain and place in baking dish. Cover with sour cream and grated cheese. Bake at 350 degrees F until browned.

Egg batter: Separate 2 eggs. Beat egg whites until stiff. Beat yolks and fold into whites.

Yields: 6 servings

BEAN BURRITOS

8 ozs. pork sausage
1 tsp. chili powder
1 med. onion, chopped
2 cups refried beans
1/4 lb. cheddar cheese, grated
1/4 lb. Jack cheese, grated
chili sauce
6 flour tortillas
oil

Cook sausage, chili powder and onion until sausage is brown and crumbly. Add beans and cheeses. Season with chili sauce. Heat tortillas on dry hot griddle. Remove from griddle and place mound of bean filling in center of each. Fold in sides and roll to enclose. Cook on hot greased skillet until browned.

Yields: 6 burritos

MEXICAN BEAN AND BEEF LOAF

2 cans (15 ozs. each) dry beans) (kidney, pinto, pink or red)
3/4 lb. ground beef
3/4 cup chopped onion
1/2 cup chopped green pepper
1 1/2 tsps. salt
1/2 tsp. chili powder
1/4 tsp. pepper
Tabasco
green pepper rings, for garnish
Spicy cheese sauce:
1 can (11 oz.) cheddar cheese soup
1/4 cup milk
2 tbs. jalapeno taco sauce

Drain beans and mash coarsely. combine beans with beef, onion, green pepper, salt, chili powder, pepper and a dash of Tabasco. Mix well. Place in medium loaf pan and bake at 350 degrees F for 1 hour. Garnish with green pepper rings and serve withspicy cheese sauce.

To prepare spicy cheese sauce: In a saucepan, combine soup, milk

and jalapeno taco sauce. Heat through. Serve over Mexican bean and beef loaf.

Yields: 6 servings

RED BEANS-AND-RICE

To prepare beans:
1 lb. (2 2/3 cups) Idaho dried red beans
6 cups water
2 tsps. salt
To finish the dish:
3 tbs. butter or other fat
1/2 cup chopped onion
1 fat clove garlic, minced
1 cup diced ham
3 tbs. flour
1 cup red table wine or tomato juice
1 cup (about) liquid from beans
1/4 tsp. powdered thyme
1/4 cup snipped parsley
cooked red beans
3 cups cooked rice, piping hot

Soak washed beans overnight in measured amount of water. Or bring to boiling point; boil 2 minutes only. Soak for 1 hour. The addition of 1/4 teaspoon soda to the soaking water helps to shorten cooking time. Do not drain. Add salt. Bring to boiling point. Cover and simmer about 2 hours or until beans are tender. Drain. Save liquid.

Cook onion, garlic and ham in butter or ham fat. Stir in flour. Cook a minute. Add red wine or tomato juice, bean liquid, parsley, and thyme. Cook slowly until smooth and thickened. Taste for seasoning. Add salt if needed. Stir in cooked beans. Heat thoroughly.

To serve: Place cooked rice in a mound on hot chop plate. Pour the bean mixture around the rice. Serve with hot cornbread sticks or squares, crisp relishes. End the meal with fruit and cheese, coffee for dessert.

Note: A meaty ham bone may be cooked with the beans (start with 1 teaspoon salt). Remove when beans are cooked. Cut off the meat and dice it to be cooked in the sauce. Canned red beans may be used. Two cans will yield about 4 cups with liquid. Use three cans if you like. Should there be any of the dish left over, gently stir the bean mixture into the rice. Place in casserole to reheat for another days' enjoyment.

Yields: variable servings

ENCHILADAS

1 cup dry Idaho red or pink beans
1/2 cup chopped onion
1/2 cup sliced ripe olives
1 can (15 oz.) tomato sauce
1 can (4 oz.) chopped green chilies
1 tsp. garlic salt
1 can (10 oz.) tortillas
1 cup grated cheddar cheese

Soak beans overnight in 3 cups water. Or, for quick soak method, add measured amount of cold water to beans, bring to boil and boil 2 minutes. Cover and let stand 1 hour. Cook in soaking liquid until tender, 1 to 1 1/2 hours. Drain. Mash beans. In a large bowl, combine mashed beans, onions, olives, 3/4 cup tomato sauce, chilies and garlic salt. Mix well. Soften tortillas according to directions on can. Place a generous portion of bean mixture along center of each tortilla. Roll up and place in baking dish. Spoon remaining tomato sauce over tortillas. Sprinkle with grated cheese. Bake at 350 degrees F for 15 to 20 minutes.

Note: Two cans (15 ounces) drained red or pink beans may be used in place of cooked dry beans.

Yields: 18 enchiladas

BEANS AND HAM, MEXICO WAY

1 lb. (2 1/3 cups) Idaho dried red or pinto beans
meaty ham bone
1 fat clove garlic, slivered and mashed with 1 tsp. salt
1 cup chopped onion
1 lg. bay leaf
1 1/2 to 2 tbs. chili powder
1 tsp. ground cumin
4 ripe tomatoes, skinned and chopped or 2 cups mashed solid pack tomatoes

Rinse beans; place in heavy kettle or Dutch oven with 6 cups cold water. Bring to boiling point; boil 2 minutes only. Add 1/4 teaspoon soda to soften water. Cover and let stand for 1 hour. Or soak overnight in measured amounts of water and soda.

To cook: Add ham end, garlic and salt, onion and bay leaf to undrained beans. Bring to boiling point; reduce heat and cover tightly. Simmer for 2 to 2 1/2 hours or until beans are tender.

Mix chili powder and cumin with a little of the bean liquid. Add to beans along with tomatoes. Cook over low heat, stirring occasionally, for about 45 minutes or longer. Or turn into a casserole with tight-fitting cover and bake in a moderate oven (350 degrees F) 45 to 60 minutes. Saltiness of the ham determines whether additional salt needs to be added. Strength and family likes decide the amount of chili powder to use.

Yields: 8 to 12 servings

PURSE STRING REFRIED BEANS

1 lb. Idaho pinto beans, soaked
1/4 lb. salt pork or bacon, diced
2 cloves garlic, minced
1 onion, chopped
chicken stock or water
salt
1/2 cup shortening

Soak beans overnight or by quick method. Drain, saving liquid. Sauté salt pork or bacon, garlic and onion until golden. Add beans. Add soaking liquid and enough chicken stock or water to cover beans. Bring to boil. Cover and simmer 2 hours or until very tender. Add more water if needed. Season to taste. Drain beans, reserving liquid. Heat shortening. Add beans and reserved liquid gradually, mashing and stirring until all beans are used. Cook until thickened.

Yields: 5 to 6 cups

FIESTA SALAD IN TORTILLA CUPS

vegetable cooking spray
1/2 lb. lean ground beef (85% lean)
1/2 cup chopped onion (about 1 med.)
2 tbs. chili powder
1/4 tsp. garlic powder
1 can (10 3/4 oz.) Campbell Healthy Request condensed tomato soup
1/4 cup water
1 cup cooked rice, cooked without salt
1 tsp. vinegar
4 flour tortillas (6 inch)
2 cups shredded lettuce
1 cup diced tomato (about 1 med.)
1/4 cup shredded reduced-fat cheddar cheese (1 oz.)

Spray 10 inch skillet with cooking spray. Heat over medium-high heat 1 minute. Add beef, onion, chili powder and garlic powder. Cook until beef is browned and onion is tender, stirring to separate meat. Spoon off fat.

Stir in soup, water, rice and vinegar. Heat to boiling. Reduce heat to low. Cook 10 minutes, stirring occasionally.

Meanwhile, in 15 x 10 inch jelly roll pan, place 4 custard cups (6 ounces), upside down. Drape 1 tortilla over each cup. Bake at 400 degrees F for 5 minutes or until edges are golden. Allow tortillas to cool on cups.

In each tortilla cup, arrange 1/2 cup lettuce. Top with 2/3 cup meat mixture, 1/4 cup tomato and 1 tablespoons cheese.

Tip: If you don't have custard cups, bake tortillas flat on baking sheet at 400 degrees F for 5 minutes or until edges are golden.

Yields: 4 servings

BLACK-EYE BURRITOS

**1 1/2 cups cooked black-eyed peas (or 1 15 oz. can), reserving 1/2 cup of liquid
4 ozs. lean ham, diced
1/4 onion, diced
dash of black pepper
8 to 19 flour tortillas, (8 inch) size (no added fat)**

Place diced ham in a skillet and heat slightly. Add diced onions and cook until onions are tender. Place the cooked black-eyed peas and bean liquid in the same pan with the onions and ham. Mash and mix ingredients, adding a dash of black pepper. Stir and fry at a medium heat for 3 to 4 minutes. Spoon mixture onto a hot tortilla, roll and enjoy!

Note: For breakfast or lunch, scramble an egg or two in the burrito ingredients just before taking them out of the skillet, and roll it up in a hot flour tortilla.

Yields: 8 to 10 burritos

FRIJOLES CON CHILES Y QUESCO

**6 to 6 1/2 cups drained, cooked, or canned lg. or baby limas
1 1/2 cups rich vegetable or meat stock
2 cans (4 ozs. each) whole or diced mild green chiles
1/2 tsp. basil or thyme
1/8 tsp. oregano
3/4 cup sour cream
1/2 lb. Jack cheese**

Spread one third of beans in shallow 2 to 3 quart ovenproof dish. Sprinkle with half of each herb. Cut whole chiles lengthwise and crosswise in 1/2 inch squares or use diced chiles from can. Cut cheese in 1/2 inch strips or coarse grate. Scatter half the chiles and one third of the cheese over the layer of beans. top with rest of beans and sprinkle with remaining cheese and chiles. Stir stock into sour cream until smooth. Liquid should almost cover beans. Bake uncovered for 30 to 45 minutes or 325 degrees F or until bubbling.

Yields: 8 to 10 servings

TENDER FAJITAS

**12 tomatillos, with husks removed
1 can (4 oz.) chopped mild green chiles, drained
1/4 cup mined cilantro
1 jalapeno pepper, minced
1 garlic clove, minced
salt and ground pepper to taste
1 package (about 1 lb.) Perdue Fit 'n Easy fresh skinless and boneless chicken breast tenderloins
1 tsp. chili powder
1 tsp. ground cumin
2 tsps. vegetable oil
1 cup shredded iceberg lettuce
1/3 cup reduced fat sour cream
4 flour tortillas (8 inch size)**

In small saucepan over medium-high heat, combine tomatillos and water to cover; bring to a boil. Reduce heat to medium; cook 5 to 10 minutes until tomatillos are just tender. Drain tomatillos; cool and dice. In medium bowl, combine diced tomatillos, chilies, cilantro, jalapeno, garlic and salt and pepper; set aside.

Sprinkle tenderloins on both sides with salt and pepper, chili powder and cumin. In large nonstick skillet over medium-high hat, heat oil; add seasoned tenderloins and sauté 1 minute on each side. Reduce heat to medium-low; cook 4 to 7 minutes longer until cooked through, turning 2 to 3 times. To serve, combine tenderloins, tomatillo mixture, lettuce and sour cream in tortillas and roll up.

Yields: 4 servings

TORTILLA ROLL-UPS

**1/2 cup lime juice
1/2 cup water
1 Anaheim chile, seeded and chopped
2 garlic cloves, minced
1 tbs. olive oil
1 package (about 1 lb.) Perdue fresh Fit 'n Easy skinless and boneless turkey cubed steaks
2 bell peppers (1 red and 1 green), seeded and cut in strips
1 onion, peeled and cut in eighths
4 flour tortillas (10 inch size), warmed
prepared salsa and/or guacamole (optional)**

In baking dish, combine lime juice, water, chile, garlic and oil. Place steaks, peppers and onion slices in lime mixture and toss to coat well. Cover and refrigerate 30 minutes or up to several hours. Place large, nonstick skillet over medium-high heat. Add steaks; brown 2 minutes on each side. Add peppers and onions; continue cooking 4 to 6 minutes, until steaks are cooked through and vegetables are tender-crisp, stirring frequently. Place a steak and vegetables on each warm tortilla. Roll tortilla, jelly-roll style, to enclose filling. Serve "roll-ups" with salsa and guacamole.

Yields: 4 servings

CATFISH STIR-FRY

2 tbs. peanut oil (or vegetable oil)
1 tbs. fresh grated ginger (or 1 tsp. ground ginger)
2 cloves garlic, crushed
4 genuine U.S. farm-raised catfish fillets, cut into thin strips
1/2 lb. bok choy (Chinese cabbage), thinly sliced (or cabbage)
4 scallions, chopped
1/4 cup roasted cashews
2 tbs. soy sauce
2 tbs. rice or cider vinegar
1/2 cup rice wine (or sherry)
1/4 tsp. crushed red pepper flakes

In a wok or large skillet heat oil and cook garlic and ginger for 2 minutes over moderately high heat; stirring to prevent burning. Add farm-raised catfish, bok choy, scallions and cashews, and continue to stir gently. When catfish begins to brown, add soy sauce, vinegar and wine. Cook for an additional 3 to 4 minutes until the catfish flakes easily. Serve over steamed rice.

Yields: 4 servings

ORIENTAL CHICKEN SALAD SANDWICHES

1 can (4 oz.) chuck chicken
2 tbs. sweet pickle relish
1 tsp. minced onion
1/3 cup non-fat mayonnaise
1/4 cup sliced water chestnuts
8 slices white bread

Mix ingredients as listed. If time permits, refrigerate chicken salad for 30 minutes.

Yields: 5 servings

EASY BEEF AND BROCCOLI STIR-FRY

1 beef top round steak, cut 1 inch thick (about 1 1/2 lbs.)
3 cups broccoli flowerets
3 tbs. each soy sauce and dry sherry
1 tbs. dark sesame oil
2 tsps. sugar
1 lg. clove garlic, minced
1/8 tsp. crushed red pepper
2 tbs. vegetable oil
1 tsp. cornstarch
1/4 cup unsalted peanuts
2 tbs. sliced green onions

Cook broccoli in boiling water 2 minutes. Drain; reserve. Cut beef top round steak in half; wrap and freeze 1/2 of the steak for another meal. Slice remaining half diagonally across the grain into 1/8 inch strips.

Combine soy sauce, sherry, sesame oil, sugar, garlic and red pepper. Place beef in plastic bag; add soy sauce mixture, turning to coat beef. Close bag securely; marinate in refrigerator 30 minutes, turning once. Remove beef from marinade; reserve marinade.

Heat vegetable oil in wok or large skillet over medium-high to high heat. Add beef; stir-fry 2 minutes. Add broccoli; continue cooking 2 minutes. Combine cornstarch and reserved marinade.

Add to beef mixture; cook, stirring until sauce boils and thickens. Sprinkle peanuts and green onions over stir-fry.

Yields: 3 servings

CHICKEN AND SHII-TAKE ALFREDO

1 package (3 1/2 oz.) Shii-take mushrooms
2 tbs. butter or margarine
3/4 cup chopped sweet red bell pepper
8 ozs. boned and skinned chicken breasts (cutlets), thinly sliced
1 cup heavy (whipping) cream
1 cup frozen green peas
3/4 tsp. salt
1/4 tsp. black pepper
1/2 cup grated parmesan cheese
4 ozs. capellini (angel hair) pasta, freshly cooked and drained

Remove stems from Shii-take mushrooms (use in stews, to flavor broths, etc.); cut each cap in 1/2, then into 4 to 6 slices; set aside.

In a large skillet melt butter. Add red pepper; cook and stir until slightly softened, about 3 minutes. Add chicken and reserved mushrooms; cook and stir until chicken is tender, about 3 minutes. Add cream, peas, salt and black pepper; boil, uncovered, until sauce is slightly thickened, about 4 minutes, stirring often. Stir in parmesan cheese. Spoon over pasta; serve immediately.

Yields: 2 to 3 servings

CHINESE CHICKEN WITH PEANUTS

4 lbs. boneless chicken breasts (or other boned chicken)
1/2 cup peanut oil
1/2 cup soy sauce
1 can (15 1/4 oz.) pineapple chunks
1 can (6 oz.) sliced mushrooms
1/2 cup minced green onion
1/2 cup dark corn syrup
1 lg. clove garlic, minced
1/4 tsp. ground ginger
1/8 tsp. red pepper
2 tsps. water
1/4 cup cornstarch
1/2 cup sherry wine
1/2 cup chopped peanuts

Cut chicken into 1 inch strips. Heat oil in skillet to 350°F. Add chicken and lightly brown. Add remaining ingredients except water, cornstarch, wine and peanuts. Reduce heat to 325°F. Cook covered for 10 minutes.

Stir water into cornstarch and add to skillet ingredients, stirring constantly. Add wine and peanuts. Cook 2 to 3 minutes more. Serve over steamed rice, Chinese noodles or toast points.
Yields: 12 to 14 servings

JAPANESE-STYLE TURKEY STEAKS

1/2 tsp. low-sodium chicken bouillon granules
2 tbs. boiling water
2 tbs. reduced-sodium soy sauce
2 tbs. dry sherry
1 tsp. ground ginger
1 clove garlic, crushed
1 lb. (3/4 inch thick) turkey breast steaks

In large, shallow glass bowl, dissolve bouillon in boiling water. Add soy sauce, sherry, ginger, garlic and turkey. Refrigerate turkey mixture 35 to 45 minutes.
Preheat grill.

Drain marinade from turkey and discard. Grill turkey 15 minutes, turning every 5 minutes, or until turkey meat is no longer pink in center.
Yields: 4 servings

GINGERED BEEF STIR FRY

1/2 lb. boneless beef sirloin steak, cut 1/2 inch thick
1 tsp. vegetable oil
1/8 tsp. each salt and ground white pepper
1/2 cup sliced fresh mushrooms
1/2 cup each sliced green onions and red pepper strips
1 tsp. minced fresh ginger
1 tsp. corn starch
1 tbs. soy sauce
1 cup hot cooked rice

Cut beef diagonally across grain into 1/8 inch slices. Heat oil in wok or medium skillet over medium-high heat. Add beef and seasonings and stir-fry until beef is browned. Add vegetables and stir-fry until vegetables are crisp.

Blend ginger, corn starch, soy sauce and 1 tablespoon water in small bowl; add to beef and cook, stirring until sauce is thickened. Serve over rice.
Yields: 2 servings

STIR-FRIED CAJUN PORK

1 lb. boneless pork loin, cut into julienne strips
4 tbs. Cajun-style seasoning (recipe follows)
1 tsp. vegetable oil
1 red bell pepper, diced
1 tart green apple, cored and diced
1/4 cup pecan pieces

Season pork strips with 2 tablespoons Cajun seasoning. Toss remaining ingredients EXCEPT OIL with 2 tablespoons seasoning, reserve.

Heat oil in non-stick skillet over medium-high heat. Stir-fry pork 2 minutes; add reserved mixture, cook and stir 2 minutes more. Serve immediately.

Cajun-style seasoning: Mix together well 3 tablespoons paprika, 1/2 teaspoon cayenne pepper, 1 tablespoon garlic powder, 2 teaspoons oregano, 2 teaspoons thyme, 1/2 teaspoon salt, 1/2 teaspoon white pepper, 1/2 teaspoon cumin, 1/4 teaspoon nutmeg.
Yields: 4 servings

VEGETABLE PORK STIR-FRY

3/4 lb. pork tenderloin, cut in strips
1 tbs. vegetable oil
1 1/2 cups sliced fresh mushrooms
1 lg. green pepper, cut in strips
1 zucchini, thinly sliced
2 ribs celery, diagonally sliced
1 cup thinly sliced carrots
1 clove garlic, minced
1 cup chicken broth
2 tbs. light soy sauce
1 1/2 tbs. cornstarch
3 cups hot cooked rice

Brown pork strips in oil in large skillet over high heat. Push meat to side of skillet; add vegetables. Stir-fry vegetables approximately 3 minutes. Combine broth, soy sauce, and cornstarch; add to skillet and cook until clear and thickened. Serve over rice.
Yields: 6 servings

CHINESE-STYLE SPARERIBS

6 lbs. pork spareribs
1/4 cup Hoisin sauce
1/4 cup water
3 tbs. dry sherry
2 tbs. honey
2 tbs. soy sauce
2 cloves garlic, minced

Cut spareribs into serving-size portions; set aside.

Place large plastic bag in large bowl. In bag, combine remaining ingredients; mix well. Add ribs, close bag tightly. Refrigerate 6 hours or overnight; turn bag several times to distribute marinade.

Drain ribs, reserving marinade. Place ribs in shallow roasting pan; cover with foil and bake in a 350 degrees F oven for 1 1/2 hours.

Uncover and brush ribs with the reserved marinade. Bake, uncovered, for 30 minutes or till done.

Yields: 6 servings

CHINESE PORK SALAD

1 lb. pork strips, marinated in 1/2 cup Oriental stir-fry
1/2 red onion, peeled and thinly sliced
2 packages (10 ozs. each) frozen pea pods, thawed and drained
1 can (8 oz.) mandarin oranges, drained
1 can (3 oz.) chow mein noodles

In large non-stick skillet, stir-fry pork and onion over medium-high heat for about 4 to 5 minutes. In a large bowl, toss all ingredients together.

Yields: 4 servings

FRIED RICE WITH PORK

3/4 lb. boneless pork loin
5 slices bacon
2 eggs, beaten
1 cup chopped fresh mush-rooms
1/2 cup thinly sliced green onion
3 cups cooked rice, chilled
1/4 cup soy sauce

Partially freeze pork. Thinly slice across the grain into bite-sized strips; set aside.

In a large skillet or wok cook bacon until crisp. Drain bacon,

reserving 3 tablespoons drippings; crumble bacon on paper toweling.

Cook eggs in 1 tablespoon hot drippings for 2 minutes or until set; remove and set aside. Add 1 tablespoon drippings to skillet. Stir-fry 1/2 of the pork till browned; remove. Stir-fry remaining pork; remove. Add the remaining drippings to skillet; stir-fry mushrooms and onion 1 minutes or until tender. Stir in bacon, egg, pork and rice; cook 2 minutes, stirring gently. Pour soy sauce over pork-rice mixture; cook 3 minutes more or until heated through.

Yields: 4 servings

GINGERED PORK WITH PEANUT SAUCE

1 lb. pork tenderloin
1 package (3 oz.) pork-flavored oriental noodles
2 tsps. vegetable oil
1/2 tsp. dry red pepper flakes
1 tsp. shredded fresh ginger
1/4 cup peanut butter
2 tbs. soy sauce
2 cups torn spinach, washed and drained
1/4 cup sliced green onions

Cut tenderloin into 1/4 inch slices, trimming as necessary; cut each slice in 1/2.

Cook noodles as directed on package. Drain and keep warm. Reserve cooking water.

Heat oil in a heavy frypan; add pork, red pepper flakes and ginger. Cook and stir until pork is done, about 4 to 5 minutes. Remove pork and keep warm. Discard cooking oil.

Blend peanut butter, 1/2 cup reserved cooking water and soy

sauce; heat and stir until hot, adding more cooking water, if needed. Toss cooked pork, noodles, spinach and green onions with peanut sauce. Serve immediately.

Yields: 4 servings

MANDARIN ORANGE PORK SALAD

1 1/4 cups wine vinegar
1/2 cup sugar
2 tbs. salt
1 1/2 tsps. black pepper
2 cups vegetable oil
4 lbs. cold roasted pork loin, cut in julienne strips
10 lbs. iceberg lettuce, torn into pieces
5 cups thinly sliced celery
5 cups red seedless grapes
2 1/2 cups sliced green onions
1/2 cup chopped fresh parsley
5 cups mandarin orange segments, well drained
48 lettuce cups
2 1/2 cups sliced and toasted almonds

Combine wine vinegar, sugar, seasonings and vegetable oil. Marinate pork in dressing a minimum of 4 hours or overnight. Toss lettuce, celery, grapes, green onions and parsley. Add dressing and pork; toss well. Carefully fold in orange segments. Serve immediately in lettuce cups topped with almonds. Portion size: 1 1/2 cups.

Yields: 48 servings

STUFFED ARTICHOKE WITH ORIENTAL NOODLE SALAD

Salad:
4 med. California arti-chokes, prepared and cooked as directed for whole artichokes
6 ozs. dried Chinese noodles, or spaghetti broken into 2 to inch lengths

1 cup cucumber, peeled and chopped
1/2 cup shredded carrots
1/2 cup shredded radishes
1/4 cup thinly sliced green onion
4 ozs. fresh snow peas, blanched and cut into thin diagonal strips
Dressing:
1/2 cup unseasoned rice wine vinegar
1/2 cup fresh orange juice
1 tbs. grated orange peel
1 to 1/2 tbs. light soy sauce (reduced sodium)
1 tsp. sesame oil
4 tsps. peanut oil
2 tbs. fresh ginger root, finely minced
2 tsps. minced garlic
1 tsp. sugar
1/8 tsp. cayenne pepper

Halve artichokes lengthwise. Remove and discard center petals and fuzzy center; set artichokes aside.

Cook pasta until done but slightly firm, rinse and set aside.

In a medium bowl whisk together dressing ingredients. In a large bowl combine pasta, cucumber, carrots, radishes, green onions and snow peas. Toss noodle mixture with half of the dressing; reserve the remaining half.

Arrange 2 artichoke halves on each plate. Spoon noodles into halves. Use reserved dressing as dip for artichoke leaves. Serve immediately.

Yields: 4 servings

PEKING PORK PASTA SALAD

1 lb. pork tenderloin, cut into 1/4 inch thick slices
1 tsp. vegetable oil
1/2 cup soy sauce
1/2 cup dry sherry
1 tsp. sesame oil
8 ozs. fusilli or corkscrew pasta, cooked and drained
1 cup sliced green onion, including some green tops
1/2 cup diced green pepper

1/4 cup toasted almond slices
8 ozs. fresh spinach leaves, washed and drained

In a non-stick frypan, heat vegetable oil over medium-high heat. Add pork and stir-fry quickly. Remove pork from pan and place in a large bowl.

Combine soy sauce, sherry and sesame oil. Pour 1/2 over pork strips and toss well. Cover and chill 1 hour.

Arrange pasta mixture on spinach leaves, top with pork and garnish with almonds. Serve remaining soy sauce mixture on side.

Yields: 6 servings

PORK AND RED CHILE STIR-FRY

1 lb. lean boneless pork loin, cut into thin slices
1 tsp. vegetable oil
2 cloves garlic, minced
3/4 lb. fresh green beans, cut into 2 inch lengths
2 tsps. sugar
2 tsps. soy sauce
2 sm. red chile peppers, thinly sliced
1 tsp. shredded fresh ginger
1 tsp. sesame oil
1 tsp. rice vinegar

Heat oil in a non-stick pan; add pork strips and garlic and cook and stir until lightly browned. Add green beans; stir-fry until the beans and pork are tender, about 5 minutes. Push the meat and beans to 1 side of the frypan. Add sugar, soy sauce, red pepper and ginger; stir to dissolve sugar. Add sesame oil and vinegar. Stir to coat meat and beans. Serve immediately with cooked rice or shredded lettuce.

Yields: 4 servings

PORK TERIYAKI

1 lb. pork tenderloin, cut into 6x1/2x1/8 inch strips
2 tbs. sliced green onion

1 tbs. brown sugar
1/2 tsp. ginger
1 clove garlic, minced
1/2 cup soy sauce
1/4 cup dry sherry

Combine all ingredients except pork strips, mix well. Add pork to marinade, cover and marinate in refrigerator at least 1 hour. Thread meat onto skewers. Broil or grill, turning frequently, 4 to 5 minutes. Serve with rice, if desired.

Yields: 4 servings

TERIYAKI CHOPS

2 1/4 cups soy sauce
3/4 cup dry sherry
1/4 cup sugar
3 tbs. black pepper
2 tbs. garlic powder
1 1/2 cups vegetable oil
12 center cut bone-in pork chops (4 ozs. each)

Combine soy sauce, sherry, sugar and seasonings; stir well. Blend in oil. Pour marinade into pan. Place pork chops in single layer in marinade, turning once to coat both sides. Marinate in refrigerator a minimum of 4 hours or overnight. Drain off marinade, discard.

Bake chops in single layer: Conventional oven at 400 degrees F for 10 to 12 minutes; Convection oven at 350 degrees F for 9 to 11 minutes, or until chops are brown, tender and juicy. Portion size: 1 4 ounce chop.

Yields: 12 servings

SINGAPORE SAMPLINGS

1 1/2 lbs. boneless pork loin, sliced into 4x1x1/8 inch strips
8 wooden skewers
1/4 cup soy sauce
3 tbs. rice vinegar
1 tbs. grated fresh ginger or
1 tsp. dry ginger
1 clove garlic, minced
1/2 tsp. crushed red pepper peppered tofu (recipe follows), if desired

Soak skewers for 20 to 30 minutes in water. Thread pork onto skewers. Place in a 12x9 inch baking dish. Combine remaining ingredients and pour over skewers, turning to coat. Marinate at room temperature for 30 minutes, turning once or twice. Broil 6 inches from heat for 10 minutes, turning to cook all sides. Baste occasionally with remaining marinade. Serve with peppered tofu, if desired.

Peppered tofu: Heat 1 tablespoon sesame oil in a frypan, add 1/2 teaspoon dried red pepper and 1 thin slice fresh ginger. Cook and stir over medium heat for 2 to 3 minutes. Stir in 1 tablespoon oyster sauce; add 8 ounces tofu, cubed, and stir to heat through and coat with sauce.

Yields: 6 servings

SWEET AND SOUR PORK

1 lb. boneless pork loin
1 tbs. vegetable oil
1 med. green pepper, cut into 1 inch pieces
1 med. onion, cut into thin wedges
1 can (15 1/4 oz.) pineapple chunks in juice
1/4 cup firmly packed brown sugar
1/4 cup white wine vinegar
2 tbs. cornstarch
2 tbs. soy sauce
hot cooked rice (optional)

Partially freeze pork. Cut across the grain into 2 1/2 x 2 1/4 inch strips; set aside. Preheat a wok or large skillet over high heat; add oil. Stir-fry green pepper and onion in hot oil for 2 to 3 minutes or till crisp-tender. Remove from wok. Add more oil, if necessary. Add 1/2 the pork to wok; stir-fry until browned. Remove pork; stir-fry the remaining pork. Return all pork to wok; keep warm.

Drain pineapple, reserving juice. In a small saucepan combine the juice, brown sugar, vinegar, cornstarch and soy sauce. Bring to a boil; cook about 1 minute or

till thickened, stirring constantly.

Return green pepper and onion to wok. Stir in pineapple and the thickened pineapple juice mixture. Cook and stir until heated through. Serve with rice, if desired.

Yields: 4 servings

SWEET'N SOUR TUNA RICE SALAD

3 tbs. red wine vinegar
2 tsps. granulated sugar
1/4 tsp. salt
1/4 to 1/2 tsp. pepper
8 ozs. drained, canned water-packed tuna, broken into chunks (reserve liquid)
2 cups cooked long grain white or brown rice
2 cups chopped peeled fresh tomatoes
1 cup finely diced red onion
1 cup finely diced celery
1/2 cup chopped scallions
1/2 cup frozen peas, thawed

In a small bowl, combine vinegar, sugar, salt, pepper and 1 tablespoon of reserved tuna liquid.

In a large bowl combine remaining ingredients add vinegar mixture and toss. Let stand for 10 minutes; toss again and serve.

Yields: 4 servings

TERIYAKI SALAD KABUKI

1 head iceberg lettuce
4 half-breasts of chicken (about 2 lbs.)
8 diagonal slices zucchini, 1 inch thick
4 square (1 inch) green peppers
8 cherry tomatoes

4 mushrooms, halved
Kabuki salad dressing:
1/2 cup beef consommé
2 tbs. each soy sauce, dry sherry, and white wine vinegar
1 sm. clove garlic, minced
1/4 tsp. ground ginger

Core, rinse and thoroughly drain iceberg lettuce; chill in sealed plastic bag or plastic crisper. Prepare Kabuki dressing.

Remove skin and bones from chicken and cut each breast into thirds lengthwise. Ripple 3 strips into each of 4 bamboo skewers. Parboil zucchini and green pepper 1 minute; drain.

Arrange on 4 skewers, along with tomatoes and mushrooms. Broil or barbecue chicken skewers 5 inches from heat 10 minutes, basting well with Kabuki dressing and turning often.

Add vegetable skewers last 5 minutes chicken cooks; turn and baste with dressing often. Cut lettuce into bite-size chunks to measure 2 quarts. Arrange 1 chicken and 1 vegetable skewer on a bed of lettuce for each serving. Pass remaining dressing.

Kabuki salad dressing: combine beef consommé, salad oil, soy sauce, dry sherry, vinegar, garlic and ginger in a small jar and shake well to blend. Shake again just before serving.

Yields: 4 servings

TERIYAKI TENDERLOIN SALAD

12 ozs. pork tenderloin
1/3 cup teriyaki sauce
3/4 cup orange juice
2 tsps. cornstarch
1/4 tsp. sesame oil
few drops hot pepper sauce
2 tsps. vegetable oil
6 cups mixed greens
1 1/2 cup snap peas, cooked and chilled or 1 package (6 oz.) frozen peas
1 cup sliced fresh mushrooms
1 cup chow mein noodles

1/3 cup sliced green onion
1 tbs. toasted sesame seeds

Slice pork tenderloin into 1/4 inch slices. Brush slices with some of the teriyaki sauce; set aside. Stir together orange juice, cornstarch, sesame oil, hot pepper sauce and remaining teriyaki sauce. Set aside.

In large skillet heat oil. Stir-fry tenderloin slices over medium-high heat 2 to 3 minutes or to desired doneness. Remove meat from skillet. Add green onion to skillet. Stir in orange juice mixture. Cook and stir until slightly thickened and bubbly.

Meanwhile arrange greens on 3 dinner plates or in large salad bowls. Sprinkle with peas, mushrooms, and chow mein noodles. Arrange tenderloin slices on top. Drizzle with hot orange dressing. Sprinkle each serving with sesame seeds.

Yields: 3 servings

CHICKEN STIR-FRY

vegetable cooking spray
1 lb. skinless, boneless chicken breasts, cut into strips
1 cup broccoli flowerets
1 cup carrots cut in matchstick-thin strips (about 2 med.)
1/2 cup onion cut in wedges (about 1 med.)
1 can (10 3/4 oz.) Campbell's Healthy Request condensed cream of broccoli soup
2/3 cup water
2 tsps. low sodium soy sauce
1/4 tsp. ground ginger
4 cups hot cooked rice, cooked without salt

Spray 10 inch nonstick skillet with cooking spray. Heat over medium-high heat 1 minute. Add half of the chicken; stir-fry until browned. Remove; set aside. Repeat with remaining chicken.

Remove skillet from heat; spray skillet with cooking spray. Reduce heat to medium. Stir-fry broccoli, carrots and onion until tender-crisp.

Add soup, water, soy and ginger. Heat to boiling. Return chicken to skillet. Heat through, stirring occasionally. Serve over rice.

Yields: 4 servings

ASIAN BEEF NOODLES

1 lb. beef round tip steaks, cut 1/8 to 1/4 inch thick
1 jalapeno pepper, finely chopped
1 tbs. vegetable oil
1 package (3 oz.) beef flavor instant ramen noodles
1/4 cup steak sauce
1 med. carrot, shredded
2 tbs. chopped fresh cilantro or green onion
1/4 cup chopped peanuts

Stack beef steaks; cut into 1 x 3 inch strips. In medium bowl, combine beef, jalapeno pepper and oil; toss to coat.

Break noodles into 4 pieces; reserve seasoning packet. Cook noodles as package directs; drain.

Heat large nonstick skillet over medium-high heat until hot; stir-fry beef (1/2 at a time) 1 minute or until no longer pink. (Do not overcook.) Remove beef; keep warm.

In same skillet, combine noodles, steak sauce, carrot, cilantro and reserved seasoning. Cook over medium heat until hot, stirring occasionally. Then return beef to skillet; mix lightly. Sprinkle with peanuts.

Yields: 4 servings

ORIENTAL TURKEY

1 tbs. vegetable oil
3 med. carrots, diagonally sliced
1/4 tsp. ground ginger
1 can (10 1/2 oz.) Franco-American turkey gravy
1 tbs. soy sauce
2 green onions, sliced
1 1/2 cups cubed cooked turkey
3 cups hot cooked rice

In skillet over medium heat, heat oil. Add carrots and ginger and stirfry until tender-crisp.

Add gravy, soy sauce, and turkey. Heat through. Serve over rice.

Yields: 3 servings

BEEF STEAK STIR-FRY

1/2 lb. boneless beef round or sirloin steak
2 tsp. cornstarch
2 tsp. vegetable oil
1/2 bunch broccoli, in flowerettes
1 green bell pepper, in 1 inch strips
1/2 cup beef broth
hot cooked rice (optional)
Ginger-soy marinade:
1/2 cup beef broth
1/4 cup sherry
3 tbs. soy sauce
2 tbs. finely chopped fresh ginger
2 tbs. chopped cilantro
2 tbs. sesame oil
1 tsp. sugar
1/4 tsp. crushed red pepper

Cut beef across grain into thin strips; place in glass baking dish. Prepare marinade; pour over beef and cover. Refrigerate 30 minutes. Remove beef from marinade and stir in cornstarch; reserve.

Heat 1 teaspoon oil in nonstick skillet. Stir-fry beef strips 2 minutes. Remove beef; place in reserved marinade. Add remaining oil to skillet. Stir-fry broccoli and bell pepper for 1 minute. Add beef broth; cover skillet. Steam 2 minutes.

Uncover; add beef and marinade. Cook, stirring constantly, until sauce thickens and boils. Cook and stir 2 minutes. Using a slotted spoon, serve on two plates over cooked rice, if desired.

Ginger-soy marinade: Mix all ingredients.

Yields: 2 servings

TRADITIONAL SPAGHETTI AND MEATBALLS

1 lb. spaghetti, linguine or thin spaghetti, uncooked
Meatballs:
4 slices white bread
1/2 cup skim milk
2 lg. egg whites
8 ozs. ground turkey
8 ozs. extra lean ground beef
1/4 cup grated romano cheese
1 tbs. mined fresh basil or 1 tsp. dried basil
1 tsp. minced fresh oregano or 1/2 tsp. dried oregano
1/2 tsp. salt
1/4 tsp. pepper
Sauce:
1 recipe basic tomato sauce
1 tsp. vegetable oil, divided

Put the bread into a medium mixing bowl and pour the milk over it. Let sit 5 minutes. Add the egg whites, ground turkey, ground beef, romano cheese, basil, oregano, salt and pepper. Knead the mixture with your hands until it is smooth. To prevent sticking, dip your hands into cool water before forming each meatball. Form mixture into 30 1 1/2 inch balls.

Pour the tomato sauce into a large, heavy bottom saucepan and bring to a simmer over low heat. Warm 1/2 teaspoon vegetable oil in a large nonstick skillet. Add half the meatballs to the skillet and brown them on all sides. Spoon the meatballs into the tomato sauce. Add the remaining 1/2 teaspoon vegetable oil to the skillet and brown the rest of the meatballs, then add them to the sauce. Simmer, stirring for 20 minutes.

While sauce is simmering, prepare pasta according to package directions; drain. Transfer to a larger serving bowl. Remove bay leaves from sauce; pour sauce over pasta and serve.

Yields: 6 servings

APPLE PASTA SALAD

1 container (8 oz.) plain nonfat yogurt
1 can (8 oz.) unsweetened crushed pineapple, undrained
1/2 tsp. salt, optional
1/4 tsp. garlic powder
1/4 tsp. dry mustard
1 tsp. finely chopped crystallized ginger
1 tbs. honey
2 cups uncooked rotini pasta
1/2 cup shredded carrot
1 cup sliced celery
1/4 cup sliced green onions
1/4 cup raisins
3 cups diced, unpeeled Michigan apples (Empire, Gala, Ida Red, Jonagold, Jonathan, McIntosh, Red Delicious, Rome)

Thoroughly combine yogurt, pineapple, salt, spices, ginger and honey; refrigerate.

Cook pasta according to package directions, omitting salt. Rinse with cold water and drain thoroughly. Cool completely.

In large bowl, combine all ingredients including yogurt dressing. Chill before serving.

Yields: 8 servings

BAKED PASTA PARMESAN

1 tbs. Progresso olive oil
1 lb. ground beef
1 can (19 ozs.) Progresso minestrone soup
1 can (8 ozs.) Progresso tomato sauce
1 1/2 tsps. basil
1/2 tsp. oregano
1/4 tsp. salt
1/8 tsp. ground black pepper
1 1/2 cups (6 ozs.) 1/2 inch tube shape pasta
1/2 cup Progresso grated parmesan cheese, divided usage
1 cup (4 ozs.) shredded mozzarella cheese

Preheat oven to 375 degrees F. In a large skillet, heat olive oil until hot. Brown ground beef; drain. Add soup, tomato sauce and spices. Simmer uncovered until slightly thickened, about 10 minutes, stirring occasionally. Prepare pasta according to package directions; drain. Spoon a thin layer of the meat mixture into an 8 x 8 inch baking dish. Add the pasta and top with remaining meat mixture. Sprinkle with 1/4 cup parmesan cheese. Cover with mozzarella cheese and remaining parmesan cheese. Bake until cheese is golden brown, about 25 minutes.

Yields: 4 servings

BAKED PASTA WITH SMOKED CHICKEN

1 lb. rotini, twists or spirals, uncooked
3 ozs. sun-dried tomatoes, dry
1 tbs. blended olive oil
2 cloves garlic, minced
2 lg. shallots, finely chopped
8 ozs. assorted wild mushrooms such as oyster, shitake, cremini or portabella, sliced
8 ozs. skinless smoked chicken (breast, legs or thighs)
1 bunch fresh oregano, coarsely chopped or 1 to 2 tsps. dried oregano
8 ozs. chicken broth, skimmed of fat, or 1 bouillon cube
salt and freshly ground pepper
1/3 lb. part skim provolone cheese or mozzarella cheese, grated

Cook pasta according to package directions; drain. Soak sun-dried tomatoes in lukewarm water until soft (5 to 6 minutes). Drain and chop. Preheat oven to 400 degrees F.

Heat oil in large skillet. Add garlic and shallots and cook until lightly toasted. Add mushrooms, chicken, sun-dried tomatoes and oregano. Cook lightly.

Add chicken broth and cook 4 to 5 minutes until slightly reduced. Season with salt and pepper to taste.

Toss cooked pasta with sauce, place in an oven proof baking dish and top with cheese. Bake for 5 to 10 minutes or until cheese is melted.

Yields: 6 to 8 servings

CHICKEN AND BROCCOLI PASTA DIJON

1 lb. mostaccioli, penne or other med. pasta shape, uncooked

8 ozs. boneless, skinless chicken breast, cut into 1 inch pieces
1/2 tsp. salt
1/4 tsp. freshly ground black pepper
2 cloves garlic, minced
2 tsp. vegetable oil
3 cups broccoli florets
1 lg. red bell pepper, cut into short, thin strips
1/2 cup low sodium chicken broth
1 can (12 oz.) evaporated skim milk
1 tbs. cornstarch
3 tbs. Dijon mustard

Prepare pasta according to package directions. While pasta is cooking, toss chicken with salt, pepper and garlic. Coat a large nonstick skillet with cooking spray; place over medium-high heat until hot. Add chicken mixture; stir fry 4 to 5 minutes or until chicken is cooked through. Remove chicken from skillet and place in a medium bowl.

Add broccoli, red pepper and chicken broth to skillet. Cover; simmer over medium heat 5 to 6 minutes or until vegetables are tender-crisp. Transfer to bowl with chicken. In a small bowl, combine 1/4 cup of the milk with cornstarch, mixing until smooth. Add to skillet with remaining milk; bring to a boil, stirring constantly. Reduce heat; stir in mustard. Stir in reserved chicken mixture.

When pasta is done, drain well. Toss with chicken mixture. Serve immediately with additional freshly ground pepper, if desired.

Yields: 4 servings

ROASTED VEGETABLE LASAGNA

12 pieces lasagna, uncooked
vegetable oil cooking spray
8 ozs. mushrooms, halved
2 zucchini or yellow squash, halved lengthwise and cut crosswise into 1/2 inch pieces

2 yellow or red bell peppers, cut into 1 inch pieces
1 sm. red onion, cut into 1 inch pieces
2 tbs. balsamic vinegar
1 tsp. olive or vegetable oil
2 cloves garlic, minced
1/2 tsp. dried rosemary, crushed
1 jar (26 oz.) fat-free spaghetti sauce
1 container (15 oz.) part-skim milk ricotta cheese
1 package (10 oz.) frozen chopped spinach, thawed, squeezed dry
1 lg. egg white
1/4 tsp. hot red pepper flakes
1 cup shredded part-skim mozzarella cheese
1/4 cup grated parmesan cheese

Prepare lasagna according to package directions. While lasagna is cooking, heat oven to 425 degrees F. Coat a shallow metal roasting pan with cooking spray. Add mushrooms, squash, bell peppers and onion. In a small dish, combine vinegar, oil, garlic and rosemary; brush evenly over vegetables. Bake 15 minutes; toss vegetables. Continue baking 8 to 10 minutes or until vegetables are browned and tender.

Spoon 1 cup spaghetti sauce over bottom of 13 x 9 inch baking dish. Arrange 4 pieces of lasagna (3 lengthwise, 1 widthwise) over the sauce. Cover lasagna with 1 cup sauce. In a medium bowl, combine ricotta cheese, spinach, egg white and hot red pepper flakes. Drop half the cheese mixture by spoonfuls over sauce; arrange half of the roasted vegetables between spoonfuls of cheese mixture. Arrange another 4 pieces of lasagna over cheese and vegetables, pressing lightly; top with 1 cup sauce. Repeat layering with remaining cheese, roasted vegetables, 4 pieces of lasagna and remaining sauce.

Reduce oven temperature to 375 degrees F. Cover lasagna with foil; bake 45 minutes. Uncover;

sprinkle with mozzarella and parmesan cheese; continue baking, uncovered, 5 minutes or until cheese is melted. Let stand 10 minutes before serving.

Yields: 8 servings

LOBSTER SAUTÉ WITH LINGUINE

3 Maine lobsters (1 1/4 lbs.)
1 lb. linguine
2 cloves garlic, minced
1 1/2 cups onion, sliced
2 tbs. butter
1/2 to 3/4 cup mushrooms, sliced
1/4 cup white wine
2 cups fresh tomatoes, peeled/seeded/diced or canned, pasta-ready tomatoes
1/2 cup lobster broth
1/2 cup heavy cream or yogurt
1/2 cup scallions, cut 1/2 inch long
2 tbs. parsley, chopped
Old Bay or seafood seasoning to taste
1/4 to 1/2 cup parmesan cheese, grated

Steam lobsters (1 per every 2 persons), in one inch of water for 8 to 10 minutes. Remove, and let cool. Reserve 1/2 cup of liquid (lobster broth). After lobsters cool, pick meat out of the shells and dice in large pieces. Carefully extract claw meat and leave whole.

Cook the linguine.

In a large skillet, sauté garlic and onion in butter for 5 to 8 minutes until onions are soft. Do not allow to brown. Add mushrooms and cook water out of them, then remove and reserve. Add wine and reduce by 1/2. Add tomatoes and cook 2 to 3 minutes.

Add lobster broth and cream or yogurt and reduce by 1/4. Bring to a boil, simmer and add lobster and scallions, parsley, reserved mushrooms and Old Bay or seafood seasoning. Add parmesan cheese to thicken.

Toss 1/2 of sauce with cooked linguine. Arrange on plate, pour remaining 1/2 of sauce over each serving. Top each serving with the whole claw meat.

Yields: 4 to 6 servings

CREAMY BAKED POLENTA

1 tbs. Bertolli extra virgin or classico olive oil
1/2 cup chopped onion
6 cups water or half water and half reduced sodium chicken broth
1 1/2 cups yellow cornmeal
1 tsp. salt, or to taste
2 tbs. grated Parmigiano-Reggiano
1 cup (4 ozs.) coarsely shredded part skim mozzarella
3/4 cup skim milk

Heat the olive oil in a large broad saucepan; add the onion and cook, stirring, over medium heat, until golden, about 5 minutes.

In a separate bowl combine polenta, salt and half the water, whisk together until blended. Add to the saucepan and cook, stirring constantly, until mixture boils.

Slowly stir in the remaining water or broth. Cook, stirring, until mixture is very thick and smooth, about 20 minutes. Add the grated parmesan.

Heat oven to 350 degrees F. Lightly oil a 2 quart shallow baking dish. Pour half of the polenta into the dish. Spread with half of the cheese. Top with the remaining polenta and cheese. Pour milk over the top.

Bake until browned and bubbly, about 25 minutes. Let stand 10 minutes before serving. To serve, spoon onto a plate or cut into squares and top with the veal and mushroom ragu.

Yields: 4 to 6 servings

FETA AND BLACK-EYE PASTA TOSS

12 oz. Fusilli or med. shell pasta
3 tbs. olive oil
2 to 3 lg. garlic cloves, minced
1 can (28 oz.) diced tomatoes, drained
3 cups cooked (1 cup dry black-eyed peas makes 3 cups cooked) or 2 cans (15 ozs. each) black-eyed peas, drained
4 ozs. (1 cup) feta cheese, crumbled
2 tbs. chopped fresh basil or 1 tsp. dried basil
1/4 tsp. black pepper
pinch of crushed red pepper

Cook pasta according to package directions; drain in colander and set aside.

Add oil and garlic to pot. Cook over high heat for 30 seconds, stirring constantly. Add pasta, tomatoes, and black-eyed peas; reduce heat to medium. Stir gently until heated through, about 2 minutes. Add remaining ingredients; toss to coat thoroughly.

Yields: 6 to 8 servings

PASTA WITH WARM SALSA

8 ozs. bow tie, elbow macaroni or other med.-shaped pasta, uncooked
2 tbs. olive oil
3/4 cup chopped green onions
1 1/2 tsps. ground cumin
1 1/2 tbs. fresh lime juice
1 1/2 cups cooked (1/2 cup dry black-eyed peas makes 1 1/2 cups cooked) or 1 can (15 oz.) black-eyed peas, drained
1/4 tsp. salt

freshly ground black pepper, to taste
8 cherry tomatoes, quartered
2 tbs. chopped fresh cilantro

Prepare the pasta according to package directions, reserving 1/2 cup cooking water before draining.

Meanwhile, prepare blackeye salsa. Heat oil in saucepan over medium heat. Add green onions and cumin; cook for 2 minutes. Remove from heat and stir in lime juice. Add the black-eyed peas, salt and pepper; toss to coat. (The salsa can be made and refrigerated up to one day in advance. Reheat to continue with recipe.)

Return drained pasta and reserved cooking water to the pasta pot; add blackeye salsa. Bring to a simmer over medium heat; cook until sauce is slightly thickened and lightly coats pasta, 2 to 3 minutes. Remove from heat and gently stir in the cherry tomatoes and cilantro. Serve immediately.

Yields: 4 servings

BEEF 'N ZUCCHINI PASTA

1/2 lb. boneless beef round or sirloin steak
1 tbs. olive oil
1 lg. zucchini, pared, in 2 inch strips
1 red bell pepper, in thin strips
2 cloves garlic, finely chopped
1 tsp. dried oregano leaves
3/4 tsp. each dried rosemary and thyme
1/4 tsp. each salt and pepper
2 tbs. dry white wine
1/2 cup beef broth
1 cup hot cooked spinach linguini
3 tbs. grated parmesan and romano cheese (optional)

Cut beef across grain into thin strips. Heat 1 tablespoon oil in nonstick skillet. Stirfry zucchini, pepper and garlic in hot oil until crisp-tender. Remove and reserve. Stirfry beef 2 to 3 minutes; remove and reserve. Stir in spices and wine. Reduce wine by half. Add beef broth. Stir in vegetables and beef. Cook and stir until sauce is thickened. Divide linguini onto two plates; spoon on beef and vegetables. Sprinkle with parmesan or romano cheese, if desired.

Yields: 2 servings

THIN-SLICED PANZANELLA

3 tbs. extra-virgin olive oil
2 garlic clove, pressed or minced
1 package (about 1 lb.) Perdue Fit 'n Easy fresh skinless and boneless oven stuffer roaster thin-sliced breast
1 tsp. dried Italian herb seasoning
salt and ground pepper to taste
6 ripe Italian plum tomatoes, halved
10 to 12 fresh basil leaves, divided
1 tbs. balsamic vinegar
8 ozs. fettuccine
2 tbs. grated romano cheese
1 lg. bunch arugula, well rinsed

In small bowl, combine oil and garlic. Remove 2 teaspoons oil mixture and use to rub chicken. Sprinkle chicken with Italian seasoning, salt and pepper, refrigerate until ready to cook.

Prepare outdoor grill for cooking or preheat broiler. In food processor, combine 1 tablespoon reserved oil mixture, tomatoes, half the basil and vinegar. Pulse on and off to chop tomatoes. Season sauce with salt and pepper and set aside.

Cook pasta according to package directions. Drain and toss with remaining oil mixture, cheese and salt and pepper.

Grill or broil chicken 3 to 6 inches from heat source 1 1/2 to 2 minutes on each side until cooked through. To serve, spoon warm pasta over greens; top with chicken and tomato sauce and garnish with remaining basil leaves.

Yields: 4 servings

PRIMAVERA PASTA SALAD

1 1/2 tbs. olive oil
1 1/2 tbs. butter or margarine
1 1/2 cups broccoli florets
2 cloves garlic, minced
2 med. tomatoes, seeded and diced
3/4 cup julienne zucchini
1/2 cup julienne carrot
1/4 cup honey
1/4 cup lemon juice
1 1/2 tsps. grated lemon peel
3/4 tsp. dried basil, crushed
3/4 tsp. dried oregano, crushed
salt and pepper to taste
6 ozs. linguine or fettucine noodles, cooked
grated parmesan cheese

Heat oil and butter in large skillet over medium high heat; add broccoli and garlic and stir fry 2 minutes. Reduce heat to low and add tomatoes, zucchini, carrot, honey, lemon juice, lemon peel and seasonings. Simmer about 4 minutes or until vegetables are tender, stirring gently. Toss with noodles; cool. Sprinkle with parmesan cheese. Serve at room temperature or chilled.

Yields: 6 servings

LEAN MARATHON STUFFED POTATOES

2 med. Washington Russet potatoes
2/3 cup low-fat cottage cheese
1 tomato, chopped and drained
1/4 cup minced parsley
2 tbs. minced chives or green onions
1/4 tsp. each salt and pepper
dash dill weed, crushed
1 tbs. grated parmesan cheese

Scrub potatoes; pierce with fork. Bake at 400 degrees F 50 to 60 minutes or until tender. Remove lengthwise slice from each potato; scoop out pulp leaving a 1/4 inch shell.

Mash pulp; stir in cottage cheese, tomato, parsley, chives, salt, pepper and dill weed. Fill shell with cottage cheese mixture; sprinkle with Parmesan cheese.

Bake at 400 °degrees F 15 minutes or until thoroughly heated.
Yields: 2 servings

MAINE FISHERMAN POTATOES AU GRATIN

2 cans (3 3/4 or 4 ozs. each) Maine sardines
2 tbs. chopped onion
2 tbs. melted fat or oil
2 tbs. flour
1 tsp. salt
dash pepper
2 cups milk
1 cup shredded cheese
2 tsps. Worcestershire sauce
5 cups sliced cooked potatoes
3/4 cup soft bread cubes
2 tbs. butter or margarine, melted
paprika

Drain sardines. Cook onion in fat until tender. Blend in flour and seasonings. Add milk gradually and cook until thickened, stirring constantly. Add cheese and Worcestershire sauce. Stir until cheese melts. Arrange half the potatoes in a well-greased, 1 1/2 quart casserole. Cover with sardines and remaining potatoes. Pour sauce over potatoes. Toss bread cubes with butter and sprinkle over top of casserole. Bake in a moderate oven, 350 degrees F, for 25 to 30 minutes or until lightly browned.
Yields: 6 serving

CHILE CON QUESO WITH POTATOES

1 tsp. salt
1 lb. ground beef
1 can (28 oz.) tomatoes, cut into sm. pieces
1 can (4 oz.) chopped green chiles
1 lb. Monterey jack or Swiss cheese, grated
cayenne pepper to taste
5 med. Colorado potatoes, cubed
1/4 tsp. black pepper
1/2 cup chopped onion

Brown ground beef and onions. Drain grease and set aside. Cook tomatoes, chiles, cheese, salt and pepper over low heat until cheese melts. In a casserole, combine ground beef mixture, cheese mixture and potatoes, and bake at 375 degrees F for 1 to 1 1/2 hours.
Yields: 6 to 8 servings

POTATOES ITALIANO

2 tbs. olive oil
2 tbs. tomato paste
1 tsp. salt
2 med. cloves garlic, crushed
1 can (28 oz.) crushed tomatoes
2 tsps. dried Italian seasoning, crushed
1 tsp. dried basil, crushed
1 1/2 cups (6 ozs.) shredded fontina cheese
2 lbs. med. red Colorado potatoes unpared and thinly sliced
1 lg. onion, diced
2 tbs. minced parsley
1/4 tsp. cracked pepper

In a 5 quart Dutch oven, heat olive oil over medium heat. Add onion and garlic; sauté 3 minutes. Add tomatoes, tomato paste, parsley, Italian seasoning, basil, salt and pepper. Bring to boil. Simmer, covered, 15 minutes, stir occasionally.

Preheat oven to 400 degrees F. Spread one third of the sauce over bottom of shallow 2 quart baking dish. Arrange half of the potatoes over the sauce; sprinkle with 1/2 cup fontina cheese. Spoon half of the remaining sauce over the cheese. Cover with the remaining potatoes; sprinkle with 1/2 cup cheese. Spread remaining sauce over all.

Bake until potatoes are tender, about 45 minutes. Sprinkle with remaining 1/2 cup cheese; bake until cheese melts, about 5 minutes.

Yields: 8 servings

SHORTCUT SHEPHERD'S PIE

1 tbs. chopped onion
2 tbs. butter
1 package frozen mixed vegetables
2 cups leftover roast beef or lamb
1 cup grated cheddar cheese
4 Colorado potatoes, cooked, mashed and seasoned to taste
2 tbs. flour
1 cup evaporated milk

Cook the mixed vegetables according to package directions. Drain and add onion, flour, butter and canned milk. Cook until thickened. Stir in meat and any meat juices there may be. Heat to boiling and turn into a greased 2 quart casserole. Top the mixture with mashed potatoes and sprinkled grated cheese on top. Put under the broiler until the cheese melts. Serve at one.

Yields: 4 servings

MICRO-BAKED POTATOES WITH TOPPINGS

4 (8 ozs. each) potatoes
Classic Chicken or Dijon-Chicken Topping

Pierce potatoes with tines of fork; place in microwave on rack or paper towel. Micro-bake on high 22 minutes until potatoes are fork tender, turning once. Let stand 2 minutes. Meanwhile, prepare topping of your choice. Preheat oven to 400 degrees F. Cut potatoes in half lengthwise; place potatoes cut sides up on 10

1/2 x 15 1/2 inch jelly roll pan. Cover potatoes with topping mixture, dividing equally. Sprinkle with cheese. Heat in oven about 6 minutes or until potatoes and topping are hot and cheese is melted.

Note: Microwave-baking times are based on a 700-watt microwave. Adjust cooking times to your own oven.

Classic chicken topping: In bowl combine 1 can (11 1/2 ounce) chunk chicken in water, drained, 3 green onions, sliced, and 6 tablespoons nonfat mayonnaise dressing. Cover topping with 1/4 cup grated parmesan cheese and heat as directed.

Dijon-chicken topping: In bowl combine 1 can (11 1/2 ounce) chunk chicken in water, drained, 8 ounces (half of a 16 ounce bag) frozen broccoli, thawed, 1/4 cup nonfat mayonnaise dressing, 1 tablespoon Dijon-style mustard and 1/2 teaspoon dried tarragon or basil leaves. Season with salt and pepper. Cover topping with 1/4 cup reduced fat sharp cheddar cheese and heat as directed.

Yields: 4 servings

WARM POTATO SALAD WITH HONEY DRESSING

1/3 cup vinegar
2 tbs. vegetable oil
1/4 cup honey
1 tbs. Dijon style mustard
1/8 tsp. bottled hot pepper sauce
1 1/2 lbs. cooked sm. new potatoes, cut into halves or bite sized pieces
4 to 6 slices crisp-cooked bacon, crumbled
2 tbs. chopped parsley
2 tbs. chopped green onions
1/2 tsp. salt

Whisk together vinegar, oil, honey, mustard and pepper sauce in large skillet; mix well. Add cooked potatoes; stir gently to coat all surfaces. Cook on medium heat, stirring gently, until potatoes are heated through. Add bacon,

parsley, green onions and salt; mix well.

Yields: 4 to 6 servings

HONEY GLAZED SWEET POTATOES

1 1/2 lbs. sweet potatoes or yams, pared and quartered
2/3 cup orange juice, divided
1/2 tsp. ground ginger
1/2 tsp. ground nutmeg
1 tbs. butter or margarine
1 tbs. cornstarch
1/3 cup honey

To microwave: Combine sweet potatoes and 1/3 cup orange juice in 2 quart microwave safe baking dish; sprinkle with ginger and nutmeg. Dot with butter. Cover and microwave at high (100%) 7 to 10 minutes or until sweet potatoes are tender, stirring halfway through cooking time. In 2 cup measure, combine cornstarch with remaining orange juice and honey. Microwave at high 2 minutes or until thickened; stir every 30 seconds. Drain liquid from sweet potatoes into honey mixture. Microwave at high 1 minute. Pour sauce over sweet potatoes and microwave at high 1 minute more or until sweet potatoes are thoroughly heated.

Yields: 4 servings

HOT SALSA POTATOES

1 sm. onion, chopped
1 clove garlic, minced
1/3 cup hot chunky salsa
1 lb. lean ground beef or chicken
4 med. Colorado potatoes
1/8 tsp. chili powder
1 cup sour cream
1 tsp. oregano

In large skillet, brown beef with onion and garlic. Drain. Stir in sour cream, salsa, oregano and chili powder. Serve over hot baked potatoes.

Yields: 2 1/2 cups

POULTRY
CHICKEN & TURKEY

CHILEAN CHICKEN WITH BEANS

2 lbs. (4 rounded cups)
Idaho great northern beans
soaked in 10 cups water
1 tbs. salt
2 tbs. butter
2 frying chickens (3 lbs.
each) or 1 lg. stewing hen
1 sm. onion
3 coarse stalks celery with
leaves
4 cups boiling water
2 tsps. salt
Sauce:
5 tbs. butter or chicken fat
5 tbs. flour
3 cups chicken stock (about)
3 to 4 tsps. chili powder

Add salt and butter to beans and soaking water. Cover and cook slowly until beans are tender, about 1 1/2 hours.

Cook chicken and other ingredients in covered heavy pot until tender. When cool enough, remove bones, leaving chicken meat in fairly large pieces. Strain chicken stock, discarding celery and onion. Add the boned chicken. Set in refrigerator to cool. Lift off the fat for sauce.

For sauce: Melt butter or chicken fat in heavy saucepan. Add flour and chili powder. Cook a few minutes over low heat, stirring constantly. Remove from heat. Heat chicken in stock just enough to pour off stock. Add chicken stock gradually to butter mixture. Milk may be added to make 3 cups liquid. Cook over low heat, stirring as it thickens. Taste. Add salt as needed. Cover with a folded paper towel and tight-fitting lid. Set aside until ready to use. Then add chicken and heat over hot water or low heat.

To serve: Using a slotted spoon or wire strainer, lift hot beans onto a heated platter or into top of chafing dish. Place hot sauce and chicken over the beans.

Party idea: For an anniversary dinner or other very important occasion, this makes a remembered meal. Preceded by a toast for "many more," serve this dish with buttered broccoli over a food warmer, a colorful fruit salad mold, hot rolls.

Yields: 12 to 15 servings

CAJUN PRALINE TURKEY

1/3 cup maple syrup
1 tbs. margarine
2 slices (about 1/8 inch
thick) turkey ham, cut in
half
1 lb. turkey cutlets or slices
1 oz. Monterey jack cheese,
cut into 1/4x2 inch sticks
2 tsps. creole seasoning
1/4 cup pecans, finely
chopped
4 tbs. yogurt or sour cream

In 8 inch, microwave-safe dish combine syrup and margarine. Microwave at high (100% power) 20 to 30 seconds or until margarine is melted; set aside.

On each cutlet place a ham slice. Arrange a cheese stick at 1 end of ham-topped-cutlet. Roll cutlet up, jelly-roll style, to encase cheese. Place rolls, seam-side down, in baking dish with syrup mixture. Sprinkle each roll with 1/2 tsp. Creole seasoning.

Cover dish with wax paper. Microwave high at (100% power) 2 1/2 minutes. Rotate dish 1/2 turn and baste rolls with sauce. Sprinkle pecans over top; recover. Microwave at high (100% power) 2 1/2 minutes.

Allow rolls to stand, covered 1 to 2 minutes before serving. Top each roll with 1 tbs. yogurt or sour cream substitute, if desired.

Yields: 4 servings

MANY PEPPERED FILLETS

1 package (about 3/4 lbs.)
Perdue Fit 'n Easy fresh
skinless and boneless turkey
breast fillets
1 tbs. olive oil
salt and ground pepper to
taste
2 cups sliced bell peppers
1 cup sliced onion
2 cups hot, cooked
couscous or brown rice
1 tbs. mined fresh parsley
(optional)

Prepare outdoor grill for cooking or preheat broiler. Rub fillets with oil and lightly season with salt and pepper. Grill fillets 5 to 6 inches from heat source 3 minutes. Turn fillets over and cover with peppers and onions. Grill 5 to 6 minutes longer until turkey is cooked through. Serve with couscous tossed with parsley.

Yields: 4 servings

TURKEY SCALOPPINI

1 lb. turkey breast cutlets,
sliced 1/4 inch thick
salt and pepper
4 tsps. margarine
2 tbs. olive oil

Season cutlets with salt and pepper to taste.

In a large skillet, over medium-high heat, sauté cutlets about 2 minutes per side, or until no longer pink in thickest part of cutlet, in margarine and oil.

Garnish with a lemon wedge and parsley, if desired.

Yields: 4 servings

EASY CHICKEN AND GRAVY

4 skinless, boneless chicken
breast halves (about 1 lb.)
2 tbs. all-purpose flour
1 tbs. vegetable oil
1 can (10 1/2 oz.) Franco-
American chicken gravy
4 cups hot cooked rice

Coat chicken with flour.

In medium skillet over medium heat, heat oil. Add chicken and cook 15 minutes or until chicken is browned and no longer pink. Remove and keep warm.

Add gravy. Heat through. Serve with chicken and rice.

Herb chicken: Add 1/8 teaspoon each dried thyme leaves, crushed and pepper with gravy.

Oriental chicken: Mix 1/4 teaspoon garlic powder with flour. Add 1 tablespoon soy sauce and 1/4 teaspoon ground ginger with gravy.

Chicken paprika: Add 1/4 cup sour cream and 1/2 teaspoon paprika with gravy.

Yields: 4 servings

TURKEY RAGOUT

1 1/2 lbs. turkey thighs,
boned, skinned and cut into
1 inch cubes
1 tbs. vegetable oil

1 cup tomato, peeled and
cut into chunks
1 cup green pepper, thinly
sliced
1 clove garlic, minced
2 tbs. lemon juice
1 tsp. Italian seasoning or
1/2 tsp. basil and 1/2 tsp.
oregano
salt and pepper
2 1/2 tsps. corn starch
3 tbs. cold water

In 3 quart saucepan, over medium-high heat, sauté turkey in oil until all sides are browned. Add tomato, green pepper, garlic, lemon juice, Italian seasoning, salt and pepper. Cover, reduce heat to low and simmer 12 to 15 minutes or until turkey is no longer pink and reaches 180 to 185 degrees F.

In small bowl, mix corn starch and cold water. Stir into hot turkey mixture and cook until thickened.

Serve over rice, if desired.

Yields: 4 servings

CREAMY BAKED CHICKEN

4 lbs. chicken parts
1 can (26 oz.) Campbell's
condensed cream of mush-
room soup

In large shallow roasting pan, arrange chicken bone side down. Bake at 375 degrees F for 30 minutes.

Spoon soup over chicken. Bake 30 minutes or until chicken is no longer pink and juices run clear. Stir sauce before serving.

Tip: If desired, remove skin from chicken before baking.

Yields: 8 servings

BAKED TURKEY TENDERLOINS IN BARBECUE SAUCE

2 turkey breast tenderloins
(8 ozs. each) cut in 1/2
2 tbs. water
1/4 cup cider vinegar
1/4 cup catsup

1/2 tsp. dry mustard
1/2 tsp. Worcestershire
sauce
3 tbs. minced onion
1 clove garlic, minced or
pressed
salt and pepper to taste
1 drop Tabasco sauce

Arrange turkey pieces in a baking dish. Combine remaining ingredients and mix well. Spoon over turkey. Bake, uncovered, in preheated 350°F oven 15 to 20 minutes or until turkey turns from pink to light in color in deepest part. Baste once or twice.

Yields: 4 servings

SOUTHERN-STYLE BARBECUED CHICKEN

1 can (26 oz.) Campbell's
condensed tomato soup
1/4 cup honey
2 tsps. dry mustard
1 tsp. onion powder
8 chicken breast halves
(about 4 lbs.) skinned

In 2 quart saucepan, combine soup, honey, mustard and onion powder.

Arrange chicken on grill, directly above medium coals. Grill, uncovered, 30 minutes, turning often. Brush chicken with sauce and continue grilling 30 minutes or until chicken is no longer pink and juices run clear, turning often and brushing with sauce.

Heat remaining sauce to boiling. Serve with chicken.

Yields: 8 servings

CHICKEN AND BISCUITS

1 can (26 oz.) Campbell's
condensed cream of chicken
soup
2/3 cup milk
1/4 tsp. dried thyme leaves,
crushed
1/4 tsp. pepper
4 cups cooked cut up veg-
etables (broccoli, cauli-
flower, carrots and potatoes)

2 cups cubed cooked chicken or turkey
1 package (7 1/2 or 10 oz.) refrigerated biscuits

In 3 quart oblong baking dish, combine soup, milk, thyme and pepper. Stir in vegetables and chicken.

Bake at 400 degrees F for 15 minutes or until mixture begins to bubble. Stir. Meanwhile, cut each biscuit into quarters.

Arrange biscuits on chicken mixture. Bake 15 minutes or until biscuits are golden.

Tip: Use 1 bag (16 oz.) frozen vegetable combination (such as broccoli, cauliflower and carrots) and 1 cup diced, peeled potato. Microwave on high 8 minutes, rotating dish once during cooking. Let stand 2 minutes.

Yields: 6 servings

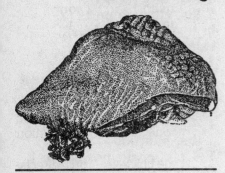

APRICOT TURKEY TENDERLOINS WITH MUSTARD SAUCE

1/3 cup dried apricots, chopped
2 tbs. raisins, chopped
1 sm. clove garlic
2 green onions, cut in 1 inch pieces
1 celery stalk, cut in 1 inch pieces
2/3 cup plain dry bread cubes
1 lb. turkey breast tenderloins
1 tbs. cornstarch
1 cup low-sodium chicken bouillon
1 tbs. country-style (grainy) mustard
1 tbs. honey
2 1/2 tsps. lemon juice

1/3 cup reduced-calorie mayonnaise

In medium-size, microwave-safe bowl combine apricots and raisins; cover with hot water. Microwave at high (100% power) 1 1/2 to 2 minutes or until fruit is soft. Drain well and set aside.

Fit food processor bowl with metal blade. With processor motor running, drop garlic through feed tube and process until garlic is minced. Through feed tube, add onion and celery. Process until finely chopped; combine with fruit mixture. Add bread cubes and cover bowl with vented plastic wrap. Microwave at high (100% power) 1 1/2 minutes.

Cut a lengthwise pocket in tenderloins, being careful not to cut all the way through to other side. Spoon 1/2 of the fruit mixture into each tenderloin pocket. Secure with toothpicks. Place in 9 inch round or square microwave-safe dish. Set aside.

In 4 cup microwave-safe measure combine cornstarch, bouillon, mustard, honey and lemon juice. Microwave at high (100% power) 1 1/2 to 2 minutes, stirring every 45 to 60 seconds. Fold in mayonnaise. Pour sauce over tenderloins. Cover with vented plastic wrap. Microwave at medium-high (70% power) 10 to 15 minutes rotating dish 1/4 turn every 4 minutes until internal temperature of tenderloins reaches 170 to 175°F. and turkey is no longer pink in thickest part.

Yields: 4 servings

CHICKEN TETRAZZINI

8 ozs. dry spaghetti
2 tbs. margarine or butter
2 cups diced mushrooms (about 6 ozs.)
1 med. onion, chopped (about 1/2 cup)
1 can (26 oz.) Campbell's condensed cream of chicken soup
1 1/4 cups milk
3/4 cup parmesan cheese

2 tbs. dry sherry (optional)
1/4 cup chopped fresh parsley or 2 tbs. dried parsley flakes
1/4 tsp. pepper
3 cups cubed cooked chicken

In 4 quart saucepan, prepare spaghetti according to package directions. Drain in colander.

In same saucepan over medium heat, in hot margarine, cook mushrooms and onion until tender and liquid is evaporated, stirring often.

Stir in soup, milk, cheese, sherry, parsley and pepper. Add spaghetti and chicken; toss to coat. Reduce heat to low. Heat through, stirring occasionally.

Yields: 6 servings

CHICKEN AND MUSHROOMS

2 tbs. cornstarch
1 can (16 oz.) Campbell's Healthy Request ready to serve chicken broth
2 tsps. prepared mustard
1 tbs. olive oil
4 skinless, boneless chicken breast halves (about 1 lb.)
2 cups sliced mushrooms (about 6 ozs.)
1 tsp. Italian seasoning, crushed
generous dash ground red pepper
2 cups hot cooked rice, cooked without salt

In small bowl, stir together cornstarch, broth and mustard until smooth; set aside.

In 10 inch skillet over medium-high heat, in hot oil, cook chicken 10 minutes or until chicken is browned on both sides. Remove; set aside.

Reduce heat to medium. In same skillet, cook mushrooms with Italian seasoning and red pepper until tender and liquid is evaporated, stirring often.

Add reserved cornstarch mixture. Cook until mixture boils

and thickens, stirring constantly. Return chicken to skillet. Reduce heat to low. Cover; cook 5 minutes or until chicken is no longer pink, stirring occasionally. Serve with rice.

Yields: 4 servings

LIGHT AND EASY LEMON BROCCOLI CHICKEN

vegetable cooking spray
4 skinless, boneless chicken breast halves (about 1 lb.)
1 can (10 3/4 oz.) Campbell's Healthy Request condensed cream of broccoli soup
1/2 cup skim milk
2 tsps. lemon juice
1/8 tsp. pepper
4 thin lemon slices

Spray 10 inch nonstick skillet with cooking spray. Heat over medium-high heat 1 minute. Add chicken; cook 10 minutes or until browned on both sides. Remove; set aside.

In same skillet, combine soup, milk, lemon juice and pepper. Heat to boiling. Return chicken to skillet. Top each chicken piece with lemon slice. Reduce heat to low. Cover; cook 5 minutes or until chicken is no longer pink, stirring occasionally.

Yields: 4 servings

BLACK WALNUT TURKEY

4 lbs. turkey parts
1 cup buttermilk
1 egg, slightly beaten
1 cup flour
1 cup ground black walnuts
1/4 sesame seed
1 tsp. paprika
1 tsp. salt
1/8 tsp. pepper
3/4 cup butter, melted
1/2 cup black walnut halves

In shallow dish, mix buttermilk and egg.

In medium bowl, mix together flour, ground walnuts, sesame seed, paprika, salt and pepper.

Dip turkey in buttermilk mixture, then in flour mixture, turning to coat sides.

In large baking pan, place melted butter; add turkey, turning to coat on all sides.

Arrange turkey in baking pan, skin side up.

Bake in 350°F oven about 1 hour and 30 minutes.

About 15 minutes before done, place walnut halves over turkey.

Yields: 8 servings

EASY BAKED CHICKEN

vegetable cooking spray
4 chicken breast halves (about 2 lbs.) skinned
1/8 tsp. garlic powder
1/8 tsp. pepper
1 can (10 3/4 oz.) Campbell's Healthy Request condensed cream of broccoli soup
1/2 cup water
4 cups hot cooked cholesterol-free noodle style pasta (about 4 cups dry), cooked without salt

Spray 2 quart oblong baking dish with cooking spray. In baking dish, arrange chicken bone side down. Sprinkle with garlic powder and pepper. Bake at 375 degrees F for 30 minutes.

In small bowl, combine soup and water; spoon over chicken. Bake 30 minutes or until chicken is no longer pink. Stir sauce before serving. Serve with pasta.

Yields: 4 servings

ZESTY CHICKEN BAKE

1 can (16 oz.) Campbell's Healthy Request ready to serve chicken broth
1 cup uncooked regular long grain rice
1/4 tsp. dried thyme leaves, crushed
1 bag (16 oz.) frozen vegetable combination (broccoli, carrots, water chestnuts and red pepper)
4 skinless, boneless chicken breast halves (about 1 lb.)
1/4 cup Marie's refrigerated lite and zesty fat free Italian vinaigrette

In 3 quart oblong baking dish, combine broth, rice and thyme. Bake at 375 degrees F for 20 minutes.

Stir in vegetables. Arrange chicken on rice mixture. Pour vinaigrette over all. Bake 30 minutes or until chicken is no longer pink and rice and vegetables are tender.

Yields: 4 servings

CHICKEN PAPRIKA

1 tbs. vegetable oil
2 lbs. chicken parts (2 breast halves, 2 legs), skinned
1 can (10 3/4 oz.) Campbell's Healthy Request condensed cream of celery soup
1/4 cup skim milk
1 tbs. paprika
1/4 tsp. garlic powder or 2 cloves garlic, minced
1/8 tsp. pepper
1/2 cup sliced onion, separated into rings (about 1 med.)
4 cups hot cooked cholesterol-free noodle style pasta (about 4 cups dry), cooked without salt

In 10 inch skillet over medium-high heat, in hot oil, cook chicken 10 minutes or until browned on all sides. Remove; set aside. Pour off fat.

In same skillet, combine soup, milk, paprika, garlic powder and pepper. Add onion. Heat to boiling. Return chicken to skillet. Reduce heat to low. Cover; cook 30 minutes or until chicken is no longer pink, stirring occasionally. Serve with noodles.

Yields: 4 servings

CHICKEN IN SAVORY LEMON SAUCE

vegetable cooking spray
4 skinless, boneless chicken breast halves (about 1 lb.)
1 can (10 3/4 oz.) Campbell's Healthy Request condensed cream of chicken soup
2 tbs. water
1/4 cup chopped sweet red pepper or green pepper
1 tbs. chopped fresh parsley
1 tbs. lemon juice
1/2 tsp. paprika
4 lemon slices for garnish

Spray 10 inch skillet with cooking spray. Heat over medium-high heat 1 minute. Add chicken; cook 10 minutes or until browned on both sides. Remove; set aside.

In same skillet, combine soup, water, pepper, parsley, lemon juice and paprika. Heat to boiling. Return chicken to skillet. Reduce heat to low. Cover; cook 5 minutes or until chicken is no longer pink, stirring occasionally. Garnish with lemon slices.

Yields: 4 servings

WEST COAST SMOKED TURKEY BREAST WITH APPLE PIE SAUCE

1 1/2 tsps. cornstarch
1/8 tsp. apple pie spice
1/2 cup apple juice
1 lg. apple, cut in 1/2 inch cubes
1 tbs. raisins
3/4 lb. smoked turkey breast, sliced

In small saucepan over medium heat, combine cornstarch, pie spice and juice. Stir in apples and raisins.

Bring mixture to boil and cook 2 to 3 minutes or until apples are tender, stirring occasionally. Do not over cook. Serve sauce over turkey slices.

Yields: 4 servings

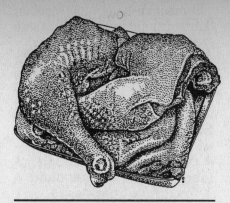

CHICKEN SUPREME

4 skinless, boneless chicken breast halves (about 1 lb.)
2 tbs. all-purpose flour
1 tbs. vegetable oil
1 can (10 3/4 oz.) Campbell's Healthy Request condensed cream of celery soup
1 cup skim milk
1/8 tsp. pepper
1/8 tsp. poultry seasoning
4 cups hot cooked rice, cooked without salt
2 tbs. chopped fresh parsley or 2 tsps. dried parsley flakes

On waxed paper, coat chicken with flour.

In 10 inch skillet, over medium-high heat, in hot oil, cook chicken 10 minutes or until browned on both sides. Remove; set aside. Pour off fat.

In same skillet, combine soup, milk, pepper and poultry seasoning. Heat to boiling. Return chicken to skillet. Reduce heat to low. Cover; cook 5 minutes or until chicken is no longer pink, stirring occasionally. Combine rice and parsley; serve with chicken.

Yields: 4 servings

MACARONI AND CHICKEN BAKE

1 tbs. olive oil
1 cup thinly sliced carrots (about 3 med.)
3/4 cup chopped onion
1 tsp. dried basil leaves, crushed
1/8 tsp. garlic powder or 1 clove garlic, minced
1 can (10 3/4 oz.) Campbell's Healthy Request condensed cream of chicken soup
3/4 cup skim milk
2 tbs. grated parmesan cheese
4 tsps. lemon juice
2 cups hot cooked corkscrew macaroni (about 1 1/2 cups dry), cooked without salt
2 cans (5 ozs. each) Swanson premium chunk white chicken, drained

In 10 inch skillet over medium heat, in hot oil, cook carrots and onion with basil and garlic powder until tender, stirring occasionally. Stir in soup, milk, cheese and lemon juice; add macaroni and chicken. Spoon into 2 quart oblong baking dish.

Bake at 400 degrees F for 20 minutes or until hot and bubbling.

Yields: 5 servings

CHICKEN DIJON

1 tbs. olive oil
4 skinless, boneless chicken breast halves (about 1 lb.)
1 can (10 3/4 oz.) Campbell's Healthy Request condensed cream of celery soup
2/3 cup water
1 tbs. Dijon style mustard
1/8 tsp. pepper
4 cups hot cooked rice, cooked without salt

In 10 inch skillet over medium-high heat, in hot oil, cook chicken 10 minutes or until browned on both sides. Remove; set aside. Pour off fat.

In same skillet, combine soup, water, mustard and pepper. Heat to boiling. Return chicken to skillet. Reduce heat to low. Cover; cook 5 minutes or until chicken is no longer pink, stirring occasionally. Serve with rice.

Yields: 4 servings

CHICKEN BROCCOLI DIVAN

1 lb. fresh broccoli, cut into spears, cooked and drained or 1 package (10 oz.) frozen broccoli spears, cooked and drained
1 cup cubed cooked chicken
1 can (10 3/4 oz.) Campbell's Healthy Request condensed cream of broccoli soup
1/2 cup skim milk
1/8 tsp. pepper
4 low-salt saltine crackers, crushed (about 2 tbs.)
1 tbs. grated parmesan cheese
1/2 tsp. paprika

In 9 inch pie plate or 2 quart oblong baking dish, arrange broccoli; top with chicken. In small bowl, combine soup, milk and pepper; pour over chicken.

In cup, combine cracker crumbs, cheese and paprika; sprinkle over chicken. Bake at 450 degrees F for 20 minutes or until hot and bubbling.

Tip: For 1 cup cubed cooked chicken, in 1 quart saucepan over medium heat, in 2 cups boiling water, cook 1/2 pound skinless, boneless chicken breasts, cubed, 5 minutes or until chicken is no longer pink.

Yields: 4 servings

HEALTHY CHICKEN PRIMAVERA

2 tbs. cornstarch
1 can (16 oz.) Campbell's Healthy Request ready to serve chicken broth
1/4 tsp. garlic powder
2 cups broccoli flowerets
1 cup carrots, diagonally sliced (about 2 med.)
1/2 cup sweet red or green pepper strips
1/4 cup onion, chopped (about 1 sm.)
2 cans (5 ozs. each) Swanson premium chunk white chicken, drained
4 cups hot cooked spaghetti (about 8 ozs. dry), cooked
1 tbs. grated parmesan cheese

In cup, stir together cornstarch and 1 cup broth until smooth; set aside.

In 2 quart saucepan over high heat, heat remaining broth and garlic powder to boiling. Add broccoli, carrots, pepper and onion. Reduce heat to medium. Cover; cook 5 minutes or until vegetables are tender-crisp, stirring occasionally.

Add reserved cornstarch mixture. Cook until mixture boils and thickens, stirring constantly. Add chicken; heat through, stirring occasionally. Serve over spaghetti. Top with cheese.

Yields: 5 servings

CHICKEN TETRAZZINI WITH A TWIST

3 cups dry twist or cork-screw macaroni
1 1/4 cups shredded zucchini (about 1 med.)
1 tbs. olive oil
1/4 cup chopped onion (about 1 sm.)
1 can (10 3/4 oz.) Campbell's Healthy Request condensed cream of mushroom soup
1/4 cup lowfat sour cream
1/4 cup skim milk
1 tbs. grated parmesan cheese
2 cans (5 ozs. each) Swanson premium chunk white chicken, drained

Cook macaroni according to package directions, omitting salt. Add zucchini for last 1 minute of cooking time. Drain in colander.

Meanwhile, in 2 quart saucepan over medium heat, in hot oil, cook onion until tender, stirring often. Stir in soup, sour cream, milk and cheese; add chicken. Reduce heat to low. Heat through, stirring occasionally.

In large bowl, toss hot macaroni mixture with chicken mixture.

Yields: 4 servings

GREEK CHICKEN

1 package (about 1 1/4 lbs.) Perdue Fit 'n Easy fresh skinless and boneless oven stuffer roaster thighs
1 1/2 tsps. dried oregano leaves
salt and pepper to taste
1 tbs. olive oil
2 cups fresh or frozen green beans
1 cup canned artichoke hearts packed in water, drained
1 cup frozen pearl onions, thawed
1 lg. garlic clove, minced
1 1/2 tsps. grated fresh lemon peel
1 cup reduced sodium chicken broth
1/2 cup white wine
2 cups hot, cooked orzo or other sm. pasta

Remove excess fat from thighs. Flatten thighs slightly and sprinkle with seasonings. In large nonstick skillet over medium-high heat, heat oil. Add thighs and cook 8 to 10 minutes until browned on both sides, turning once.

Stir in remaining ingredients; reduce heat to medium-low. Cover and simmer 10 to 15 minutes until chicken is cooked through and vegetables are tender-crisp. Serve over orzo.

Yields: 5 servings

STRAWBERRY VINEGAR

2 pints fresh strawberries
1 quart cider vinegar
1 cup sugar

Remove stems from strawberries; halve strawberries; set 1/4 cup aside. In a large bowl, place remaining strawberries. Pour vinegar over strawberries. Cover and set aside for 1 hour. Transfer vinegar and strawberries to a large sauce pot. Add sugar, bring to a boil. Reduce heat and simmer, covered, for 10 minutes. Strain out strawberry mixture, pressing out as much liquid as possible. Pour vinegar into a 1 1/2 quart jar. Add reserved strawberries. Cover tightly.
Yields: 1 1/2 quarts

ORANGE VINEGAR

1 quart white vinegar
1 cup sugar
orange peel from 1 med.
orange (orange portion only)

In a large sauce pot, place vinegar, sugar and orange peel; bring to a boil. Reduce heat and simmer, covered, for 20 minutes. Transfer vinegar and orange peel to a 1 quart jar. Cover tightly.
Yield: 1 quart

CREAMY CAESAR-STYLE DRESSING

3 lg. garlic cloves, peeled, halved
2 tsps. salt

4 anchovy fillets
1 tsp. dry mustard
2 tsps. Worcestershire sauce
2 tbs. fresh lemon juice
2 1/2 tbs. red wine vinegar
3/4 cup olive oil
1 egg, well beaten

Place the garlic in the work bowl of a food processor fitted with the steel blade and mince it. Add the salt, anchovy fillets and dry mustard. Process 10 seconds. Add the Worcestershire sauce, lemon juice and red wine vinegar and process 10 seconds. With the machine running, slowly add all the olive oil, then drizzle in the egg until a creamy emulsion has formed. Refrigerate. Let dressing stand half an hour at room temperature before tossing with greens. The dressing will keep refrigerated for about 5 days.
Yields: About 1 cup

DIETER'S SALAD DRESSING

1/2 cup California Sauterne or other white dinner wine
1 tsp. cornstarch
1 1/2 tbs. white wine vinegar
1 tbs. chopped parsley
3/4 tsp. seasoned salt
1 tsp. poppy seed

Combine Sauterne and cornstarch in small saucepan, and cook, stirring constantly, until mixture boils and clears. Remove from heat, and stir in remaining ingredients. Cool before using. Celery hearts, sliced mushrooms

and raw zucchini slices are especially good with this dressing.
Yields: About 1/2 cup

HONEY SHERRY DRESSING

3/4 cup oil
1/4 cup wine vinegar
1/3 cup honey
1 tsp. dry mustard
1/2 tsp. paprika
1/2 tsp. celery seed
1 clove garlic
1/4 cup sherry

Combine all ingredients in a jar or bowl. Shake or beat until well blended. Store, covered, in the refrigerator until needed, then shake or beat again before using. Garlic may be removed once its flavor has permeated the dressing.
Yields: About 1 1/2 cups

CHIFFONADE SALAD DRESSING

1/3 to 1/2 cup wine vinegar
1 cup salad oil
1/2 tsp. salt
1/4 tsp. ground black pepper
1 finely chopped hard-cooked egg
1 tsp. minced onion
1 tsp. chopped green pepper

Combine ingredients in a bowl or covered container; mix until well blended. Set aside to blend seasonings. Shake each time before using.
Yields: About 1 1/3 cups

SESAME SWEET DRESSING

1/2 cup vegetable oil
1/2 cup rice vinegar
1/4 cup honey
3 tbs. toasted sesame seeds
1 to 2 tbs. grated fresh gingerroot
1 sm. clove garlic, minced
3/4 tsp. sesame oil
1/8 tsp. crushed dried red pepper
salt to taste

Whisk together oil, vinegar and honey in small bowl. Add sesame seeds, gingerroot, garlic, sesame oil, red pepper and salt to taste; mix thoroughly. Dressing may be stored in refrigerator, tightly covered, for up to 1 week.
Yields: 1 1/3 cups

LIME CREAM HONEY DRESSING

1/2 cup whipping cream
2 tbs. honey
1 tsp. grated lime peel

Beat whipping cream with electric mixer in large bowl until fluffy. Drizzle in honey and beat until stiff. Fold in lime peel.
Yields: 1 cup

HONEY APRICOT DRESSING

1 can (12 oz.) apricot nectar
1/4 cup honey
2 cloves garlic, minced
1/3 cup vegetable oil
1/2 cup raspberry vinegar
1 1/2 tsps. cornstarch
1/2 tsp. ground ginger
1/4 cup minced fresh basil or 1 tbs. dried basil, crushed
1/8 tsp. salt
1/8 tsp. pepper
1 tbs. toasted sesame seeds

Whisk together apricot nectar, honey, garlic, oil, vinegar,

cornstarch, ginger, basil, salt and pepper in medium saucepan. Bring to a slow boil over medium heat. Reduce heat to low and simmer 5 minutes, stirring constantly. Cool; add sesame seeds and refrigerate tightly covered up to 10 days.
Tip: This makes an excellent dressing on both fruit and vegetable salads.
Yields: 1 to 2 cups

POPPY SEED AND HONEY DRESSING

3/4 cup mayonnaise
1/3 cup honey
2 tbs. poppy seeds
1 tbs. Dijon style mustard
salt and pepper to taste

Whisk together all ingredients in small bowl until blended. Cover and refrigerate until ready to serve.
Tip: This dressing is delicious with green salads or fruit salads.
Yields: 1 1/3 cups

HONEY ORANGE DRESSING

1/2 cup plain yogurt
1/4 cup honey
1/4 cup mayonnaise
3/4 tsp. grated orange peel
1/4 tsp. dry mustard
3 tbs. orange juice
1 1/2 tsps. vinegar

Whisk together yogurt, honey, mayonnaise, orange peel and mustard in small bowl until blended. Gradually mix in orange juice and vinegar. Cover and refrigerate until ready to serve.
Tip: This may be served with both fruit and vegetable salads.
Yields: About 1 cup

HONEY LEMON DRESSING

1/4 cup honey
3 tbs. lemon juice
2 tbs. vegetable oil

1/2 tsp. dried basil, crushed
salt and pepper to taste

Whisk together honey, lemon juice, oil, basil, salt and pepper in small bowl until blended.
Tip: This dressing adds zest to mixed greens or a seafood salad.
Yields: About 1/2 cup

HONEY MUSTARD DRESSING

3/4 cup mayonnaise
1/3 cup vegetable oil
1/4 cup honey
1/4 cup lemon juice
1 tbs. minced fresh parsley
1 tbs. prepared mustard
1 tsp. pepper
1/2 tsp. minced onion flakes

Whisk together mayonnaise, oil, honey, lemon juice, parsley, mustard, pepper and onion flakes in small bowl until smooth and creamy. Cover and refrigerate until ready to serve.
Tip: This dressing is wonderful on tossed salad greens, spinach or with chicken or seafood salads.
Yields: 2 1/2 cups

BEAN SALAD FRANCAISE

1/2 cup Idaho red beans
1/2 cup Idaho pinto beans
1/2 cup Idaho Great Northern beans
3/4 cup sliced celery
1/2 cup sliced radishes
1/2 cup diced cucumber
1/4 cup sliced green onion
1/4 cup olive or salad oil
2 tbs. lemon juice
1 tbs. tarragon vinegar
1 clove garlic, minced
1/2 tsp. salt
fresh ground black pepper
lettuce
skewered cubed cold meat and vegetables

Soak and cook beans according to directions. Drain and cool beans. Combine beans and vegetables. Beat together oil, lemon juice, vinegar, garlic and seasonings. Pour dressing over beans and toss to coat thoroughly. Chill for 2 hours. Serve on lettuce-lined plate garnishing with skewered cold meat and vegetables.

Yields: 6 servings

THREE-BEANS SALAD

2 cups Idaho lg. white Great Northern beans, home-cooked or canned
2 cups Idaho red or kidney beans, home-cooked or canned
2 cups canned green beans Italian or French (tomato-free) dressing

Drain beans and place in separate bowls. Carefully stir in a savory tomato-free garlic-flavored French or Italian dressing. Cover the bowls and refrigerate overnight and the next day until nearly time to be used. To serve, combine in chilled bowl the three beans, dressing and all, with some minced sweet onion or onion rings and thin-sliced celery. Add some diced cheddar cheese if desired. Toss together gently. Dress up the edge of the bowl with crisp cold salad greens of your choice.

Yields: 6 to 8 servings

IDAHO'S CENTENNIAL SALAD

cooked Idaho Great Northern (lg. white) beans
thin-sliced celery
chive dressing
whole garlic black pepper (fresh ground in your pepper mill)
slivers of swiss and cheddar cheeses
boiled or baked ham
sliced hard cooked eggs
crisp salad greens
Chive dressing:
1/2 cup undiluted evaporated milk

1/2 cup salad oil
3 tbs. cider vinegar or red wine vinegar
1 tsp. salt
1 tsp. granulated sugar
1/2 tsp. dry mustard
1/4 tsp. coarse-grind black or white pepper
2 tbs. frozen chopped chives

Soak washed beans overnight or boil 2 minutes; let stand 1 hour. Simmer in soaking water until tender, adding 1 teaspoon salt for each cup of beans. Drain, reserving the liquid to use as soup along with some of the beans. Better cook plenty. One cup dried beans will give about 2 cups cooked beans plus liquid. Allow about 1/2 cup cooked beans for each salad serving. Chill beans before adding salad dressing and celery. Then stir in enough thin sliced celery to add crunchiness, add fresh ground pepper and enough dressing to coat the beans. Chill well in the bowl in which the salad is to be served. Just before serving, tuck crisp salad greens around the edges of the bowl. Arrange the slivers of cheese, ham, and chicken or turkey if desired, in alternate clumps atop the bean salad, with hard cooked egg slices or thin sliced radishes as a center garnish.

To make chive dressing: Combine all ingredients in a pint jar with a tight-fitting cover and shake until well blended. Chill thoroughly to mellow the flavors.

Yields: 4 to 6 servings

IDAHO'S CHEF SALAD

cooked or canned Idaho Great Northern (lg. white) beans
thin sliced celery
chive dressing
whole black pepper (fresh ground in your pepper mill)
slivers of swiss and cheddar cheeses, boiled or baked ham, chicken or turkey
sliced hard cooked eggs
crisp salad greens

Chive dressing: In a pint jar with a tight-fitting cover, place 1/2 cup each undiluted evaporated milk and salad oil, 3 tablespoons cider vinegar and red wine vinegar, 1 teaspoon each salt and granulated sugar, 1/2 teaspoon dry mustard 1/4 teaspoon coarse-grind black or white pepper, 2 tablespoons frozen or freeze-dried chives. Shake until well-blended. Chill thoroughly to mellow the flavors.

To cook beans, soak washed beans overnight or boil 2 minutes; let stand 1 hour. Simmer in soaking water until tender, adding 1 teaspoon salt for each cup of beans. Drain, reserving the liquid to use as soup along with some of the beans. Drain, reserving the liquid to use as soup along with some of the beans. Better cook plenty. One cup dried beans will give about 2 cups cooked beans plus liquid. Allow about 1/2 cup cooked beans for each salad serving.

Chill beans and salad bowl before adding salad dressing and celery. Then stir in enough thin sliced celery to make for crunchiness, add fresh ground pepper and enough dressing to coat the beans. Chill well in the bowl in which the salad is to be served. Just before serving, tuck crisp salad greens around the edges of the bowl. Arrange the slivers of cheese, ham, and chicken or turkey if desired, in alternate clumps atop the bean salad, with hard cooked egg slices or thin sliced radishes as a center garnish.

Yields: 6 to 8 servings

HEARTY BEAN AND SAUSAGE SALAD

1 can (15 1/2 oz.) dark red kidney beans, or 1 2/3 cups cooked kidney beans
1 can (15 1/2 oz.) garbanzo beans, or 1 2/3 cups cooked garbanzo beans
1 can (15 oz.) Great Northern beans, or 1 2/3 cups cooked Great Northern beans

93

1 avocado
2/3 cup coarsely chopped onion
1 cup diced cucumber
1 lg. tomato, diced
1/2 lb. fully cooked Polish sausage
1/2 cup salad oil
1/4 cup white wine vinegar
1 tsp. sugar
1 tsp. salt
1 tsp. dry mustard
1/2 tsp. dried tarragon
1/4 tsp. pepper
1/8 tsp. paprika
lettuce

Drain beans. Peel and pit avocado. Reserve 2 slices for garnish. (Dip in lemon juice to prevent discoloration). Dice remainder. Mix beans with avocado, onion, cucumber, and tomato. Thinly slice sausage and mix with vegetables. Combine oil, vinegar and seasoning in jar. Cover and shake until blended. Toss salad with dressing. Chill. To serve, place in lettuce-lined bowl. Garnish with avocado slices.

Yields: 6 to 8 servings

BEAN SALAD PLATTER

1 can (15 oz.) pinto beans
1 can (15 oz.) cooked dry lg. lima beans
1 can (7 oz.) water pack solid white tuna
1/4 lb. Swiss cheese, cut in julienne strips
1 cucumber, scored and sliced
tomato wedges
lettuce or curly endive
Lemon-oil dressing:
1/2 cup salad oil
3 tbs. lemon juice
1/2 tsp. salt
1/4 tsp. sugar
1/4 tsp. dry mustard
1/8 tsp. pepper
2 tbs. chopped parsley

Drain beans and combine with dressing. Refrigerate several hours. Drain beans, reserving marinade. Arrange beans, tuna, cheese, cucumber and tomato on lettuce-lined platter. Serve with reserved marinade, if desired.

To prepare dressing: Combine all ingredients and mix until well blended.

Yields: 10 appetizer servings or 6 main dish servings

SPECIAL BLACK-EYE SALAD

3 cups cooked black-eyed peas (or 2 15 oz. cans)
1 cup fresh artichoke hearts, thawed or canned (not in oil)
3/4 cup finely diced red onion
1 cup chopped celery
Dressing:
1/4 cup vinegar
1 1/4 tbs. olive oil, preferably extra-virgin
1 tbs. reduced sodium chicken stock, defatted
1 tsp. Worcestershire sauce
dash Tabasco sauce
salt and pepper, to taste

Quarter artichokes and combine in a large bowl with black-eyed peas, onions and celery. For the dressing, either use your favorite bottled lowfat vinaigrette dressing or in a small bowl mix together vinegar, oil, chicken stock, Worcestershire and Tabasco sauces. Pour over the blackeye mixture and toss until all ingredients are coated.

Serve over your favorite greens.

Yields: 4 servings

WARM SALAD VALENCIA

1 package (about 1 1/4 lbs.) Perdue Fit 'n Easy fresh skinless and boneless oven stuffer roaster thighs
3 tbs. olive oil, divided
1 tsp. dried thyme leaves
salt and ground black pepper to taste
2 red bell peppers, quartered and seeded
3 tbs. orange juice
1 tbs. grainy Dijon mustard
1 tbs. balsamic vinegar
1 tbs. fresh lemon juice
1 head Boston or bibb lettuce
1 head frisse or curly chicory
2 orange, peeled and sectioned
2 tbs. thinly sliced scallions

Prepare outdoor grill for cooking or preheat broiler. Remove excess fat from thighs. Rub chicken with 1 tablespoon oil; season both sides with thyme, salt and pepper. Grill or broil chicken 6 to 8 inches from heat source 25 to 30 minutes until cooked through, turning once. Slice chicken, reserving juices; set aside. Place bell peppers on edge of grill or on broiler pan. Cook 5 to 10 minutes until tender, turning occasionally. Remove peppers from heat; slice and set aside.

Meanwhile, in small saucepan on side of grill or over low heat combine orange juice, mustard, vinegar and lemon juice. Whisk in remaining oil and any juices from chicken; bring to a simmer. Season mixture with salt and pepper to taste.

To serve on dinner plates, arrange greens and orange sections; top with chicken and pepper slices. Drizzle dressing over salad. Sprinkle with scallions and serve immediately.

Yields: 5 servings

FESTIVE LAYERED PASTA SALAD

1 package Suddenly Salad Caesar pasta salad mix (1 package Suddenly Salad creamy macaroni salad mix can be used; increase mayonnaise to 1/2 cup)
1/3 cup mayonnaise
1/2 cup sliced celery
2 green onions (with tops), sliced
2 cups bite-size pieces salad greens
2 lg. tomatoes, chopped (about 2 cups)

1 1/2 cups chopped fully cooked smoked ham, turkey or chicken
1 cup shredded cheddar cheese (4 ozs.)

Prepare salad as directed on package—except stir mayonnaise into seasoning mixture. Stir celery and onions into finished salad. Layer salad greens, tomatoes, ham, cheddar cheese and pasta salad in 2 to 2 1/2 quart glass bowl or casserole. Garnish with tomato wedges if desired. Refrigerate any remaining salad.

High altitude directions (3500 to 6500 feet): Boil pasta and vegetables 16 minutes.

Yields: 8 to 10 servings

MAINE SARDINE CAESAR SALAD

3 cans (3 3/4 or 4 ozs. each) Maine sardines
1 clove garlic, peeled and quartered
1/2 cup salad oil
1 1/2 cups croutons
1 sm. onion, thinly sliced
8 cups salad greens
1/2 tsp. salt
dash pepper
1 egg, cooked 1 minute
2 tbs. lemon juice
1/3 cup grated parmesan cheese
2 tomatoes, cut in wedges

Drain sardines and cut into large pieces. Add garlic to oil and let stand at least 1 hour. Remove garlic from oil. Gradually pour 1/4 cup of garlic oil over croutons, mixing lightly until all of the oil is absorbed. Separate onion slices into rings. Combine onion rings, salad greens, salt, and pepper. Pour remaining 1/4 cup of garlic oil over salad greens. Toss lightly. Break egg into salad. Add lemon juice and mix thoroughly. Add cheese, croutons, and sardines. Toss lightly. Garnish with tomato wedges.

Yields: 6 servings

FRENCH QUARTER SALAD

1 1/2 cups lg. limas (cooked or canned)
1 hard cooked egg
1/2 cup diced celery
3 tbs. sliced dill pickle
1 cup mayonnaise
2 tsp. lemon juice
1 tsp. prepared mustard
dash hot pepper sauce
1 tbs. chopped parsley
lettuce cups

Drain limas, rinse and chill. Dice egg and combine with limas, celery and pickle. Mix together mayonnaise, lemon juice, mustard, pepper sauce and parsley, and blend with bean mixture. Salt to taste. Arrange lettuce cups on individual salad plates and spoon in salad mixture. Serve ice cold.

Yields: 6 servings

CURRIED SALAD BOMBAY

1 package (about 1 1/3 lbs.) Perdue Fit 'n Easy fresh skinless and boneless turkey breast
1/2 cup reduced sodium chicken broth
1/2 cup reduced fat mayonnaise
1/2 cup plain low fat yogurt
1 tbs. peach or mango chutney
2 to 3 tsps. curry powder
salt and ground pepper to taste
1 red apple, unpeeled, cored and sliced
1 green apple, unpeeled, cored and sliced

3/4 cup red and/or green seedless grapes
2 tbs. snipped fresh chives
curly green or bibb lettuce

In deep 2 quart microwave safe utensil, place turkey breast and broth. Cover with plastic wrap and microwave at high (100% power) 3 minutes. Reduce power to medium (70% power) and microwave 7 minutes.

Turn breast over; re-cover with plastic wrap and microwave at medium-high 7 minutes longer. Allow to stand, covered with aluminum foil, 10 minutes, and if time allows, cool breast in broth.

In medium bowl, combine mayonnaise, yogurt, chutney, curry, salt and pepper.

Remove turkey from broth and cut into small cubes; add to mayonnaise mixture. Add apples, grapes and chives; toss gently to coat ingredients with dressing. Serve salad on a bed of lettuce.

Yields: 6 servings

FIVE BEAN SALAD

1 can (16 oz.) green beans
1 can (16 oz.) wax beans
1 can (16 oz.) garbanzo or lima beans
1 can (16 oz.) kidney beans
1 can (16 oz.) peas
1/2 cup chopped cauliflower
1/2 cup chopped celery
1/2 cup chopped onion
1/2 cup chopped green pepper
1/2 cup chopped pimiento
1 1/2 cups sugar
1/2 tsp. paprika
1 cup cider or white vinegar
1/2 cup salad oil

Drain beans and peas; place in a large bowl. Add cauliflower, celery, onion, green pepper and pimiento. In a small bowl combine sugar, paprika, vinegar and oil. Pour over vegetables; mix well. Cover and refrigerate 12 hours or longer.

Yields: 2 1/2 quarts

DUTCH SPINACH SALAD

6 cups fresh spinach, torn
into bite sized pieces
1/4 cup chopped onion
4 slices bacon, diced
1/4 cup wine vinegar
1 tbs. sugar
1 tsp. salt
1/4 tsp. ground black pepper

Place spinach and onion in a large serving bowl; set aside. In a skillet sauté bacon until crisp; remove from heat. Stir in vinegar, salt and black pepper. Bring to the boiling point. Slowly pour hot dressing over spinach and onion; toss and serve at once.

Yields: 4 to 6 servings

ICICLE RADISH SALAD WITH HONEY SESAME DRESSING

3 cups washed and torn
fresh spinach
1 cup julienne icicle radishes
1 cup julienne carrots
1 cup fresh bean sprouts
(optional)
Honey sesame dressing:
1/2 cup vegetable oil
1/2 cup rice vinegar
1/4 cup honey
3 tbs. toasted sesame seeds
1 to 2 tbs. grated fresh
gingerroot
1 sm. clove garlic, minced
3/4 tsp. sesame oil
1/8 tsp. crushed dried red
pepper
salt to taste

Arrange vegetables on serving platter. Spoon on desired amount of honey sesame dressing.

To prepare dressing whisk together oil, vinegar and honey in small bowl. Add sesame seeds, gingerroot, garlic, sesame oil, red pepper and salt to taste; mix thoroughly. Dressing may be stored in refrigerator, tightly covered, for up to 1 week.

Yields: 6 servings

CHINESE SPINACH TOSS

3 to 4 cups fresh bean
sprouts or 2 cans (16 ozs.
each) bean sprouts, well
drained
1/3 cup honey
1/3 cup white wine or rice
vinegar
2 tbs. vegetable oil
2 tsps. soy sauce
1 to 2 tsps. grated fresh
gingerroot
6 cups washed and torn
fresh spinach
1 cup diced peeled jicama
1 cup crisp Chinese noodles

Place bean sprouts in large glass or ceramic bowl. Combine honey, wine, oil, soy sauce and gingerroot in small bowl; pour over bean sprouts. Cover and refrigerate at least 1 hour, tossing occasionally. Just before serving, add spinach and jicama; toss gently to coat. Top each serving with noodles.

Yields: 6 servings

HARVEST CIDER SALAD

3 cups apple cider, divided
1/4 cup honey
2 envelopes unflavored
gelatin
1 can (6 oz.) frozen lemonade concentrate, thawed
2 lg. red apples, cored and
diced
1/4 cup chopped celery
1/4 cup chopped walnuts or
pecans

Blend 2 cups cider and honey in large bowl. Combine remaining 1 cup cider with gelatin in small saucepan; let stand 5 minutes. Cook and stir gelatin mixture over very low heat until gelatin is dissolved. Remove from heat and add to honey-cider mixture.

Pour lemonade concentrate over diced apples in another large bowl; stir to coat all sides to prevent darkening. Remove apples with slotted spoon and set aside. Stir lemonade into honey-cider mixture. Refrigerate mixture until

it begins to get thick and syrupy. Stir in apples, celery and nuts. Pour into 1 1/2 quart mold and refrigerate until firm.

Yields: 8 servings

HONEY VINAIGRETTE SALAD

1/2 cup berry flavored or
balsamic vinegar
1/4 cup honey
olive oil
favorite fresh herb
mixed greens or fruit

Combine vinegar and honey in small bowl; mix well. When ready to serve, drizzle 2 to 3 tablespoons vinegar mixture, 1 to 2 tablespoons oil and 1 tablespoon chopped fresh herb over 8 cups mixed greens. Toss to coat greens.

Or, drizzle 1 to 2 tablespoons vinegar mixture, 1 tablespoon oil and 2 to 3 tablespoons chopped fresh mint over 4 cups mixed fruit; mix well. Tip: Select flavor of vinegar and honey to complement salad. Vinegar and honey mixture may be stored in covered jar for future use.

Yields: 4 to 6 servings

CAESAR SALAD

12 cups torn romaine lettuce leaves
6 tbs. Egg Beaters 99% egg
product
1/4 cup corn oil
1/4 cup lemon juice
1 tsp. Grey Poupon Dijon
mustard
2 cloves garlic, minced
1/4 tsp. black pepper
grated parmesan cheese

Place lettuce in large salad bowl, set aside.

In small bowl, whisk egg product, oil, lemon juice, mustard, garlic and pepper until well blended. Pour over lettuce, tossing to coat well. Serve with parmesan cheese if desired.

Yields: 8 servings

SALSA
& RELISHES

APRICOT CHUTNEY

4 cups dried California apricot halves (3 bags, 6 ozs. each)
3 cups cider vinegar
4 cups onion wedges (3 lg. onions)
1 cup chopped candied ginger
2 tbs. salt
1 tbs. minced garlic
1 tsp. Tabasco
3 cups brown sugar (packed)
3 cups sugar
2 cups water
3 cups seedless-golden raisins
2 tbs. whole mustard seed

Cut apricot halves in 1/2 . Combine all ingredients in kettle. Bring to boil, then simmer slowly, uncovered, until thickened, about 1 hour, stirring often.

Portion into sterilized jars; seal at once. If desired, process in boiling water bath for 15 minutes.
Yields: about 13 (1/2 pints)

DRIED CHERRY RELISH

1 1/2 cups dried tart cherries
1/2 cup red wine vinegar
1/4 cup balsamic vinegar
1 tbs. butter or margarine
1 lg. red onion, finely chopped
2 tbs. granulated sugar
1/4 tsp. salt, or to taste
1/8 tsp. ground black pepper

In a medium bowl, combine cherries, red wine vinegar and balsamic vinegar. Let soak 30 minutes.

Heat butter in a large skillet. Add onion; cook 5 minutes, or until onion is soft. Add sugar; mix well. Cook, stirring occasionally, over low heat 10 minutes.

Add cherries with soaking liquid to onion mixture. Simmer, uncovered, 10 to 15 minutes, or until almost all the liquid is evaporated. Season with salt and pepper. Serve warm. Relish may be prepared ahead of time and refrigerated; reheat before serving.
Yields: about 2 cups; 12 servings as a relish

CRISP AND SPICY CABBAGE RELISH

1 1/2 cups packaged coleslaw mix
1/4 cup chopped red onion
1/4 cup chopped green or red bell pepper
Dressing:
1 1/2 tsps. dark sesame oil
1/2 to 1 jalapeno pepper, seeded, finely chopped
1 clove garlic, crushed
1/8 to 1/4 tsp. pepper
2 tbs. sugar

2 tbs. white wine vinegar
Perfect grilled burgers:
1 1/2 lbs. lean ground beef
salt and pepper (optional)
6 hamburger buns, split

In medium bowl, combine coleslaw mix, onion and bell pepper.

In small saucepan, heat oil over medium-low heat until hot. Add jalapeno pepper, garlic and pepper; cook and stir 1 minute. Add sugar and vinegar; cook and stir 30 seconds or until sugar is dissolved.

Pour hot dressing over cabbage mixture; toss to coat. Cover and refrigerate 1 hour or overnight, if desired. Serve with perfect grilled burgers.

Perfect grilled burgers: Shape ground beef into six 1/2 inch thick patties.

Place patties on grid over medium coals. Grill 7 to 9 minutes or until no longer pink and juices run clear, turning once. Season with salt and pepper, if desired, after turning.

Serve grilled burgers on buns.

Cook's Tip: Thinly sliced green cabbage may be substituted for packaged coleslaw mix.
Yields: 1 1/2 cups

TANGY OLIVE SALSA

1 cup tomatoes, peeled, seeded and diced
1/3 cup fresh parsley, chopped
1/4 cup yellow bell pepper, chopped
2 tbs. Greek olives, pitted
2 tbs. fresh lime juice

1 1/2 tbs. capers, drained
1 1/2 tbs. olive oil
1 1/2 tsps. fresh basil, chopped
1 tsp. balsamic vinegar
dash cayenne pepper
dash black pepper

In medium-size bowl combine tomato, parsley, yellow pepper, olives, lime juice, capers, oil, basil, vinegar, cayenne and black pepper. Cover and refrigerate for at least 1 hour to allow flavors to blend.

Yields: 8 servings

SWEET AND SPICY SALSA

3/4 cup fresh pineapple, peeled, cored and cut into 1/4 inch cubes
1/2 cup red bell pepper, cut into 1/4 inch pieces
1/2 cup yellow bell pepper, cut into 1/4 inch pieces
1/2 cup red onion, finely chopped
1/2 cup cilantro, finely chopped
1 jalapeno, seeded and minced
2 tbs. fresh lime juice
1 1/2 tsps. brown sugar
dash salt
dash pepper

In medium-size bowl combine pineapple, red and yellow peppers, onion, cilantro, jalapeno, lime juice, brown sugar, salt and pepper. Cover and refrigerate 30 minutes before serving.

Yields: 8 servings

ONION MANGO CHUTNEY

1 cup chopped onion
1 cup cubed fresh mango or papaya
1/3 cup dark seedless raisins
2 tbs. minced candied ginger
2 tsps. grated lime rind

3 tbs. freshly squeezed lime juice
1 cup granulated sugar
1/2 cup light brown sugar
6 tbs. cider vinegar
3/4 tsp. mustard
3/4 tsp. cumin
3/4 tsp. fennel seeds
1 tsp. minced garlic
1/4 tsp. salt

Combine all ingredients in 10 inch skillet, bring to boil then simmer uncovered until thickened, about 30 minutes, stirring occasionally. The chutney will keep for up to 3 weeks in the refrigerator.

Yields: 2 cups

PAPAYA SALSA

1 ripe papaya
1 sm. red bell pepper
1 sm. red onion
6 tbs. fresh lime juice
1/4 cup pineapple juice
1/4 cup chopped fresh cilantro
1 clove garlic finely chopped
1 scotch bonnet pepper
salt and pepper to taste

Peel, seed and coarsely dice papaya. Slice bell pepper and onion into short thin strips. Finely dice the scotch bonnet. In a large bowl combine all ingredients, mix well.

Yields: 4 servings

HOT FRUIT RELISH

4 Chiquita bananas
4 tbs. butter or margarine
2 1/2 cups unsweetened pineapple chunks
6 tbs. brown sugar

Melt butter in heavy skillet. Peel bananas, cut into thirds and sauté lightly. Add pineapple and sugar. Cook over low heat until fruit is hot and sauce is bubbly. Sprinkle with diced candied ginger.

Note: This relish complements almost any entree but is

particularly good with ham, pork, or poultry.

Yields: 4 servings

TWO BEAN RELISH

3/4 cup Idaho red beans
3/4 cup Idaho Great Northern beans
1 cup vinegar
3/4 cup sugar
1 1/2 tsps. salt
1 tsp. mustard seeds
1/2 med. onion, thinly sliced
1 med. cucumber, coarsely chopped
2 tbs. cornstarch
3/4 cup water

Cook beans as directed. To cook beans combine with 4 cups cold water. Bring to boil, simmer 2 minutes. Remove from heat; cover and let stand 1 hour. Bring beans to boil again and simmer 1 hour or until beans are tender. Drain well. Combine vinegar, sugar, salt, mustard seeds, onion and cucumber in saucepan. Bring to boil; simmer 5 minutes. Dissolve cornstarch in water. Stir into vinegar mixture; cook, stirring constantly until mixture boils for 1 minute. Pour over beans, stirring to mix well. Cover and refrigerate overnight, stirring occasionally.

Note: Canned red or Great Northern beans may be used, if desired.

Yields: about 5 cups

HONEY CRANBERRY RELISH

1 med. orange
1 package (12 oz.) fresh or frozen whole cranberries
3/4 cup honey

Quarter and slice unpeeled orange, removing seeds. Coarsely chop orange and cranberries. Place in medium saucepan and stir in honey. Bring to a boil over medium high heat and cook 3 to 4 minutes. Cool.

Yields: 2 1/4 cups

CATFISH STEW

4 lbs. genuine U.S. farm-raised catfish, cut in 3 inch pieces
1 cup vegetable oil
1 cup flour
2 onions, chopped
6 scallions, chopped
1/2 cup parsley
1 cup chopped celery
1 can (16 oz.) whole tomatoes, drained and chopped
1 can (6 oz.) tomato paste
3 cloves garlic, minced
1 lemon, sliced
3 bay leaves
1/2 tsp. thyme
1/4 tsp. ground cloves
1/4 tsp. allspice
1/4 tsp. mace
2 1/2 qts. fish stock
1/2 cup dry red wine
1/4 tsp. cayenne pepper

Heat the oil in a large pot. Add the flour and stir to make a roux (mixture used to thicken sauces, soups). Add the onion, scallions, parsley, garlic and celery and cook until vegetables are soft, about 3 to 4 minutes. Add the tomatoes and the tomato paste. Add the bay leaves, thyme, allspice, mace, cloves, lemon slices, red wine, cayenne and black pepper. Mix well. Add the fish stock. Simmer for 45 minutes to an hour; stir to prevent sticking.

Rub the farm-raised catfish pieces with a mixture of salt, pepper and cayenne pepper. Add to the pot and continue to cook for another 20 to 30 minutes until fish is tender.

Yields: 8 servings

BEEF MINESTRONE SOUP

1 lb. beef round tip steaks, cut 1/8 to 1/4 inch thick
3 cups water
1 package (10 ozs.) frozen mixed vegetables
1 can (14 1/2 ozs.) Italian-style diced tomatoes, undrained
1/2 cup uncooked ditalini pasta or elbow macaroni
2 tsps. instant beef bouillon granules
1/2 tsp. dried basil leaves
grated parmesan cheese (optional)

In 3-quart saucepan, combine water, vegetables, tomatoes, pasta, bouillon and basil. Bring to a boil; reduce heat to low. Simmer, uncovered, 10 minutes or until pasta is tender.

Meanwhile stack beef steaks; cut lengthwise in half and then crosswise into 1 inch wide strips.

Stir beef into simmering soup. Immediately remove from heat. Cover and let stand 5 minutes. Serve immediately; sprinkle with cheese, if desired.

Yields: 4 servings

STEAK AND VEGETABLE SOUP

1 lb. boneless beef top sirloin steak, cut 3/4 inch thick
1 can (13 3/4 to 14 1/2 ozs.) ready-to-serve beef broth
1 1/2 cups water

1 lg. onion, chopped
1/2 lb. all-purpose potatoes, cut into 1/2 inch pieces
1/2 lb. baby carrots
1 cup frozen peas
1/4 cup chopped assorted fresh herbs (parsley, chives, thyme, basil)
2 tbs. balsamic vinegar
2 tsps. vegetable oil
1/2 tsp. coarse grind black pepper

Trim fat from beef steak. Cut steak lengthwise into three strips and then crosswise into 1/2 inch thick pieces.

In large saucepan, combine broth, water, onion, potatoes, carrots and peas. Bring to a boil; reduce heat to low. Simmer, uncovered, 15 minutes or until vegetables are tender. Stir in herbs and vinegar.

Meanwhile in large nonstick skillet, heat oil over medium-high heat until hot. Add beef (1/2 at a time) and stir-fry 2 to 3 minutes or until outside surface is no longer pink. (Do not overcook.) Season with pepper. Place equal amount of beef into 4 individual soup bowls.

To serve, ladle vegetables and broth mixture over beef. Serve immediately.

Yields: 4 servings

SAVORY VEAL STEW

2 1/2 lbs. veal for stew, cut into 1 inch pieces
1/3 cup all-purpose flour
1/2 tsp. salt
1/2 tsp. pepper
3 tbs. olive oil

1 lg. onion, coarsely chopped
3 lg. cloves garlic, crushed
1 can (13 3/4 to 14 1/2 ozs.) ready-to-serve chicken broth
2 tsps. dried thyme leaves
1 package (1 lb.) baby carrots
1 lbs. sm. new red potatoes, cut in half
1 cup frozen peas

In medium bowl, combine flour, salt and pepper. Add veal; toss to coat. In Dutch oven, heat 1/2 the oil over medium heat until hot. Add 1/2 the veal and brown evenly, stirring occasionally. Remove veal. Repeat with remaining veal and oil.

In same pan, add onion and garlic; cook and stir 1 minute. Gradually stir in broth and thyme. Return veal to pan. Bring to a boil; reduce heat to low. Cover tightly and simmer 45 minutes.

Stir in carrots and potatoes. Cover and continue cooking 30 minutes or until tender.

Skim fat from cooking liquid. Stir in peas; heat through.

Cook's Tip: To prepare in oven, use covered, ovenproof Dutch oven or roasting pan. After adding veal to onion mixture, cook in 325 degrees F oven; cooking time remains the same.

Yields: 8 servings

SOUTHWESTERN BEEF STEW

1 1/4 lbs. well-trimmed beef tip roast, cut into 1 inch pieces
1 tbs. vegetable oil
1/2 cup coarsely chopped onion
1 lg. clove garlic, minced
1 1/2 tsps. dried oregano leaves
1 tsp. ground cumin
1/2 tsp. each crushed red pepper and salt
4 med. tomatoes, chopped and divided (about 4 cups)
1/2 cup water

1 can (4 ozs.) whole green chilies
1 tbs. cornstarch
1/4 cup sliced green onion tops

Heat oil in Dutch oven over medium-high heat. Add beef pieces, onion and garlic; cook and stir until beef is browned. Pour off drippings.

Combine oregano, cumin, red pepper and salt; sprinkle over beef. Add 3 cups of the tomatoes and the water; stirring to combine. Reduce heat; cover tightly and simmer 1 hour and 55 minutes or until beef is tender, stirring occasionally.

Drain green chilies; reserve liquid. Cut chilies into 1/2 inch pieces; add to beef mixture. Combine cornstarch and reserved liquid; gradually stir into stew and cook, uncovered, until thickened. Stir in remaining tomatoes; garnish with green onion tops.

Yields: 4 servings

SAN FRANCISCO MINESTRONE

1/4 lb. salt pork or chunk bacon
1 med. onion, chopped
1 clove garlic, minced
5 cups water and 1 cup meat stock (or 6 cups water and 2 bouillon cubes)
1 cup dry lg. limas
1 tsp. salt
1 carrot, sliced
1 turnip, halved and slivered
2 cups sliced celery
1/2 bay leaf
1/4 tsp. dried basil
1 1/2 cups canned stewed tomatoes
1 cup chopped spinach
2 cups shredded cabbage
1/4 cup uncooked rice
grated parmesan or romano cheese

To prepare this soup the way Italian chefs do, cut pork in cubes and fry with onion and garlic until lightly browned. Put water and

meat stock in a large soup kettle. Add washed dry limas, the browned pork mixture, and bring to a boil. Next add carrot, turnip, celery, bay leaf and basil, and boil gently for 1 1/2 hours. Add tomatoes, spinach, cabbage and rice and cook 1/2 hour longer until rice is done. Taste, add salt if needed. Serve in tureen. Ladle into individual bowls, with grated cheese on top.

Yields: 6 to 8 servings

WESTERN BEEF SOUP

1/2 lb. boneless beef round or sirloin steak
1 tbs. vegetable oil
1 sm. onion, chopped
2 cloves garlic, finely chopped
1 can (14 1/2 oz.) peeled tomatoes, chopped
1/2 cup whole kernel corn, frozen
1 can (4 oz.) diced green chiles
2 tbs. chopped fresh cilantro
3/4 cup beef broth
1/2 tsp. ground cumin
1 corn tortilla, in strips
2 tbs. chopped green onion

Cut beef across grain into thin strips. Heat 1/2 tablespoon oil in large skillet. Stirfry beef in hot oil 2 to 3 minutes. Remove and reserve. Add remaining oil to skillet. Stirfry onion and garlic until onion is limp. Stir in remaining ingredients except beef, tortilla strips and green onion. Heat to boiling; reduce heat and cover. Simmer 5 minutes. Add beef. Simmer 3 minutes. Arrange tortilla strips in soup bowls; spoon in soup. Sprinkle with green onion.

Yields: 2 servings

BABY LIMA CHOWDER

3 1/3 cups, drained cooked or canned white baby limas
2 ozs. salt pork
1/2 cup chopped onion
2 tbs. butter or margarine

2 tbs. flour
2 cans (6 1/2 ozs.) minced clams
1 1/2 cups milk
1 1/2 cups half and half
1/2 tsp. Worcestershire sauce
cayenne pepper and salt
1/2 cup sliced green onion

Puree the cooked beans with their cooking liquid, adding enough water to make 1 to 1 1/2 cups. Cut salt pork into 1/2 inch cubes and fry until lightly browned. Remove salt pork and sauté chopped onion in the fat. Don't brown. Add butter; blend in flour. Drain clams; save the broth and add water to make 1 cup. Stir clams, broth, milk, half and half, Worcestershire sauce and a dash of cayenne into onion mixture. Cook and stir until thickened. Add pureed beans and salt pork. Heat thoroughly but do not boil. Salt to taste and garnish with green onion. Serve in individual bowls with oyster crackers.
Yields: 6 to 8 servings

SHEEPHERDER'S HEARTY SOUP

1/2 cup chopped celery
1/4 cup diced onion
2 tbs. butter or margarine
2 tbs. flour
1 cup water
2/3 cup milk
dash of bottled hot pepper sauce
3 1/3 cups drained, cooked or canned white baby limas
1 can (16 oz.) whole kernel corn
1 can (8 oz.) tomatoes, crushed
3/4 cup shredded Jack cheese
1/4 tsp. salt
1/8 tsp. pepper

Sauté celery and onion in butter. Blend in flour. Add water and milk. Cook, stirring until thickened and smooth. Add beans, corn (with its liquid), tomatoes and cheese. Heat

thoroughly, but do not boil. Season to taste with salt, pepper and hot sauce. Serve with wedges of sheepherder's or sour dough bread.
Yields: 6 to 8 servings

CHILI BEAN SOUP

1 lb. pink, red or pinto beans
6 to 8 cups boiling water
1 tsp. garlic salt
1 tsp. onion salt
1/4 tsp. each thyme and marjoram
1 can (10 1/2 oz.) beef or chicken broth
1 can (16 oz.) stewed tomatoes
1 package (1 5/8 oz.) chili seasoning mix or 1 can (7 to 10 ozs.) green chile salsa

Rinse, sort and soak beans. Drain and empty them into a large pot. Add boiling water, garlic and onion salt, thyme, and marjoram. Cover and simmer until beans are tender (about 2 1/2 to 3 hours). Don't let beans boil dry. Add hot water as needed. Spoon out 3 cups of the cooked beans to use another day in another way. Mash rest of beans with their liquid. Add remaining ingredients, plus 1 cup hot water. Heat at least ten minutes to blend flavors.
Note: Those spooned-out beans make a great salad. Just cool them, cover with French dressing.
Yields: 5 to 6 cups soup

CHICKEN VEGETABLE SOUP

1 tbs. olive oil
1/2 cup sliced carrot
1/2 cup coarsely chopped celery (about 1 stalk)
1/8 tsp. garlic powder or 1 clove garlic, minced
2 cans (16 ozs. each) Campbell's Healthy Request ready to serve chicken broth
1/4 cup dry orzo (rice-shaped pasta)

1 cup cubed cooked chicken
1 tbs. chopped fresh parsley or 1 tsp. dried parsley flakes

In 2 quart saucepan over medium heat, in hot oil, cook carrots and celery with garlic powder until tender-crisp, stirring often.
Add broth and orzo. Heat to boiling. Reduce heat to low; cook 15 minutes or until orzo is tender, stirring occasionally.
Add chicken and parsley; heat through, stirring occasionally.
Tip: For 1 cup cubed cooked chicken, in 1 quart saucepan over medium heat, in 2 cups boiling water, cook 1/2 pound skinless, boneless chicken breasts, cubed, 5 minutes or until chicken is no longer pink.
Yields: 5 servings

RUSSIAN HILL BEAN BORSCHT

2 cups grated raw beets
1 med. onion
7 to 8 cups clear, strong beef broth
1 to 1 1/2 cups cooked or canned California pink or red kidney beans
2 cups shredded cabbage
1 tbs. butter
1 tbs. lemon juice
pepper and salt to taste
sour cream

Wash and pare two large beets; grate coarsely (easy if you leave 3 or 4 inches of stems for handles). Chop onion, add with beets to boiling broth, and cook 15 to 20 minutes. Add cabbage and drained beans; cook 10 minutes. Don't overcook. Add butter, lemon juice, pepper and salt. Serve with a spoonful of sour cream.
Yields: 6 to 8 cups

PINTO STUFFED PEPPERS

2 cups dried Idaho pinto beans
6 cups water
2 tsps. salt
4 slices crisp bacon, crumbled
2 cups grated cheddar cheese
2 tomatoes, chopped
1/2 cup white wine
1/4 cup chopped green onions
8 green peppers

To cook beans: Add cold water and soak overnight. Or, for quick soak method, add measured amount of cold water to beans, bring to boil and boil 2 minutes. Cover and let stand 1 hour. Add 1 teaspoon salt per cup dry beans. Cook in soaking liquid until tender, 1 to 1 1/2 hours. Drain. One cup dry beans will yield approximately 2 1/2 cups cooked beans.

For stuffed peppers: In a large bowl, mash cooked beans. Add bacon, cheese, tomatoes, wine and onions; mix together. Slice tops off peppers; remove seeds and inner portions. Parboil peppers for 3 minutes in salted water. Drain and fill with bean mixture. Place in greased pan and bake in 400 degrees F oven for 25 minutes, or until peppers are tender.

Note: Leftover bean stuffing may be used as topping for open-face broiled sandwiches. Especially delicious on whole wheat bread.
Yields: 8 servings

CROWD PLEASING VEGETABLE CASSEROLE

1 can (26 oz.) Campbell's condensed cream of mushroom soup
1 1/2 cups shredded Swiss cheese (6 ozs.)
2/3 cup sour cream
1/4 tsp. pepper
2 bags (16 ozs. each) frozen vegetable combination (broccoli, carrots and cauliflower), cooked and drained
2 cans (about 2 1/2 ozs. each) or 1 can (6 oz.) French fried onions

In large bowl, combine soup, 1 cup cheese, sour cream and pepper. Stir in vegetables and half of the onions. Spoon into 3 quart oblong baking dish.

Bake at 400 degrees F. Stir. Sprinkle remaining 1/2 cup cheese and onions over vegetable mixture.

Bake 2 minutes or until hot and bubbly and onions are golden.
Yields: 12 servings

BROCCOLI MUSHROOM CHICKEN

6 cups cut up broccoli (about 1 lb.), cooked and drained or 1 bag (16 oz.) frozen broccoli cuts, thawed and drained
8 skinless, boneless chicken breast halves (about 2 lbs.)
1 can (26 oz.) Campbell's condensed cream of mushroom soup
2/3 cup milk
1/4 tsp. pepper
8 cups hot cooked rice

In 3 quart oblong baking dish, arrange broccoli; top with chicken. In medium bowl, combine soup, milk and pepper. Pour over chicken.

Bake at 400 degrees F for 30 minutes or until chicken is no longer pink. Stir sauce before serving.

Tip: To thaw broccoli, microwave on high 10 minutes, stirring once during heating.
Yields: 8 servings

GREEN BEAN BAKE

1 can (26 oz.) Campbell's condensed cream of mushroom soup
1 cup milk
2 tsps. soy sauce
1/4 tsp. pepper
2 bags (16 ozs. each) frozen cut green beans, cooked and drained
2 cans (about 2 1/2 ozs. each) or 1 can (6 oz.) French fried onions

In 3 quart oblong baking dish, combine soup, milk, soy and pepper. Stir in green beans and half of the onions.

Bake at 350 degrees F for 25 minutes. Stir. Sprinkle remaining onions over green bean mixture.

Bake 5 minutes or until hot and bubbling and onions are golden.

Variation: Substitute 4 cans (about 16 ozs. each) cut green beans, drained for frozen green beans.
Yields: 10 servings

CHICKEN BROCCOLI STUFFING BAKE

1 can (26 oz.) Campbell's condensed cream of mushroom soup
1 1/2 cups milk
1 package (14 oz.) Pepperidge Farm cubed herb seasoned stuffing
3 cups cubed cooked chicken or turkey
2 packages (10 ozs. each) frozen chopped broccoli, thawed and drained
2 stalks celery, finely chopped (about 1 cup)
1 cup shredded Swiss cheese (4 ozs.)

In large bowl, combine soup and milk. Stir in stuffing, chicken, broccoli and celery. Spoon into 3 quart oblong baking dish.
Bake at 375 degrees F for 35 minutes. Sprinkle with cheese. Bake 5 minutes or until cheese is melted.

Yields: 8 servings

VEGETABLE ROTINI

5 cups dry corkscrew macaroni
2 bags (16 ozs. each) frozen vegetable combination (broccoli, carrots and cauliflower)
1 can (26 oz.) Campbell's condensed cream of chicken soup
1 package (3 oz.) cream cheese or cream cheese with chives, softened
1 cup milk
1/2 cup grated parmesan cheese
2 tbs. Dijon style mustard (optional)
1/8 tsp. pepper

In 6 quart Dutch oven, prepare macaroni according to package directions. Add vegetables for the last 5 minutes of cooking time. Drain in colander.
In same Dutch oven over low heat, gradually stir soup into cream cheese; add milk, parmesan cheese, mustard and pepper. Heat until cream cheese is melted, stirring often. Add macaroni and vegetables; toss to coat. Heat through, stirring occasionally.

Yields: 14 servings

GARDEN VEGETABLE TWISTS

1 tbs. olive oil
1 cup chopped broccoli
1 cup thinly sliced carrots (about 3 med.)
1 tsp. dried basil leaves, crushed
1/2 tsp. garlic powder
1 can (10 3/4 oz.) Campbell's Healthy Request condensed cream of celery soup
1 cup skim milk
2 tbs. grated parmesan cheese
2 cups cooked corkscrew macaroni (about 1 1/2 cups dry), cooked without salt
2 cups cubed cooked chicken

In 10 inch skillet over medium heat, in hot oil, cook broccoli and carrots with basil and garlic powder until tender, stirring often.
Stir in soup, milk and cheese; add macaroni and chicken. Reduce heat to low. Heat through, stirring occasionally.
Tip: For 2 cups cubed cooked chicken, in 2 quart saucepan over medium heat, in 4 cups boiling water, cook 1 pound skinless, chicken breasts, cubed, 5 minutes or until chicken is no longer pink.

Yields: 4 servings

CHICKEN BROCCOLI VEGETABLE SAUTÉ

vegetable cooking spray
4 skinless, boneless chicken breast halves (about 1 lb.)
1 cup broccoli flowerets
1 cup sliced mushrooms (about 3 ozs.)
1/2 cup thinly sliced carrots (about 1 med.)
1 can (10 3/4 oz.) Campbell's Healthy Request condensed cream of broccoli soup
3/4 cup skim milk
1/4 tsp. dried thyme leaves, crushed

Spray 10 inch nonstick skillet with cooking spray. Heat over medium-high heat 1 minute. Add chicken; cook 10 minutes or until browned on both sides. Remove; set aside.
Remove skillet from heat; spray skillet with cooking spray. Reduce heat to medium. Add broccoli, mushrooms and carrots; cool until tender, stirring often.
Add soup, milk and thyme. Heat to boiling. Return chicken to skillet. Reduce heat to low. Cover; cook for 5 minutes or until chicken is no longer pink, stirring occasionally.

Yields: 4 servings

CHUCKWAGON LIMAS

4 sm. onions
cooking oil
4 cups cooked or canned lg. limas
1/2 tsp. salt
1/2 tsp. pepper
1 tsp. sage
1 1/2 cups grated American cheese
1/2 cup light cream
4 to 5 slices bacon

Peel and slice onions thin. Sauté in oil until transparent. Spoon half of the cooked limas into buttered baking dish. Sprinkle with salt, pepper and sage. Layer onion slices over beans. Add remainder of beans and sprinkle with 1 cup cheese. Pour in cream. Lay halved bacon slices on top. Bake 30 to 40 minutes at 350 degrees F until bacon is cooked. Top with remaining cheese and return to oven a few minutes to melt cheese.

Yields: 4 to 6 servings

GERMAN COLE SLAW

1 1/2 lbs. green cabbage, finely chopped (5 cups)
1 med. onion, chopped fine
1 med. green pepper, chopped fine
1/2 cup sugar
1/2 cup cider or white vinegar
1/2 cup salad oil
1 tsp. salt
1/2 tsp. ground black pepper
1/2 tsp. celery seed

In a large bowl place cabbage, onion and green pepper. In a small saucepan combine sugar, vinegar and oil; bring to the boiling point. Immediately pour over vegetables. Add salt, black pepper and celery seed; mix well. Cover and refrigerate 12 hours or longer.

Yields: 4 cups

COPPER DOLLARS

2 lbs. carrots
1 lg. onion
1 lg. green pepper
1 cup sugar
1 can (10 3/4 oz.) condensed tomato soup
3/4 cup cider or white vinegar
1/2 cup salad oil
1 tsp. Worcestershire sauce
1 tsp. prepared mustard
salt and black pepper to taste

Slice carrots 1/4 inch thick. Cook carrots in 1 inch boiling water, covered, until tender, 10 to 15 minutes. Drain and cool. Slice and separate onion into rings. Slice green pepper into 1/4 inch

wide strips. In a large bowl place carrots, onion and green pepper along with remaining ingredients; mix well. Cover and refrigerate 12 hours or longer. Keeps for several days in the refrigerator.

Yields: 8 cups

OVERNIGHT CUCUMBER PICKLE

5 firm med. sized cucumbers (3 lbs.)
1 3/4 tsps. salt
2 1/2 cups cider vinegar
2 cups sugar
2 tsps. mustard seed
1 tsp. celery seed
1 tsp. ground ginger
1 tsp. turmeric

Slice cucumbers 1/2 inch thick (makes about 10 cups); place in a large bowl. Sprinkle with salt, mix well. Let stand for 1 hour. Drain well. In a large sauce pot combine vinegar, sugar, mustard seed, celery seed, ginger and turmeric; bring to a boil. Add cucumbers, simmer, covered, until crisp-tender, about 10 minutes. Pour into a container with a tight fitting lid. Refrigerate overnight before serving.

Yields: 3 quarts

BEES IN THE GARDEN COLESLAW

1 head green cabbage, shredded
1 med. green pepper, diced
1/2 cup diced sweet red pepper
1/2 cup mayonnaise
1/3 cup honey
2 tbs. vinegar
1/2 tsp. salt
1/2 tsp. dry mustard
1/2 tsp. celery seeds
1/4 tsp. black pepper

Toss cabbage and peppers in large bowl. Combine mayonnaise, honey, vinegar, salt, mustard, celery seeds and black pepper in medium bowl, then toss with

cabbage mixture. Mix well; cover and refrigerate until thoroughly chilled.

Yields: 8 to 10 servings

HONEY NUT SQUASH

2 acorn squash (about 6 ozs. each)
1/4 cup honey
2 tbs. butter or margarine, melted
2 tbs. chopped walnuts
2 tbs. raisins
2 tsp. Worcestershire sauce

Cup acorn squash lengthwise into halves; do not remove seeds. Place cut side up in baking pan or on baking sheet. Bake at 400 degrees F 30 to 45 minutes or until soft. Remove seeds and fibers.

Combine honey, butter, walnuts, raisins and Worcestershire sauce; spoon into squash. Bake 5 to 10 minutes or until lightly glazed.

To microwave: Cut acorn squash lengthwise into halves and remove seeds. Microwave according to manufacturer's directions. Combine honey, butter, walnuts, raisins and Worcestershire sauce; spoon into squash. Microwave at high (100%) 30 seconds or until thoroughly heated and slightly glazed.

Yields: 4 servings

SWEET AND SOUR ZUCCHINI

4 sm. zucchini, thinly sliced
1/2 to 3/4 cup honey
1/2 cup white wine vinegar
1/3 cup vegetable oil
1/4 cup chopped green bell pepper
1/4 cup diced celery
1 tbs. chopped onion
1 tsp. salt
1 tsp. black pepper

Combine zucchini, honey, vinegar, oil, bell pepper, celery, onion, salt and black pepper in large glass or ceramic bowl. Cover and refrigerate overnight. Drain and serve chilled or at room temperature.

Yields: about 2 quarts

HONEY KISSED WINTER VEGETABLES

2 to 2 1/2 cups pared seeded 1/2 inch winter squash cubes
1 turnip, pared and cut into 1/2 inch cubes
2 carrots, pared and cut into 1/2 inch slices
1 sm. onion, cut into quarters
1/4 cup honey
2 tbs. butter or margarine, melted
1 tsp. grated orange peel
1/4 tsp. ground nutmeg

Steam squash, turnip, carrots and onion on rack over 1 inch of boiling water in large covered skillet about 5 minutes or until tender. Drain. Combine honey, butter, orange peel and nutmeg in small bowl. Drizzle over vegetables and toss to coat in heated serving dish.

Yields: 4 to 6 servings

CRUNCHY BABY LIMA AND CHEDDAR SLAW

3 cups shredded cabbage
1 tbs. minced green onion
1 2/3 cups drained, cooked or canned white baby limas
1 red apple, unpeeled, cored and diced
4 ozs. cheddar cheese, cubed
1 tbs. lemon juice
1/8 tsp. garlic salt
romaine leaves
Creamy dressing:
1 cup sour cream
1/4 cup mayonnaise
2 tbs. vinegar
1 tsp. sugar
1/4 tsp. Worcestershire sauce

Combine cabbage, onion and garlic salt; add 1/4 cup creamy dressing and toss lightly. Sprinkle apple with lemon juice. Combine cabbage mixture, beans, apple and cheese in a salad bowl and mix well with a little more dressing, if needed, to coat all ingredients. Edge the bowl with romaine spears and offer to guests for self service.

Creamy dressing: Combine all ingredients and mix well.

Yields: 4 to 6 servings

HONEY GLAZED CARROTS

3 cups sliced carrots
1/4 cup honey
2 tbs. butter or margarine
2 tbs. chopped fresh parsley or 2 tsps. dried parsley flakes
1 1/2 to 2 tsps. prepared mustard (optional)

Heat 2 inches of salted water in medium saucepan to a boil over high heat. Add carrots and return to a boil. Reduce heat to medium high. Cover and cook 8 to 12 minutes or until carrots are crisp tender. Drain carrots; return to saucepan. Stir in honey, butter, parsley and mustard, if desired. Cook and stir over low heat until carrots are glazed.

Yields: 6 servings

SWEET BAKED RED ONIONS

3 lg. red onions (about 3 lbs.)
1/3 cup honey
1/4 cup water
3 tbs. butter or margarine, melted
1 tsp. paprika (Sweet Hungarian paprika is preferred.)
1 tsp. ground coriander
1/2 tsp. salt
1/8 tsp. ground red pepper

Peel onions and cut crosswise into halves. Place cut side down in shallow baking dish just large enough to hold all onions in a single layer. Sprinkle with water; cover with foil. Bake at 350 degrees F 30 minutes. Combine honey, 1/4 cup water, butter, paprika, coriander, salt and red pepper in small bowl. Remove onions from oven and turn cut side up. Spoon half of mixture over onions. Bake, uncovered, 15 minutes more. Baste with remaining honey mixture; bake 15 minutes more or until tender. Serve with poultry or pork.

Yields: 6 servings

SWEET-SOUR RED CABBAGE

1 tbs. butter or margarine
1/2 cup wine vinegar
1/4 cup honey
1 tsp. salt
1 med. head (8 cups) red cabbage, shredded
2 apples, cored and diced

Melt butter in large nonstick skillet or stainless steel saucepan over medium heat. Stir in vinegar, honey and salt. Add cabbage and apples; toss well. Reduce heat to low; cover and simmer 45 to 50 minutes.

To microwave: Place shredded cabbage in 3 quart microwave safe baking dish. Add apples, butter and vinegar. Cover and cook on high (100%) 15 minutes. Stir in honey and salt. Cover and cook on high 10 minutes.

Yields: 4 to 6 servings

STIR-FRY RICE AND VEGETABLES

3 tbs. vegetable oil
1 bunch green onions, bulbs

and tops chopped separately
1 med. sweet potato, pared, halved lengthwise and thinly sliced
1 sm. green bell pepper, cut into thin strips
2 carrots, thinly sliced
1 zucchini, thinly sliced
2 cups cooked brown rice
1 cup bean sprouts
1 cup fresh mushrooms, sliced
1/4 cup honey
1/4 cup soy sauce

Heat oil in wok or large, heavy skillet over medium high heat. Stir fry onion bulbs, sweet potato, bell pepper, carrots and zucchini until barely tender. Add rice, sprouts, mushrooms and onion tops. Cook quickly until heated through. If necessary, add more oil. Combine honey and soy sauce in cup. Pour over mixture and stir. Serve immediately.

Yields: 6 to 8 servings

HOT AND SWEET MARINATED MUSHROOMS

1/3 cup honey
1/4 cup white wine vinegar
1/4 cup dry white wine or vegetable broth
2 tbs. vegetable oil
1 tbs. soy sauce
1 tbs. sesame oil
1 clove garlic, minced
1 sm. green onion, chopped
1 tsp. grated fresh ginger-root
1/2 tsp. grated orange peel
1/4 tsp. ground red pepper
1 lb. fresh sm. button mushrooms
parsley sprigs and orange wedges for garnish (optional)

Combine honey, vinegar, wine, vegetable oil, soy sauce, sesame oil, garlic, green onion, gingerroot, orange peel and red pepper in small saucepan. Cook and stir mixture over low heat until hot.

Place mushrooms in heatproof bowl; pour hot marinade over mushrooms. Cover and marinate 3 hours in refrigerator, stirring occasionally. Arrange mushrooms in serving dish; garnish with parsley sprigs and orange wedges, if desired.

Yields: 4 to 6 servings

CURRIED BAKED BEANS

1 lb. sm. dry white beans
6 cups water
1 tsp. salt
2 med. apples, cored, pared and diced
1/2 cup golden raisins
1 sm. onion, minced
1/3 cup sweet pickle relish
2/3 cup honey
1 tbs. prepared mustard
1 tsp. curry powder (or to taste)

Combine beans, water and salt in large saucepan. Let stand overnight. Bring to a boil over high heat. Reduce heat to low and simmer 2 hours, adding water, if needed. Drain beans, reserving liquid. Combine beans with remaining ingredients. Pour into 2 1/2 quart casserole. Add enough bean liquid to barely cover. Bake, covered, at 300 degrees F 1 hour. Remove cover; bake about 30 minutes, adding more liquid, if needed.

Yields: 8 servings

VEGETABLE LASAGNA

2 cups lowfat cottage cheese (1% milkfat)
1 package (10 oz.) frozen chopped spinach, thawed
1 cup shredded carrot
1/2 cup Egg Beaters 99% egg product
2 tbs. minced onion
1 tsp. Italian seasoning
2 cups no salt added spaghetti sauce
1 cup shredded part-skim mozzarella cheese (4 ozs.)
2 tbs. grated parmesan cheese

In medium bowl, combine cottage cheese, spinach, carrot, egg product, onion and Italian seasoning; set aside.

Spread 1/2 cup spaghetti sauce over bottom of greased 13 x 9 x 2 inch baking dish. Layer 3 noodles and 1/3 each of the spinach filling and remaining sauce; repeat layer twice.

Sprinkle top with mozzarella cheese and parmesan cheese; cover. Bake at 375 degrees F for 20 minutes. Uncover; bake 25 minutes more. Let stand 10 minutes before serving.

Yields: 8 servings

VEGETARIAN CHOWDER

1 lb. white beans (lg. or baby limas, sm. whites or Great Northerns)
1 cup chopped onion
1 1/2 cups chopped celery
1/4 cup butter or margarine
1/4 cup flour
1 1/2 tsps. flour
1/8 tsp. pepper
3 cups milk
1 can (16 oz.) tomatoes
1 can (16 oz.) whole kernel corn
1/4 lb. Monterey jack cheese or sharp cheddar

Rinse, sort and soak beans. Drain. In large kettle cook beans in 6 to 8 cups hot water with 1 1/2 tsp. salt. Cook until tender (about 1 hour for limas; about 2 to 2 1/2 hours for small whites and Great Northerns).

Don't drain. Meanwhile, cook onion and celery briefly in butter in a 1 1/2 quart saucepan. Blend in flour, salt and pepper.

Stir in milk and bring mixture to boil. Add to beans and their liquid, along with remaining ingredients. Heat all to boiling.

For extra zip, add a few dashes of bottled hot sauce.

Leftover bean soups freeze beautifully.

Package in serving-sized containers for convenience.

Yields: 12 servings

GLOSSARY

ABBREVIATIONS

tsp. = teaspoon
tbs. = tablespoon
oz. = ounce
lb. = pound
sm. = small
med. = medium
lg. = large

ALTERNATIVE INGREDIENTS

Butter:
1 cup less 3 tbs. shortening for 1 cup butter.

Unsweetened Chocolate:
3 tbs. cocoa plus 1 1/2 tsps. oil for 1 oz. unsweetened chocolate.

Whole Egg:
2 egg yolks for 1 whole egg (in baking).

Cornstarch:
2 tbs. flour for 1 tbs. cornstarch.

All Purpose Flour:
7/8 cup (1 cup less 2 tbs.) unsifted all-purpose flour for 1 cup sifted all-purpose flour.

Sifted Cake Flour:
7/8 cup (1 cup less 2 tbs.) sifted all-purpose flour for 1 cup sifted cake flour.

Sour Milk or Butter Milk:
1 tbs. lemon juice or vinegar plus enough milk to make 1 cup for 1 cup sour milk or buttermilk.

Fresh Milk:
1/2 cup evaporated milk plus 1/2 cup water for 1 cup fresh milk.

Granulated Sugar:
1 cup brown sugar, packed for 1 cup granulated sugar, or 1/2 cup maple syrup plus 1/4 cup corn syrup, and reduce liquid by 1/4 cup for 1 cup granulated sugar, or 1 cup honey plus 1/4 to 1/2 tsp. baking soda, and reduce liquid by 1/4 cup for 1 cup gran. sugar.

Honey:
3/4 cup sugar plus 1/4 cup liquid for 1 cup honey

Bouillon:
1 tsp. instant soup mix plus 1 cup boiling water for 1 cup bouillon.

BREAD BAKING

• Bread and rolls taste better and smell home-baked when heated just before serving. Warm in a 400 degrees F oven for 5 to 10 minutes, wrapped in tinfoil.

• To freshen rolls, place in a paper bag, seal bag and heat in hot oven for 15 minutes.

• Brown sugar kept in the bread box keeps bread moist and keeps brown sugar from hardening.

• Instead of wrapping loaves of bread for freezing, package two to six slices, making it easier to defrost the amount of bread needed, leaving the rest of the loaf fresh.

• Bread is less subject to mold if stored in the refrigerator, but turns stale more quickly.

• If bread browns too quickly while baking, cover with brown paper for the last few minutes.

• An ideal place to raise yeast dough is on top of the refrigerator; also near, but not on the range. Keep dough covered with a cloth to protect from drafts during rising.

• Heat raisins in oven before adding to muffins or breads, and they will be more evenly distributed. Just wash them, then spread out on a flat pan. Cover and heat at 350 degrees F until they puff up.

• To get the full flavor from raisins, cut them with scissors after heating.

• Muffin tins may be lined with paper liners to avoid greasing of pans.

• When scalding milk, first rinse saucepan with cold water, to prevent sticking. The top of a double boiler is an ideal place to heat milk without danger of boiling or scorching.

• Yeast breads freeze extremely well. If glazing is desired, freeze them first, and when needed, heat and glaze.

• Making yeast dough? You don't have to bake it all the same day. Place dough in the refrigerator once it is mixed. The top should be well greased, then covered with wax paper, then a damp cloth. Be sure to keep the cloth damp. If made with milk and at least 1/4 cup sugar, it will keep about 3 days. If made with water, it will keep about 5 days. Cut off as much dough as you need at a time.

• For a highly glazed crust on yeast breads, brush with beaten egg yolk before baking.

• For a soft and tender crust, brush with soft butter or shortening while still warm. Cover with a towel to soften crust.

COOKING TERMS AND DEFINITIONS

Appetizer: A small serving of food or beverage served before, or as the first course of a meal.

Au Gratin: With a cheese topping or crust.

Bake: To cook in oven by dry heat.

Barbecue: To roast on a rack over coals or on a spit, usually basting with a sauce.

Baste: To spoon liquid or fat over food while it cooks, to add flavor and prevent drying of the surface.

Batter: A mixture of flour, liquid, etc. which can be beaten or stirred.

Beat: To mix with a brisk, regulation motion that lifts mixture over and over, making the mixture smooth and introducing air.

Blanch: To immerse in boiling water, then draining and rinsing with cold water, generally in order to loosen skin or set color.

Blend: To thoroughly mix two or more ingredients.

Boil: To cook in steaming liquid in which the bubbles are breaking on the surface (212 degrees F).

Braise: To brown food in a small amount of hot fat, then cooking tightly covered either in the oven or in top of the stove, in a small amount of liquid.

Bread: To coat food in flour, egg and crumbs.

Broil: To cook over or under direct heat.

Broth: Liquid in which meat or poultry has been simmered.

Canape: A tiny piece of bread, or a cracker, which is topped with an appetizer.

Capons: A castrated male chicken, which grows large and has tender meat.

Chill: To allow to become thoroughly cold.

Chop: To cut fine or coarse pieces with sharp knife.

Coat: To cover with a thin film, e.g. flour, crushed nuts, crumbs, etc.

Compote: Stewed fruit which has been slowing cooked in a sugar syrup to keep its natural shape.

Cool: To let stand at room temperature until no longer warm.

Cream: To work foods until soft and fluffy, ordinarily applied to mixing of sugar and shortening.

Creole: A tomato sauce which is well seasoned and contains celery, onions, green peppers, etc.

Crouton: Cubes of toasted or fried bread used in soups, in garnishes, in salads, etc.

Cube: To cut into pieces with six equal square sides.

Cut In: To combine solid fat with dry ingredients using two knives, pastry blade, etc.

Deep-Fry: To cook food in a deep layer of hot fat.

Deviled: Prepared with hot seasonings or spices.

Dice: To cut in very small cubes.

Dissolve: To mix a dry substance with liquid until it is in a solution.

Dot: To scatter bits (e.g. butter) over a food which is to be cooked.

Dough: A mixture of liquid, flour, etc. which is stiff enough to be handled or kneaded.

Dredge: To coat with flour.

Drippings: Fat and juice resulting from cooking meat or poultry.

En Brochette: Cooked on a skewer.

Fillet: Long thin boneless strip of fish or meat.

Flake: To break lightly into small pieces with a fork.

Fold In: To cut down through the center of a batter to the bottom with the edge of a spatula, and to lift the bottom to the top, repeating until foods are blended.

Frost: To cover with icing.

Fry: To cook in hot fat.

Garnish: To decorate food for eye and taste appeal using contrasting colors of food.

Giblets: The liver, heart and gizzard of poultry.

Glaze: To coat a food with syrup or jelly to give a luster.

Grate: To reduce food to small particles by rubbing against a grater.

Grind: To crush in a food chopper. Hors d'Oeuvres: A variety of appetizers.

Knead: To work dough with a pressing motion, accompanied by folding and stretching.

Leavening: Ingredients which make soda, baking powder, yeast.

Mash: To reduce to a soft pulpy state.

Melt: To liquefy by applying heat.

Meringue: A stiffly beaten mixture of egg whites, sugar and flavoring.

Mince: To cut or chop food into very small pieces (rather than chopping).

Mix: To combine two or more ingredients, usually by stirring.

Mocha: Coffee flavor, or a combination of chocolate and coffee.

Pan-Broil: To cook meat on a hot dry surface, pouring off grease as it accumulates.

Pan-Fry: To cook in a small amount of fat in a skillet.

Parboil: To boil until partially cooked. Cooking is generally competed by another method.

Pare: To cut off outside covering, e.g. carrots, potatoes.

Partially Set: To chill to consistency of unbeaten egg whites.

Peel: Strip off outside covering, e.g. oranges, bananas.

Pit: To remove pit or seeds from fruit.

Poach: To cook in simmering liquid to cover, retaining original shape of food.

Pot-Roast: To cook less tender cuts of meat in a little liquid, with or without browning first.

Preheat: To heat to desired temperature before placing food in oven.

Puree: To press cooked food through a sieve, making it a smooth, thick mixture.

Render: To free fat from connective tissue on low heat until fat melts and can be drained off.

Roast: To cook by dry heat, usually in the oven.

Sauté: To cook in a small amount of fat on low heat.

Scald: To heat to temperature just below boiling point.

Sear: To brown surface rapidly at high temperature.

Sift: To press through a sieve.

Simmer: To cook in liquid at a temperature just below boiling.

Skewer: A long pin of wood or metal on which food is placed and held in shape while cooking.

Skim: To remove film that forms.

Sliver: To cut or shred into long, thin pieces.

Stew: To cook covered in a small amount of simmering or boiling water for a long time.

Stock: The liquid in which meat, poultry, fish or vegetables have been cooked.

Toast: To brown food by the application of direct heat.

Torte: A rich cake, usually made of crumbs, nuts, eggs, etc.

Toss: To lightly mix ingredients without mashing.

Until Set: Until a liquid has become firm.

Whip: To beat rapidly to increase volume by the incorporation of air.

DIETING TIPS

- Follow the three B's while cooking: Boil, bake or broil.
- Trim all visible fat from foods. One tbs. of fat contains about 100 calories.
- Steer clear of fried foods.
- Use non-stick pans — they do not require fat for cooking.
- Use a low-calorie cooking spray instead of butter or fat when sauteing.
- Do not use gravies or cream sauces.
- To remove fats from braised foods, soups, etc. refrigerate. The fat which congeals on the surface can be easily removed.
- Eat slowly and chew well.
- Sit down when eating. Do not eat while standing or talking on the telephone.
- Weigh yourself regularly and often.
- Diet silently.
- Skim milk and buttermilk contain the same calories — 87 per 8 oz. serving — nearly half the amount in whole milk.
- Buy tuna which is packed in spring water rather than oil.
- Buy skim milk cheeses.
- Substitute dry cottage cheese (pot cheese) for cream cheese in recipes.
- Four to five tbs. sugar equals 1 tsp. liquid sweetener.
- Use cornstarch instead of flour to thicken your low-cal sauces.
- Canned fruit may be substituted for fresh if all the syrup is drained off and the fruit is washed well under cold water.

FOOD EQUIVALENTS

Apples:
- 1 pound **equals** 3 medium (3 cups sliced)

Butter (and other fats):
- 1 lb. **equals** 2 cups
- 1/2 lb. **equals** 1 cup
- 1/4 lb. **equals** 1/2 cup

Cheese:
- 1 lb. cottage cheese **equals** 2 cups
- 8 oz. pkg. cottage cheese **equals** 1 cup
- 8 oz. pkg. cream cheese **equals** 1 cup (1/2 lb.)

- 1 lb. American or Cheddar **equals** 3 to 4 cups grated

Chocolate (unsweetened):
- 1 square **equals** 1 oz. or 1 tbs. when melted
- 1/2 lb. **equals** 8 1 oz. squares

Coffee:
- 1 lb. - 80 tbs. (40 servings)

Cream:
- 1/2 pint coffee cream **equals** 6 to 8 servings of cream
- 1/2 pint (1 cup) whipping (OR 1 pkg. dessert topping) **equals** 2 cups when whipped

Dates:
- 1 lb. whole **equals** 1 1/2 to 1 3/4 cups pitted and cut up

Eggs:
- 5 whole eggs **equals** 1 cup
- 8 to 10 egg whites **equals** 1 cup
- 12 to 14 egg yolks **equals** 1 cup

Flour:
- 1 lb. all-purpose **equals** 4 cups, sifted
- 1 lb. cake & pastry flour **equals** 4 1/2 cups, sifted

Ice Cream:
- 1 quart **equals** 4 to 6 servings

Lemon:
- 1 medium - juice **equals** 2 to 3 tbs.
- 1 medium - rind **equals** 1/2 to 1 tbs.

Milk:
- 1 quart **equals** 4 cups (American) OR 5 cups (Canadian)
- 1 pint **equals** 2 cups

Nuts:
- 1 lb. almonds (in shell) **equals** 1 1/4 cups nutmeats
- 1 lb. pecans **equals** (in shell) **equals** 1 1/2 cups nutmeats
- 1 lb. peanuts (in shell) **equals** 2 cups nutmeats
- 1 lb. walnuts (in shell) **equals** 1 3/4 cups nutmeats

Orange:
- 1 medium - juice **equals** 5 to 6 tbs.
- 1 medium - rind **equals** 1 to 2 tbs.

Raisins:
- 1 lb. **equals** 3 cups

Sugar:
- 1 lb. granulated sugar **equals** 2 cups
- 1 lb. confectioner's sugar **equals** 3 1/2 cups, sifted
- 1 lb. brown sugar **equals** 2 1/4 cups, firmly packed
- 1 lb. powdered sugar **equals** 2 1/3 cups

FREEZER STORAGE TIMES

Meats:
- Beef — 8 to 12 months
- Hamburger (minced meats) — 4 to 6 months
- Beef or calves liver — 3 to 4 months
- Lamb — 8 to 12 months
- Poultry (whole) — 6 to 8 months
- Broilers & cut-up poultry — 4 to 6 months
- Turkey — 6 to 8 months
- Giblets (except liver) — 2 to 3 months
- Poultry livers — less than 1 month
- Veal — 6 to 8 months
- Hot Dogs — 2 to 3 months

Fresh Vegetables:
Vegetables should be scalded before freezing. Place in a wire basket and immerse in boiling water for no more than 4 minutes. Then cool immediately by plunging vegetables into ice water. Drain, wrap and freeze immediately.

- Asparagus (in 2 inch pieces) 6 to 8 months
- Beans, green or wax — 8 to 12 months
- Broccoli — 12 months

- Brussel Sprouts — 8 to 12 months
- Carrots (sliced) — 12 months
- Carrots (small whole) — 12 months
- Cauliflower — 12 months
- Corn on the Cob — 8 to 12 months
- Peas — 12 months
- Spinach — 12 months

Fruits:
Raspberries, cranberries, and blueberries may be frozen without sugar or syrup. Wash well and pack. Freeze immediately. — 12 months

Strawberries: Wash well, slice if desired. Sprinkle with sugar (use 1 lb. to approximately 4 to 5 lbs. berries) and mix gently. — 12 months

Cantaloupe and watermelon: Fruit should be ripe and firm. Dissolve 1/3 cup sugar and 1/3 cup orange juice in 2 cups boiling water. Cool to 70 degrees. Pour over fruit which has been cut into balls or cubes. — 6 to 8 months

Sandwiches:
Use butter instead of mayonnaise as a spread. Day-old bread is best. Fillings containing jelly, salad dressing and mayonnaise make bread soggy. Ideal fillings: salmon, tuna, cream cheese, Cheddar cheese, cooked egg yolks (whites tend to become rubbery), peanut butter – less than 1 month

Egg yolks or Egg whites:
To freeze yolks, add 2 tbs. sugar or 1 tsp. salt to each cup of yolks. Nothing need be added to the whites. Never freeze eggs in the shell. — 8 to 12 months

Cheese:
- Wrap well in tinfoil. It may crumble after long storage, but flavor will not change.
- Cheddar and processed cheese — 6 to 8 months
- Cream cheese — 2 months
- Cottage cheese — 2 weeks

Butter:
- Wrap well in foil — 6 to 8 months
- Milk — 2 weeks
- Ice Cream — 2 to 4 weeks

Cakes:
- Frosted — 2 months
- Unfrosted — 3 to 4 months
- Fruit — 8 to 12 months
- Pies (baked or unbaked) 2 to 3 months
- Bread and rolls — 2 to 3 months
- Cookies (baked or unbaked) 9 months

FREEZING TIPS

- Freezer temperature should be no higher than 0 degrees F.
- Freeze foods as quickly as possible by placing them directly against the sides of the freezer.
- Label foods for easy identification. Write the name of the food, number of servings, and date of freezing. Different colors of freezing tape are a good idea.
- Arrange freezer into sections for each food, space permitting.
- FREEZER WRAPPINGS: heavy duty aluminum foil, transparent wrap, plastic bags, freezer bags.
- FREEZER CONTAINERS: plastic ice cream containers, empty coffee cans, oven-proof casseroles, jars (leave air space a top to allow for expansion during freezing).
- If you are short of freezing containers, line the containers with plastic bag, fill with desired food, and let freeze solid. Then remove plastic bag from container. This method is ideal when using casseroles as the container, for food may be removed from the plastic bag when needed, and heated in the original container.
- When freezing meals, quart containers can hold 4 servings, pint containers, 2 servings.
- Use wide-mouth containers for freezing to avoid the necessity of complete defrosting before removal.

- To prevent sticking, spread food to be frozen (berries, hamburgers, cookies, etc.) on a cookie sheet and freeze until solid. Then remove to plastic bags and store.
- DO NOT RE-FREEZE MEATS, etc. However, once it has been cooked, you may freeze the food again, as this is not considered refreezing.
- Undercook foods which must be heated before serving to avoid a warmed-over taste.
- Slice meats before freezing. They will thaw more quickly.
- You may cook meat, poultry and fish while still frozen. Increase cooking time.
- Never stuff poultry or roasts before freezing.
- Do not unwrap meat when thawing.
- Thawing of meat and poultry: allow 2 to 2 1/2 hours per pound at room temperature, and 5 to 6 hours per pound in the refrigerator. Coffee retains that fresh-ground taste when stored in the freezer.
- If you need a lot of ice cubes, make the required amount in advance, and store in plastic bags.
- Do not freeze celery, lettuce, cucumbers, carrots or raw tomatoes.
- Rice hardens when frozen.
- To cook frozen vegetables, do not thaw them before cooking to avoid loss of Vitamin C. Cook minimum time in as little water as possible.
- Mashed and stuffed potatoes freeze well. However, omit potatoes from stews, soups, etc. that are to be frozen as cooked potatoes become mushy when frozen in liquid.
- Cakes which have been frozen, dry out more quickly when thawed than those which are freshly baked.
- Cake defrosts in approximately 2 hours at room temperature. Thaw without unwrapping.
- The cookie crumb crust of cheese cake becomes soggy when frozen.

- To freeze an unbaked fruit pie, do not pierce the top crust to prevent fruit from drying out. For easiest handling, freeze unwrapped just until frozen; then wrap immediately.
- To bake a frozen pie, remove from freezer, unwrap, make several slits in top crust and pop into the oven. Allow 15 to 20 minutes extra baking time.
- To freeze a baked fruit pie, first cool it thoroughly at room temperature, then wrap and freeze.
- Foods containing macaroni, spaghetti, or rice tastes warmed-over when thawed and re-heated, so add these ingredients when reheating rather than before freezing.

Defrost baked pies at 400 degrees for 10 to 15 minutes.

HOW TO MEASURE

Dash = less than 1/8 tsp.
3 tsp. = 1 tbs.
4 tbs. = 1/4 cup
5 1/3 tbs. = 1/3 cup
8 tbs. = 1/2 cup
10 2/3 tbs. = 2/3 cup
12 tbs. = 3/4 cup
16 tbs. = 1 cup
1 cup = 8 oz.
1 cup = 1/2 pint
2 cups = 1 pint
2 pints = 1 quart
4 cups = 1 quart
4 quarts = 1 gallon
8 quarts = 1 peck
4 pecks = 1 bushel
2 tbs. = 1 liq. oz.
16 oz. = 1 pound

INGREDIENT EQUIVALENTS

- Bread crumbs **equals** 3 oz. **equals** 1 cup

- Butter or shortening **equals** 1 lb. **equals** 2 cups

- Cheese **equals** 1 lb. **equals** 4 cups grated

- Chocolate **equals** 1 oz. **equals** 4 cups grated

- Coconut (shredded) **equals** 1 lb. **equals** 6 cups

- Cottage cheese **equals** 1 lb. **equals** 2 cups

- Cream cheese **equals** 3 oz. pkg. **equals** 6 2/3 tbs.

- Eggs (whole) **equals** 4 to 6 **equals** 1 cup
- Eggs (white) **equals** 8 to 10 **equals** 1 cup
- Eggs (yolk) **equals** 12 to 14 **equals** 1 cup

- Flour: all purpose **equals** 1 lb. **equals** 4 cups unsifted
- Flour: cake **equals** 1 lb. **equals** 4 1/2 cups unsifted
- Flour: whole wheat **equals** 1 lb. **equals** 4 cups

- Marshmallows **equals** 1 lb. **equals** 4 cups (64)

- Raisins **equals** 1 lb. **equals** 2 cups packed

- Sugar: brown **equals** 1 lb. **equals** 2 cups packed
- Sugar: confectioners **equals** 1 lb. **equals** 4 cups sifted
- Sugar: granulated **equals** 1 lb. **equals** 2 cups

- Whipping Cream **equals** 1/2 pint **equals** 2 cups whipped

SAFE COOKING- FOOD COOKING TEMPERATURES

Courtesy of the National Live Stock and Meat Board

Before You Cook
- Keep raw meat, poultry and fish and their juices from coming into contact with other foods during preparation, especially foods that won't be cooked. Wash your hands and all utensils and surfaces with hot soapy water after contact with raw meat.

- Never chop fresh vegetables or salad ingredients on a cutting board that was used for raw meat without properly cleaning it first. If possible, use a separate cutting board for the sole preparation of raw meat, poultry and fish.
- Carefully wash cutting boards with hot soapy water and then sanitize with a solution of household bleach and water (check bleach label for directions).
- Regularly clean refrigerator surfaces with hot soapy water.
- Thaw foods only in the refrigerator or microwave oven; never leave out at room temperature. When you thaw in a microwave, finish cooking immediately.
- Use a covered non-metallic container to marinate meat, poultry and seafood. Place it in the refrigerator, not on the kitchen counter. Discard the leftover marinade that was in contact with the raw meat, or bring to a rolling boil for 1 minute before using on cooked meat.
- Thoroughly rinse poultry and seafood in cold water and check for any off odors before cooking.
- Wash all fresh fruits and vegetables with cold running water—using a brush to scrub, if necessary.

Fresh Beef, Veal, Lamb
- Ground products like hamburger (prepared as patties, meat loaf, meatballs, etc.)- 160 degrees F, Cook until no longer pink
- Non-ground products like roasts and steaks-
Medium rare-145 degrees F
Medium-160 degrees F
Well done-170 degrees F

Fresh Pork
- All cuts including ground product
Medium- 160 degrees F
Well done- 170 degrees F

Poultry
- Ground chicken, turkey- 165 degrees F

- Whole chicken, turkey-Medium, unstuffed-170 degrees F Well done- 180 degrees F
- Whole bird with stuffing- 180 degrees F
- Stuffing 165 degrees F
- Poultry breasts, roasts- 170 degrees F
- Thighs, wings- Cook until juices run clear

Ham
- Fresh, raw leg- 160 degrees F
- Fully cooked, to reheat- 140 degrees F
- Cook roasts to 5 degrees F below the recommended internal temperature for doneness. The temperature will continue to rise about 5 degrees F during standing time (allow 10-15 minutes).
- Roast meat or poultry in oven temperatures of 325 degrees F or above. Avoid long, low temperatures when cooking meats, which may encourage bacterial growth before cooking is complete.
- Never partially heat foods and then refrigerate or set aside to finish cooking later. Partially-cooked foods may not reach a temperature high enough to destroy bacteria.
- Cook ground beef until no longer pink. Beef roasts and steaks should be well-browned on the surface, but the interior will be slightly pink when cooked to 145 degrees F (medium rare).
- When basting grilled meats, brush sauce on cooked surfaces only. Be careful not to contaminate fully cooked meats by reusing leftover marinade or adding sauce with a brush previously used on raw meats. Bring marinades to a rolling boil for 1 minute for safe use on cooked meats.
- Stir, rotate and cover foods when microwaving for even cooking. Check temperature with a "quick read" thermometer in at least three spots, and follow recommended standing times outside the microwave so the food completes cooking.